100 PRACTICE TESTS

GRADE 3

LANGUAGE

MATHEMATICS

SOCIAL STUDIES

SCIENCE

CANADIAN CURRICULUM PRESS

Forward Learning

100 Practice Tests, Grade 3

ISBN: 978-1-4876-0621-3

Éditions Caractère inc. © 2016 French edition
Authors: Colette Laberge and Stéphane Vallée
Original creative: Bruno Paradis and Atelier typo jane – André Vallée
Original cover design: Bruno Paradis/Cyclone Design
Selected Illustrations: Agathe Bray-Bourret, Julien Del Busso, Hugo Desrosiers,
Alexandre Bélisle, and Daniel Rainville

Telegraph Road Entertainment © 2020 English edition
The Telegraph Road Entertainment 2020 English edition, published under license from
Éditions Caractère inc., is translated and adapted from the original.
Co-authors: Vin Sriniketh and Barbara Snow, B.Ed.
Translation: Valerie Cunningham-Reimann
Editorial Team: Vin Sriniketh, Jessica Anne Carter, Emily Leahy (Intern)
Interior colour design and layout; adaptation of the original creative: Selena Revoredo
with creative consultant, Michael P. Brodey
Layout and adaptation of original cover: Selena Revoredo

Printed in Canada

Canadian Curriculum Press is an imprint of Telegraph Road Entertainment.

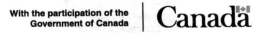

With the participation of the
Government of Canada | Canadä

Dear parents:

The 100 Practice Tests series is meant for you, parents who want to help their children progress on their learning path. The book is divided into four sections covering key concepts from the curriculum taught in Language, Mathematics, Social Studies and Science in Canadian schools. Unlike the typical comprehensive workbook, *100 Practice Tests* is structured to highlight the most important topics being taught in the classroom. Your child will have the opportunity to thoroughly review every significant lesson learned during the school year. However, you do not need to follow the sections in strict order. Your child can choose to work first on the topics already covered in class. That way, this book can truly complement your child's school learning. For homeschooled children, *100 Practice Tests* can also serve as a test book to gauge learning.

The exercises included in the book are varied and stimulating. They encourage an active learning approach and partake in the philosophy behind the educational program taught in Canadian schools. Encourage your child to attempt all questions, even the more challenging ones, to enhance her or his thinking and problem-solving abilities.

As your child works through the book, you will notice that the tests follow this pattern: Test 1 leads to Test 2 on the same topic, where your child is able to review the work done and confirm that she or he is indeed ready to move on to the next topic and its accompanying tests and exercises. Essentially, each topic has two tests and this format continues up to Test 100. With your guidance and this book to reinforce school learning, your child will be better prepared for the classroom, especially for quizzes and tests.

Enjoy the journey!

Sincerely,

The Canadian Curriculum Press Team

LANGUAGE

Grammar, Spelling and Alphabetical Order

Sentence and Punctuation

Synonyms and Antonyms

Homophones, Homonyms and Rhyme

Fact vs Opinion, Vocabulary

Reading Comprehension: Main Idea, Sequencing

Writing and Paragraph Writing

CANADIAN CURRICULUM PRESS

Forward Learning

TEST 1

1. Place the following words in alphabetical order on the lines below.

dinner	water	right	jug
vein	crayon	art	queen
octagon	shell	house	erase
television	frog	lamp	umbrella
paper	ball	gate	zipper
	neck	mat	

a) Art

b) Ball

c) Crayon

d) Dinner

e) Erase

f) frog

g) gate

h) house

i)

j) Jug

k)

l)

m) Mat

n) Neck

o) Octagon

p) Paper

q) queen

r)

s) Shell

t) television

u) Umbrela

v) Vein

1. Write each group of words below in alphabetical order. The first one is done for you.

a) soup can begin paddle

<u>begin can paddle soup</u>

b) best world hopeful concert

<u>best concert hopeful world.</u>

c) computer thunder delight race

<u>Computer delight thunder race.</u>

d) piece half hobby reward

<u>half hobby piece reward</u>

e) monster math mask moon

<u>Mask Math monster moon</u>

f) purple polite quickly quiet

<u>polite purple quickly quiet</u>

DICTIONARY

g) dictionary dock dark deep

<u>dark deep dictionary dock</u>

h) addition automatic address astronaut

<u>addittion address astronaut automatic</u>

Exercises | Language

2. Place these first names in alphabetical order.

Martha	Karina	Lydia	Alexander
Quinn	Bill	Paul	Oliver
Danny	Marika	Catherine	Aliya
Samantha	Joey	Mary	Ram
Justine	Iqbal	Jeremy	Tony
Gina	Kevin	Joan	Lalita

a) Alexander

b) Aliya

c) Bill

d) Catherine

e) Danny

f) Gina
Iqbal.

g) Jeremy
Joan, Joey

h) Justin

i) Karina

j) Kevin
Lalita, Lydiya, Marika

k) Martha

l) Mary

m) Oliver

n) Paul

o) Quinn

p) Ram

q) Samantha

r) Tony

s)

t)

u)

v)

w)

x)

3. Rewrite each word list in alphabetical order.

Hint: Look at the second letter of each word.

a) break, band, bear, board, black

band , _bear_ , _black_ , _board_ , _break_

b) cry, car, cup, cop, chord

car , _chod_ , _cop_ , _cry_ , _cup_

c) sap, special, simple, shallow, stick

sap , _shallow_ , _simple_ , _special_ , _stick_

d) great, gold, gym, gum, girl

girl , _gold_ , _great_ , _gum_ , _gym_

e) team, tackle, track, time, tyre

tackle , _team_ , _time_ , _track_ , _tyre_

f) road, right, real, rude, racket

Racket , _real_ , _right_ , _road_ , _rude_

g) home, heart, hat, hurt, hip

Hat , _heart_ , _hip_ , _home_ , _hurt_

h) pram, please, pail, pear, post

Pail , _pear_ , _please_ , _post_ , _pram_

Exercises

Language

TEST 2

1. Place the following words in alphabetical order:

| book | author | index | page | dictionary |
| library | edition | series | chapter | ending |

a) _author_

b) _book_

c) _chapter_

d) _dictionary_

e) _edition_

f) _ending_

g) _index_

h) _____

i) _____

j) _____

2. Circle each list of first names that is in alphabetical order.

(a) Fabio, Fanny, Flynn, Fred, Fritz

b) Delphine, Delvina, Diana, Dylan, Debbie

(c) Cathy, Charles, Christine, Cora, Crystal

d) Sam, Sheila, Steffi, Samantha, Shan

e) Lori, Lyle, Lara, Lux, Lata

(f) Marlene, Matt, Mike, Mina, Myrtle

(g) Ram, Rebecca, Riley, Ruby, Ryan

h) Pam, Phoebe, Patricia, Penelope, Philip

1. Write the words below in alphabetical order on the lines.

elephant	tomato	toe	shoe	jacket	magic
baby	flower	fall	fellow	lower	ice
joke	possible	pass	laugh	hat	orange
yellow	yell	out	girl	ink	train
		eraser	magnificent		

a) baby
  elephant

b) eraser
  fall, fellow, girl

c) flower

d) hat
  ice

e) ink
  Jacket

f) Joke
  laugh, lower, magic

g) Magnificent
  orange

h) out

i) Pass
  Possible, shoe, Tomato

j) toe
  train

k) yell

l) yellow

m) Shoe

n)

o)

p)

q)

r)

s)

t)

u)

v)

w)

x)

y)

z)

Exercises

Language

2. Help the dog find its bone by following the letters in alphabetical order.

3. Rewrite each word list in alphabetical order.

Hint: Look at the third letter of each word.

a) demand, debit, detail, decorate, dentist

debitate , _decorate_ , _demand_ , _dentist_ , _detail_

b) basket, barbecue, bandage, balloon, bath

balloon , _bandage_ , _barbecue_ , _basket_ , _bath_

c) pen, pet, pest, pedal, peel

pedal , _peel_ , _pen_ , _pest_ , _pet_

d) trot, trip, treasure, try, train

train , _treasure_ , _trip_ , _trot_ , _try_

e) send, sea, sell, set, seep

sea , _seep_ , _sell_ , _send_ , _set_

f) ready, rescue, red, reply, record

Ready , _record_ , _red_ , _reply_ , _rescue_

g) child, cheer, chain, chocolate, chute

Chain , _cheer_ , _child_ , _choclate_ , _chute_

h) lip, list, linger, limb, light

light , _limb_ , _linger_ , _lip_ , _list_

TEST 3

1. Complete the sentences correctly with _a_, _an_ or _the_.

a,e,i,o,u

a) ~~The~~ An _____ elephant was at the zoo.

b) Where would you find _____ a _____ bird?

c) Melanie made _____ a _____ loaf of bread.

d) Choose _____ a n _____ interesting book.

e) Did your class go on _____ a _____ field trip?

f) I want to see _____ a _____ movie tomorrow.

g) Did you eat _____ a ~~n~~ _____ cookie?

h) I had _____ a _____ egg for breakfast.

2. Choose the correct article to complete each sentence and write it on the line.

a) Hurry, _____ the _____ (the/an) bus is here.

b) Julie has _____ an _____ (an/a) orange cat.

c) Did you see _____ ~~an~~ The _____ (an/the) yellow bird on that tree?

d) _____ ~~A~~ The _____ (The/A) principal spoke to _____ ~~the~~ ~~a~~ the (a/the) students of the school.

e) He saw _____ a n _____ (a/an) airplane in the sky.

f) How was _____ the _____ (the/a) school trip?

1. Circle the phrase with the correct article in each pair. One is done for you.

Hint: *a/an* is used before a general countable noun (example: *a* bird) and *the* before a non-countable noun (example: *the* water) or a specific countable noun (example: *the* birds on that tree) or plural nouns (example: *the* boys); nouns starting with a vowel are a special case (example: *an* eraser).

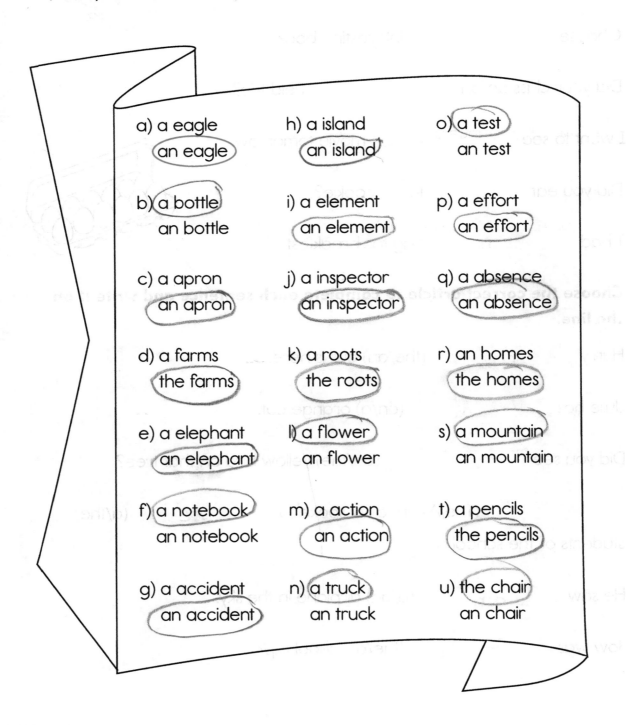

a) a eagle
an eagle

b) **a bottle**
an bottle

c) a apron
an apron

d) a farms
the farms

e) a elephant
an elephant

f) **a notebook**
an notebook

g) a accident
an accident

h) a island
an island

i) a element
an element

j) a inspector
an inspector

k) a roots
the roots

l) **a flower**
an flower

m) a action
an action

n) **a truck**
an truck

o) **a test**
an test

p) a effort
an effort

q) a absence
an absence

r) an homes
the homes

s) **a mountain**
an mountain

t) a pencils
the pencils

u) **the chair**
an chair

Exercises

Language

2. Read the story below and fill in the missing articles. Use the word bank, if you need help.

| an | a | the | a | the | a | the | a | a | the |

Once upon _____a_____ time, there was _____a_____ beautiful princess who lived in a castle on _____a_____ island. Every day, she walked down to the shore and gazed over the water at the village on the other side and wished she could go for a visit. One day, a small boat appeared on the shore and _____the_____ princess climbed inside. It sailed across the lake to the village, where the princess got to meet many new people and a duck.

The princess was so happy at _____the_____ village that she forgot to go home. The sky became dark and all the villagers went home for their dinner. Suddenly, the princess was left alone in the village with the duck. "Oh, Mr. Duck!" the princess said. "I had _____a_____ wonderful time today, but I miss my home."

Mr. Duck gave a quack and set off down _____a_____ path. The princess decided to follow the duck. Eventually, they arrived at the shore and the princess gave _____a_____ happy laugh when she saw _____the_____ boat. She and the duck got in the boat and sailed back to the castle, where they lived happily ever after, with many more trips to _____the_____ village.

3. Circle the correct articles.

a) Emma saw (an/**the**) bird fly out (**an**/the) window.

b) Do you want (a/**an**/the) ice cream cone?

c) I would like (**an**/a/the) apple for (an/**a**/the) snack.

d) Meghan sharpened (a/**the**) pencils.

e) I saw (**a**/an) otter at the zoo.

f) Earth is (a/**the**) third planet from (a/**the**) sun.

4. Choose the sentences that have the correct articles.

a) Did you see the eagle flying above a trees?

b) Mary went to the store to buy a DVD.

c) An ostrich is a large bird that cannot fly.

d) Maple syrup is a best thing to have on pancakes!

e) Tommy adopted a dog from the animal shelter.

f) Kayla had a orange and the apple.

1. Write three sentences each for *a*, *an* and *the*.

a) a: I saw a author at the library.
A boy came to my house. It is a
sunny day.

b) an: I have an umbrella. This orange
is an tasty orange. This apple is an
tasty apple.

c) the: the mall is very crouded. The
shops in the mall are just
resturants. I got a hundred bullets
for the nerf gun i have

1. Write *a*, *an* or *the* as needed before each of the following words. The first one is done for you.

a) _an/the_ idea

b) _a/the_ ✓ boat

c) _the_ ✗ lemons

d) _a n/the_ ✓ computers

e) _an/the_ apple ✓

f) _an/the_ orange ✔

g) _a/the_ ✓ sea otter

h) _and/athe_ ✗ oval

i) _a/the_ cup ✓

j) _a/the_ ✓ drum

k) _the/an_ ✓ eraser

l) _a/an_ ✗ apology

m) _an/the_ ✓ airplane

n) _the/an_ ✓ episode

o) _the/a_ ✓ friend

p) _a/the_ ✓ birds

q) _the/a_ ✓ flowers

r) _the/a_ ✓ books

Exercises

Language

2. Follow the articles through the maze to the Finish.

Start

an	a	can	his	her	it
not	the	to	him	she	he
me	a	be	the	the	a
they	an	an	a	my	a

Finish

3. Help the picky frog find his way across the pond to the rock.

Hint: He only hops on lily pads with the correct article.

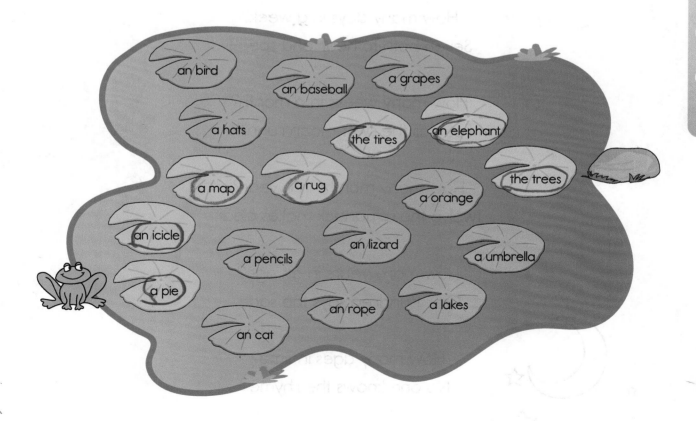

4. Read the poem below and circle all the articles.

How Many Seconds? – Christina Rossetti

How many seconds in a minute?
Sixty, and no more in it.

How many minutes in an hour?
Sixty for sun and shower.

How many hours in a day?
Twenty-four for work and play.

How many days in a week?
Seven both to hear and speak.

How many weeks in a month?
Four, as the swift moon runn'th.

How many months in a year?
Twelve the almanack makes clear.

How many years in an age?
One hundred says the sage.

How many ages in time?
No one knows the rhyme.

JULY						
SU	MO	TU	WE	TH	FR	SA
						1
2	3	4	5	6	7	8
9	10	11	12	13	14	15
16	17	18	19	20	21	22
23	24	25	26	27	28	29
30	31					

Exercises

Language

(handwritten top margin: su ← boy → Anurag. / boy / Common)

1. Circle the nouns in the following sentences. The first one is done for you.

(handwritten: Common → boy / Propernou → Anu. / Pronoun —)

a) The (cat) chased the (bird).

b) A (woman) talked on the (telephone).

c) The (house) was painted green.

d) The (boy) rode his (bicycle).

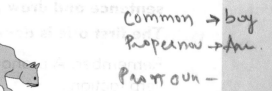

2. Underline the common nouns, circle the proper nouns, and place an X on the pronouns in the following text. One of each is done for you.

My <u>friend</u> (Tara) moved to (Thunder Bay, Ontario.)

Since ~~she~~ left, ~~I~~ have often sent ~~her~~ emails.

~~I~~ miss ~~her~~ and ~~her~~ dog, (Milo.) This summer,

~~I~~ will visit ~~her~~ and ~~we~~ will go walking along

the <u>shore</u> of the (Current) River. ~~I~~ have

many things to tell ~~her~~ when ~~we~~ meet.

Language

27

Exercises

Language

1. **Choose the correct pronoun from the word bank to complete each sentence and draw a line from the pronoun to the noun it replaces. The first one is done for you.**

Remember: A pronoun replaces the noun that is the subject (doer) of the verb (action).

~~we~~	you	~~he~~	~~she~~	~~I~~	~~they~~

a) The king put people in prison. ___He___ was a bad king.

b) The people were afraid of this bad king. ___they___ were scared.

c) The girl was ready to board the airplane. ___she___ put on her backpack and walked to the gate.

d) My name is Mark. ___I___ am glad to meet you.

e) Anita and I had a great time at the park. ___we___ really enjoyed ourselves!

f) Jim, you had a lot of fun with your friends yesterday. Did ___you___ play soccer with them?

2. **Fill in the blanks with *he, she, it* or *they* in the following sentences.**

a) My sister has a nice red dress. ___she___ loves it.

b) My mother and my grandmother were born in Canada. ___they___ are Canadians.

c) My friends are travelling abroad. ___they___ are visting Iceland.

d) A lioness hunts at night. ___it___ feeds its family.

e) Gorillas sleep in nests. ___it___ change nests every night.

f) I love watching an action movie. ___it___ is thrilling.

g) My music teacher, Mr. Roberts, sings in a choir. ___she___ has rehearsals every Saturday.

3. Replace each noun in bold with the correct pronoun from the word bank. The first one is done for you.

they	he	it	he

Eric is a young boy who lives in Victoria. ___He___ draws each day in his blue

notebook. ___it___ is very dear to **Eric**. ___He___ does not want to lose it

and takes good care of his notebook. Today, Eric drew his **friends** from

school. ___they___ are happy to see his nice drawings.

4. Circle the nouns that are the subjects of the following sentences. To help you, first underline the verb (action) and then identify the subject (doer of the action).

Ex.: The ⟨children⟩ <u>eat</u> fruit salad.

a) ⟨Bella⟩ <u>loves</u> her white goat.

b) ⟨Flowers⟩, ⟨grass⟩ and ⟨hay⟩ <u>grow</u> in the fields.

c) My ⟨grandmother⟩ often <u>tells</u> me the same story.

d) ⟨Jack⟩ and ⟨Mary⟩ would really like to have a bike.

e) In this story, fairies are nice.

5. Answer true or false.

a) A proper noun always starts with a capital letter. _____

b) A proper noun can contain more than one word. _____

6. **Underline the proper nouns and circle the common nouns in the following sentences and copy them to the correct column below. The first sentence is done for you.**

Remember: common nouns are general names for things (example: chair), while proper nouns name specific people, places or animals (example: Anna, New York, Snoopy) and always start with a capital letter.

a) Malika is my sister.

b) Mark lived in Montreal before moving to England.

c) The Titanic hit an iceberg.

d) I love chocolate ice cream.

e) My dog's name is Rex.

f) I will go play at Fountain Park after school.

Common Nouns	Proper Nouns
sister	Malika
Iceberg	Mark
dog	Montreal
I	England
	Titanic
	Rex

TEST 6

1. Write a proper noun for each common noun.

a) city _Toronto_

b) country _Canada_

c) person (female) _Ankita_

d) person (male) _Anurag_

e) store _Walmart_

f) movie _sonic_

g) street _Tiller trail_

h) pet _Tommy_

2. Choose two common nouns from the above list and write them in a sentence.

I live in Toronto, Canada. I love watching movies.

3. Write a sentence including three proper nouns, one for a person, one for a place, and one for an animal.

My name is Aarav and I live in Toronto Canada, me and my pet Tommy love going on walks.

4. Replace the underlined noun in each sentence with the correct pronoun from the word bank.

they	he	it	she	we

a) Where is <u>the book</u>?

Where is it

b) <u>Adam</u> went home.

he went home

c) <u>Anne</u> loves her hat.

She loves her hat

d) <u>Nick and Roger</u> went to the park.

They went to the park

e) <u>Nicole and I</u> play the piano.

we play the piano

1. **Read the following letter and find the proper nouns. Correct them so that they start with capital letters and write them in the correct columns below. The first few are done for you.**

Hello jackie,
(J)

I want to thank you for inviting me to your house in hamilton last weekend. *(H)*
I enjoyed our walk around that beautiful pond. Your dog, max, made me laugh *(M)*
when he tried to bite your horse, cinnamon. *(C)*

On my way back to toronto, I spoke to a girl named paula. She studies *(T)* *(P)*
medicine at the university of toronto. She was very interesting. I wonder what I
will do in the future. I am waiting to hear from you!

emily

Places	People	Animals
Hamilton	Jackie	Max
Toronto	Paula	Cinnamon

2. **Rewrite the following sentence using lowercase and uppercase letters correctly. It is started for you.**

MARY AND HER DOG CANDY ARE WALKING ON GRANVILLE
STREET IN VANCOUVER.

Mary and her dog Candy are walking
on Granville street in Vancouver

3. **Read the following story. Circle each pronoun (he, she, they, it, etc.) and draw a line to the noun it replaces. The first one is done for you. Then, write them in the chart below as shown.**

One day, a boy and his father planned on going fishing. They went to find their gear. They looked in the garage for the fishing rods. They found them. Then they looked for their boots. The boy asked his mother to help find his boots. She found them. The boy went looking for his hat. He found it. The father looked for his fishing net. He found it. They were ready to go. Wait a minute — where are the car keys? The father found them! Off they went.

Pronoun	Noun it replaces
They	a boy and his father
They	They looked for fishing rods
The	They looked for their boots
The	She found them
They	he found it
The	Where are the car keys
He	looking for his hat
Off	father found them
go	were ready

4. Rewrite the following sentences using the correct pronoun in place of the underlined noun. Use the word bank for help.

he	she	they	it

Example: <u>The house</u> is blue.

__It is blue.__

a) <u>My sister</u> likes her bicycle.

_____

b) <u>The farmer</u> rode his horse into the stable.

_____

c) <u>The tree</u> is tall.

_____

d) <u>The dogs</u> barked loudly.

_____

5. Complete each sentence with the correct pronoun from the word bank. The first one is done for you.

I	you	he	she	it	we	~~they~~

a) Yes, the students are here. _____They_____ are in the classroom.

b) I have to be responsible as _____ am the oldest.

c) Do you know Marge? _____ is the most popular girl in school.

d) My brother and I go to school daily by bus. _____ are waiting for the bus now.

e) You went to the park yesterday. What did _____ do there?

f) I don't like Jim. _____ is always mean to me.

g) Don't touch that shoe! _____ is dirty.

TEST 7

1. **Place the following words in the correct columns. Make sure they match up. The first pair is done for you.**

~~flowers~~	mat	puppy	lady	feet	men
foot	lamps	man	hands	hand	candy
books	mats	child	cookie	ladies	puppies
book	lamp	cookies	children	~~flower~~	candies

Singular	Plural
flower	flowers

1. Use ten of the words from the previous page in sentences of your own.

Remember: Singular means one, and plural means more than one.

a) _____

b) _____

c) _____

d) _____

e) _____

f) _____

g) _____

h) _____

i) _____

j) _____

2. Make the nouns below plural (more than one).

Remember: For most nouns, you only have to add an 's' at the end for the plural, but some nouns are different. One of those is done for you.

a) knife   knives

b) toy _____

c) letter _____

d) kitten _____

e) car _____

f) dog _____

g) tomato _____

h) phone _____

i) shoe _____

j) house _____

k) jug _____

l) horse _____

m) woman _____

n) bike _____

o) map _____

p) stair _____

q) key _____

r) glass _____

s) pizza _____

t) chair _____

u) table _____

v) wife _____

w) potato _____

x) leaf _____

y) ball _____

z) child _____

3. Usually, the letter "s" is added to the end of a word to change it to the plural form. There are some exceptions. Use the word bank to help you write the plural form of these exceptional nouns. One is done for you.

babies	children	feet	men	~~potatoes~~	
boxes	crises	foxes	mice	teeth	wolves
buses	families	knives	stories	wives	women

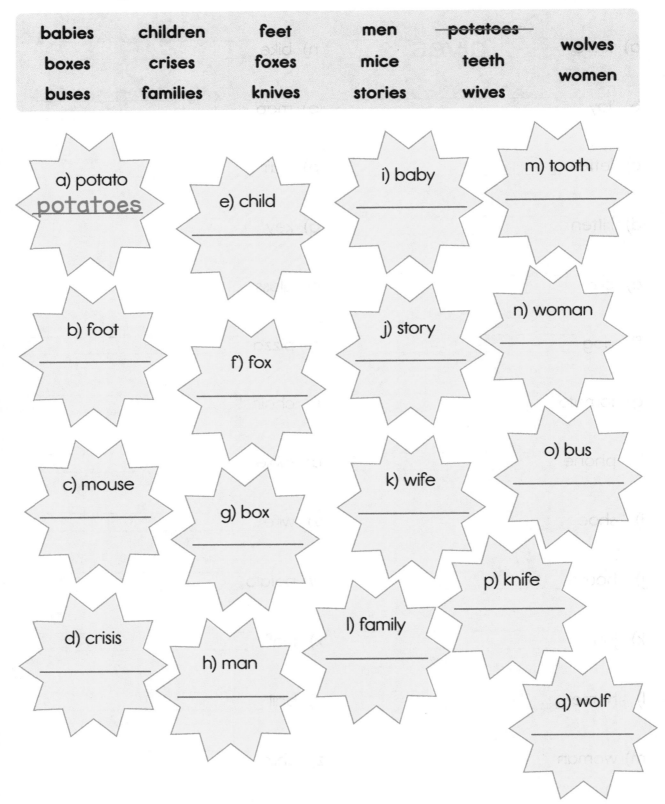

a) potato
potatoes

b) foot
_____

c) mouse
_____

d) crisis
_____

e) child
_____

f) fox
_____

g) box
_____

h) man
_____

i) baby
_____

j) story
_____

k) wife
_____

l) family
_____

m) tooth
_____

n) woman
_____

o) bus
_____

p) knife
_____

q) wolf
_____

Exercises

Language

TEST 8

1. Read the following words. Correct the plural or singular forms of the nouns to match the articles or adjectives.

a) a planes _____

b) two cherry _____

c) ten mouse _____

d) three leaf _____

e) all the child _____

f) many bus _____

g) a few orange _____

h) one men _____

i) a keys _____

j) two shoe _____

2. Make the following nouns plural.

a) goose _____

b) boat _____

c) mouse _____

d) shoe _____

e) table _____

f) man _____

g) boy _____

h) cat _____

i) head _____

j) telephone _____

k) fox _____

l) camera _____

m) book _____

n) lady _____

o) friend _____

p) army _____

3. Rewrite these words in the singular form.

a) numbers: _____

b) pages: _____

c) cars: _____

d) stories: _____

e) children: _____

f) teams: _____

g) men: _____

h) teeth: _____

i) pens: _____

1. Write the plural form for each of these nouns.

a) knife
_____

g) date
_____

n) head
_____

u) man
_____

o) foot
_____

b) bird
_____

h) mouse
_____

v) potato
_____

c) eraser
_____

i) movie
_____

p) lion
_____

w) dish
_____

q) tooth
_____

d) child
_____

j) blueberry
_____

x) word
_____

r) tie
_____

e) story
_____

k) fox
_____

s) star
_____

y) shoe
_____

l) boy
_____

f) monkey
_____

m) baby
_____

t) spoon
_____

z) shirt
_____

2. Write the plural form of each noun below.

a) knife _____

b) prize _____

c) half _____

d) tomato _____

e) foot _____

f) woman _____

g) shelf _____

h) bracelet _____

i) child _____

j) cup _____

k) scissors _____

l) wire _____

m) niece _____

n) house _____

o) boy _____

p) lighter _____

q) dress _____

r) hammer _____

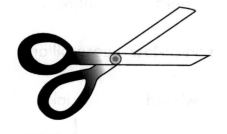

3. Follow the path of the nouns in the <u>masculine singular</u> form to get to the Finish. The first few have been done for you.

Start

king	boy	pens	paws	light	window
squirrels	man	queens	finger	stars	daughter
ear	host	couch	moons	eye	widowers
spoon	lion	house	ship	months	walk
smiles	father	thought	lakes	lions	aunt
boys	uncle	tiger	hospital	suits	ducks
phone	walls	prince	departure	plane	flowers
mice	feet	emperor	grandfather	bird	woman
songs	printers	glasses	actor	feather	foxes
paper	computers	lioness	nephew	crocodiles	accidents
tree	girl	apple	waiter	bull	plates
curtains	cow	chewing gum	books	husband	television
oranges	necklace	drawers	horses	hero	tigress
file	table	chairs	flute	son-in-law	caterpillars
piano	leaf	notes	pear	wizard	buck

Finish

Exercises

Language

TEST 9

1. Circle the verb in each sentence.

a) Cedric (went) to the grocery (store).

b) Anne and Marie (go) to the park.

c) He (studied) for the math test yesterday.

d) Stephanie (plays) the piano.

e) Lolita (gave) the book to me.

f) It (snowed) yesterday.

g) My mother (baked) my favourite cookies.

h) I (love) chocolate ice cream.

2. Indicate at what time the action of each sentence below occurs. Place an X in the correct column.

	Past	Present
Steven played in the orchestra at school.	X	
Jim went to Italy this summer.	X	
Nadine is watching television.		X
We play outside all day.		X
I read a book yesterday.	X	
Do you want to go for a swim?		X

1. **Underline the verb (action word) in each sentence.**

a) We <u>ate</u> at the restaurant. (Past)

b) The students <u>studied</u> the continents. (Past)

c) They <u>like</u> the party. (Past)

d) The pirates <u>looked</u> for treasure. (Past)

e) Please <u>don't</u> be late for school. (Present)

f) The seagulls <u>flew</u> through the air. (Past)

g) The whale <u>swam</u> in the water. (Past)

h) The birds <u>built</u> a nest. (Past)

i) The children <u>wrote</u> a letter. (Past)

2. **Change the verbs in the following sentences from the past to the present. One is done for you.**

a) The boy bought a candy.

   <u>The boy buys a candy.</u>

b) The lady baked cookies.

   _____

   _____

c) The teacher told a story.

   _____

   _____

d) I played a song.

   _____

   _____

e) The student packed his books.

   _____

3. Underline the verbs in the following sentences. Then, write whether the action happens in the past or present. The first one is done for you.

a) The kids <u>skipped</u> Halloween. _____ past _____

b) My uncle <u>was</u> in Florida. _____ past _____

c) Carol <u>picks</u> apples. _____ present _____

d) We <u>see</u> the CN Tower from the window of our room. _____ present _____

e) I <u>created</u> a website on cars. _____ past _____

f) She <u>finished</u> her project on time. _____ Past _____

g) She <u>visited</u> us last year. _____ past _____

h) I <u>want</u> some water. _____ present _____

i) I am <u>scared</u> of ghosts. _____ present _____

j) I <u>am</u> a girl. _____ Present _____

k) I <u>served</u> pasta for dinner. _____ Past _____

4. Write a sentence where the action happens in the present.

I am watching a movie

5. Write a sentence where the action happens in the past.

I was a good swimer

Exercises

Language

6. **Circle the sentence that matches each picture.**

a)

Mark plays hockey.
Mark pays for his book.

e)

The man sits.
The man swims.

i)

The father washes the dishes.
The father dries the dishes.

b)

The child sleeps.
The child talks.

f)

Sarah drinks.
Sarah eats.

j)

Joshua thinks.
Joshua eats.

c)

The lady smiles.
The lady cries.

g)

The mother sleeps.
The mother reads.

k)

Nathan talks.
Nathan sleeps.

d)

The boy reads.
The boy runs.

h)

Rick sings.
Rick sits.

l)

Anna sits.
Anna paints.

Exercises

Language

7. Use the verbs in the word bank to complete the sentences below. The first one is done for you.

cries	~~pays~~	skate	takes	watches
listens	puts	slide	walks	writes

a)

The girl __pays__ for her book.

b)

The girl _____ because she is sad.

c)

The girl _____ TV.

d)

The boy _____ to music.

e)

My cousin _____ in his workbook.

f)

My brother _____ the dog.

g)

The boys _____ down the hill.

h)

My friends _____ on the ice rink.

i)

Andy _____ his pyjamas on.

j)

Carla _____ the bus to school.

8. Circle the verbs in the sentences below. The first one is done for you.

a) Mary (eats) pizza every Friday.

b) Robert is a (fast) runner.

c) Justin (wants) an apple.

d) Bianca (bought) a new coat.

e) Sam (listens) to music.

f) Don't (close) the door.

g) That (was) a good movie.

9. Read each sentence below. Is it in the past tense or the present tense? Place an X in the correct column. The first one is done for you.

	Past	Present
a) I am a good dancer.		X
b) Laura was with us yesterday.	X	
c) Susan is reading a book at this moment.		X
d) They gave a present to their father last week.	X	
e) Claudio went to Italy last year.	X	
f) Benjamin wrote a letter last night.	X	
g) I am leaving the house.		X

1. Rewrite the following story in the past tense.

Jennifer is a doctor. She likes helping people get better. She works in a big hospital. One day, she sees a young girl trip and fall as she crosses the street. Jennifer quickly takes her to the hospital. She cleans the scrapes on the girl's arms and legs. She puts a special ointment on them and bandages them. Then, she talks cheerfully with the girl till her mother comes to pick her up. The girl tells her mother on the way home that she wants to become a doctor when she grows up.

Jennifer was a doctor. She liked helping people get better. She works in a big hospital. One day, she sees a young girl trip and fall as she crossed the street. Jenniffer quicly taked her to the hospital. She cleaned the scrapes on the girls arms and legs. She puts a special ointment on them and bandaged them. The girl told her mother on the way home that she wants to become a doctor when she grows up.

1. Underline the verbs. One is done for you.

shoe   story   ~~fixing~~

eating   yanked   underlined

sleeping   running   table

notebook   see   looking

2. Rewrite the following text, changing all verbs to the present.

Max watched television while doing his homework. His mom told him it was not a good idea. He agreed and turned off the television. He turned on the radio to listen to music. His dad came and told him it was really not a good idea. Max agreed and turned off the radio. He understood and did his homework in silence.

_____

_____

_____

_____

_____

_____

3. **Choose the correct verb to complete each sentence below in the past tense. The first one is done for you.**

a) The birds (fly, flew) away.

__The birds flew away.__

b) A terrible tsunami (hit, hits) Indonesia yesterday.

c) My neighbour (planted, plants) beautiful flowers.

d) Jack (sees, saw) a deer on the side of the road.

e) They (watched, watch) television all night long.

f) We (finish, finished) our homework very quickly.

4. **Use the following verbs in sentences.**

a) walked:

b) walks:

c) talked:

d) talks:

5. **Find the following verbs in the word search puzzle. The words can be up to down, left to right, or diagonal.**

walk	look	choose	smile	laugh
like	stop	play	follow	cry
ran	bought	eaten	win	bite
threw	shake	fill	water	loved
wrote	read	jump	dance	moved
turned	skipped	opened	shout	say

```
F I L L C H O O S E J U M P T
O T T C O M O V E D L O O K E
A R S H A K E P E A T E N S U
U S L R A T U R N E D R A N F
R L W R O T E S A Y L O V E D
E L B O S A I O P E N E D B M
A L A G D K L A U G H P F L W
D L U U T W I L I K E T O R I
A B I T E H A P C R Y I L O N
E U D H S O R T P E M H L I G
W E E I H L T E E E R E O R U
S A A E O L S V W R D D W E C
W N L I U B O U G H T P L A Y
U N B K T D A N C E M P T X S
T M S T O P H O S M I L E E L
```

6. Circle the verb in each list that correctly matches the picture. The first one is done for you.

a)

basket (skate) shoes

b)

surf   heart   eye

c)

hay   tray   play

d)

cry   sad   baby

e)

smile   squirrel   moon

f)

clock   tie   minute

g)

shuffle   elf   short

h)

star   brush   red

i)

eat   air   black

j)

knife   outside   wake up

k)

girl   dress   boy

l)

blow   country   wall

7. **Place an X in the correct column to show whether each sentence is set in the past or the present. One is done for you.**

	Past	Present
a) Please, don't do that.		X
b) Thomas was a great dancer when he was young.		
c) William joined us later in the evening.		
d) My friends were at my birthday party yesterday.		
e) Emily went shopping last weekend.		
f) Jim watches a good movie.		
g) Gabrielle and Rachel did their chores last night.		

8. **Underline each sentence that has a verb in the past tense.**

a) My friends are nice.

b) My friends went to the movie theatre without me.

c) She walked beside me.

d) The taxi is at the front door.

e) Did you like the song?

9. **Underline the verb (action word) in each sentence.**

a) He cried.

b) He sleeps.

c) We stopped.

d) She laughed.

e) She sang.

f) She eats.

g) They danced.

h) They read.

Exercises

Language

1. Rewrite each sentence using the <u>feminine and plural</u> noun for each of the underlined words.

a) The <u>king</u> is tired.

_____

_____

b) My <u>nephew</u> is fixing the car.

_____

_____

c) The <u>waiter</u> was very nice to the <u>man</u>.

_____

_____

d) The <u>hero</u> saved the <u>boy</u>.

_____

_____

e) The <u>bull</u> glared at the <u>gander</u>.

_____

_____

f) The <u>husband</u> spoke to the <u>father</u>.

_____

_____

g) The <u>landlord</u> is not home.

_____

_____

h) The <u>grandfather</u> spoke to his <u>son</u>.

_____

_____

i) The <u>prince</u> waved to the crowd.

_____

_____

Language

1. **Write the feminine and plural forms of each noun below. Use the word bank on the next page if you need help. One is done for you.**

Noun	Plural noun	Feminine noun
uncle	uncles	aunt
king		
lion		
grandfather		
policeman		
husband		
grandson		
bull		
man		
stepfather		
peacock		
rooster		
buck		
wizard		
son		
fox		
nephew		
prince		

Exercises

Language

Noun	Plural noun	Feminine noun
emperor		
gander		
gentleman		
brother		
father		
boy		
hero		

Exercises

Language

daughter   empress   heroine   goose   lady   mother   ~~uncles~~

policemen   bulls   ganders   brothers   heroes   sons   vixen

boys   ~~aunt~~   roosters   witch   kings   peahen   girl

granddaughter   princess   gentlemen   wife   grandsons   foxes

cow   queen   lioness   grandfathers   princes   doe   woman

stepfathers   nephews   peacocks   men   lions   emperors

sister   wizards   stepmother   hen   grandmother

policewoman   husbands   fathers   niece   bucks

2. Complete each sentence by choosing the correct noun (singular or plural) and writing it on the blank line.

a) The white _____ (lamb/lambs) lives on the farm.

b) The busy _____ (farmer/farmers) milks the cows.

c) The wild _____ (wolf/wolves) howl in the forest.

d) The striped _____ (zebra/zebras) are dazzling.

e) The school _____ (bus/buses) carry children to school.

f) My sister had an _____ (orange/oranges) for her breakfast.

g) I visited a haunted _____ (house/houses) in Scotland.

h) My best _____ (friend/friends) has brown eyes.

i) The _____ (gem/gems) are in the safe.

j) The _____ (actresses/actress) in this movie is my sister.

k) The woman who served us dinner at the restaurant last night was a _____ (waiter/waitress).

TEST 12

1. **Find the following singular, plural, masculine and feminine nouns in the word search. The words can be up to down, left to right, or diagonal.**

goose	gander	boy	girl	man	woman
wizard	witch	uncle	aunt	bull	cow
stone	stones	stapler	staplers	box	boxes
pencil	pencils	rock	rocks	cap	caps
knife	knives	guard	guards	nephew	niece
		father	mother		

```
P G M S T O N E S S C W O S A S G V P C
A A F R N I E C E S S N I T K P A I W C
I O W O M A N L I E O E K T O A R E R E
V D G F E O W K S U N C L E C R C A P L
A H O A E N X T E L E U G X D H L B B T
S T O B O X D T I G L G N K G E C T U S
A B S E E P C R O C K S I A W T K R L O
H L E L N E P H E W K U S R E U T F L I
P P B O Y S A R F A T H E R G A N D E R
N A E C N P T W K E H M O T H E R R C N
O H B A H E N A I U S G L E N S A H S R
S O R N O N E C P Z H T R I I C A V T H
L B A G E C E O L L A G U A R D A N A S
E C N P O I S E P L E R R O C K H A P F
E C R S E L S T O N E R D N S E P N L P
E O G U A R D S V T F U S B O X E S E D
G L I A O N X E C S T U I A U N T E R S
S P T R M L O A S W D P W M A N D U R S
P E N C I L S S O N C O W K N I V E S A
P B I K N I F E F R O T B E N C A P S E
```

1. Make the following nouns plural. Remember, "plural" means more than one. The first one is done for you.

Singular	Plural
cat	cats
book	
mouse	
shoe	
goose	
strawberry	
activity	
daisy	
fork	
gift	
elf	
roof	
wheel	
owl	
computer	
carrot	

Exercises

Language

2. Choose any five nouns from the previous page and use its singular and plural words in sentences of your own.

a) singular: _____

_____

   plural: _____

_____

b) singular: _____

_____

   plural: _____

_____

c) singular: _____

_____

   plural: _____

_____

d) singular: _____

_____

   plural: _____

_____

e) singular: _____

_____

   plural: _____

_____

Exercises

Language

3. Match each masculine noun on the left to the correct feminine noun on the right.

priest	duchess
duke	mother
father	goddess
prince	priestess
god	princess
uncle	wife
son	niece
husband	girl
boy	aunt
nephew	daughter

4. Choose any three nouns from above and use their masculine and feminine words in sentences of your own.

a) masculine: _____

_____

feminine: _____

_____

b) masculine: _____

_____

feminine: _____

_____

c) masculine: _____

_____

feminine: _____

_____

Exercises

Language

1. Underline the adjectives in the following text.

The Crow and The Fox

Perched on the low branch of a <u>tall</u> tree, a crow was eating a <u>delicious</u> piece of cheese. Just then, a <u>clever</u> fox came, <u>attracted</u> to the mouth-watering smell of the cheese.

"Hello, Mrs. Crow," he said. "You have <u>beautiful</u> feathers. They are the most <u>shiny</u> feathers I have ever seen. And so <u>soft</u> too!"

The <u>conceited</u> crow was so happy at the <u>flattery</u> and could not keep quiet. She answered, "Thank you, Mr. Fox, so kind of you!"

However, when Mrs. Crow opened her mouth to speak, the cheese fell to the ground and the <u>clever</u> fox ate the <u>delicious</u> cheese.

2. Find a synonym for each of the following adjectives.

a) delicious: _tasty_

b) beautiful: _nice_

c) friendly: _kind_

d) clever: _smart_

e) costly: _expensive_

f) small: _little_

3. Find an antonym for each of the following adjectives.

a) scared: _brave_

b) beautiful: _ugly_

c) sad: _happy_

d) tiny: _large_

e) small: _Big_

f) soft: _hard_

Adjectives are describing words. They tell more about a person, place or thing. For example: in *fluffy cloud*, *fluffy* tells what the cloud is like.

1. Write one sentence for each adjective.

a) blue: A color wich is used for degsins

b) happy: being in a good mood

c) hard: feeling presuarised so much

d) large: A thing wich is so big

e) sad: A dab mood

2. Use each adjective below to describe a person, in a sentence of your own.

a) beautiful: This is a beutiful day

b) excited: I am exited for my gift

c) helpful: These people are helpful

d) kind: People are here

e) tall: This statue is tall

f) thoughtful: This person is thoughtful

3. **Use each adjective below in a sentence of your own, to describe a feeling.**

a) angry: Today my family was angry.

b) bored: I was bored during the light show.

c) confused: I was confused what was going on at fest

d) grumpy: My dog was grumpy today

e) lonely: I felt lonely when I switched schools

f) friendly: The locals at swilserland were freindly

g) happy: Today is a happy day

h) lively: I feel so lively after playing cricket

4. **Use each adjective below in a sentence of your own, to describe the size of something.**

a) big: That house his realy big

b) narrow: This hallway is realy narrow

c) small: The painting is realy small compare to others

d) wide: this field is wide and opene

e) large: That fireplace is realy large

f) thin: My friend is realy thin

g) short: That tree is very short

h) tall: one of my friend is as tall a 8th grader

5. Replace each underlined word with its antonym (word that has the opposite meaning). The first one is done for you.

a) Mario <u>likes</u> attending dance shows.

Mario ___hates___ attending dance shows.

b) My neighbour's dog is very <u>friendly</u>.

My neighbour's dog is very _unfriendly._

c) When it is too <u>cold</u>, we play <u>inside</u>.

When it is too _hot_, we play _outside_.

d) I am so <u>happy</u> to be on vacation.

I am so _sad_ to be on vacation.

e) Lea's hair is too <u>long</u>.

Lea's hair is too _short_.

f) The movie that I saw yesterday was very <u>interesting</u>.

The movie that I saw yesterday was very _boring_.

g) My dad's moustache is <u>black</u>.

My dad's moustache is _white_.

h) I <u>remembered</u> that day.

I _forgot_ that day.

Choose from the word bank to complete questions 1 & 2:

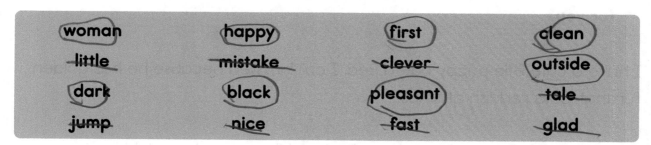

woman   happy   first   clean

little   mistake   clever   outside

dark   black   pleasant   tale

jump   nice   fast   glad

1. **Write the antonym of each of the following words.**

a) light _Dark_

b) dirty _clean_

c) inside _outside_

d) unpleasant _pleasant_

e) last _first_

f) sad _happy_

g) white _black_

h) man _Woman_

2. **Find a synonym for each of the following words.**

a) cheerful _glade_

b) story _tavle_

c) quick _fast_

d) good _nice_

e) smart _clever_

f) leap _Jump_

g) fault _mistake_

h) small _little_

3. **Underline the adjectives in the following sentences.**

a) Anastasia is wearing a beautiful red dress.

b) Terry has long, black, curly hair.

c) We have a beautiful home.

d) I am a tall girl.

e) My friend Zoe's cat is very smart.

f) You have a wonderful jacket.

Language

1. Underline the adjectives in the following story. The first one is done for you.

I have a <u>cute</u> little puppy called Red. I call him Red because he has golden fur that looks reddish at times.

One sunny afternoon this summer, Red and I went to the neighbouring beach to play. I tried teaching him to chase my beach ball, but he was so excited that he chased his stubby tail instead.

We enjoyed swimming together in the warm blue water. We can't wait to go to that lovely beach again!

2. Circle the adjectives within the underlined words.

a) <u>The cute kittens</u> were born yesterday.

b) <u>The majestic African lions</u> live in the zoo near my house.

c) <u>The little monkeys</u> lost <u>their delicious bananas</u>.

d) <u>The striped zebra</u> runs around its cage all day.

3. Match each antonym to its partner.

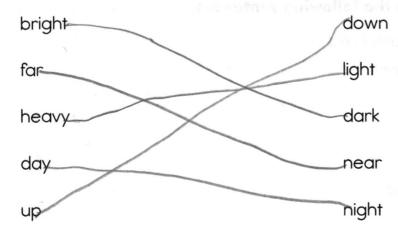

bright   down

far   light

heavy   dark

day   near

up   night

4. Complete the story by choosing and adding adjectives from the following word bank or add your own words — be as silly as you like!

slippery	fuzzy	tiny	many
shiny	big	teensy-weensy	sparkly
amazing	bigger	one	exciting
blue	biggest	five	invisble
yellow	huge	billions	lucky
polka-dot	enormous	some	angora
striped	teeny	several	dark
crazy	different	soft	comfortable

The Costume Shop

In our town, we have no ordinary costume shop. Some people say it's

___crazy___ or even downright ___amazing___! There are

___some___ wizard robes covered with ___several___ sparkles. The

___dark___ gorilla suits feel as ___soft___ as a(n) ___comfortable___

sweater. The ___lucky___ princess gowns are so ___shiny___ that you

might need to wear ___five___ sunglasses to look at them. There are

___some___ wigs, ___striped___ shoes, ___invisible___ wands,

___sparkly___ hats, and many other _____ things. You should stop

by there next Halloween!

69

5. Write down three words and their antonyms on the lines below.

a) _____Dark_____ is the opposite of _____bright_____.

b) _____good_____ is the opposite of _____bad_____.

c) _____Strong_____ is the opposite of _____weak_____.

6. Draw a line from each word to its synonym. You can consult a dictionary if you are unsure of the meaning of a word.

loyal	angry
mad	icy
draw	sketch
delicious	horrible
awful	faithful
loving	tasty
cold	caring

7. Read the story below. Then, trace an arrow from each underlined adjective to the noun it is describing. The first one is done for you.

One early morning I woke up, looked out my window, and saw

aliens in our backyard. After their shiny, silver spaceship landed, I watched

three huge aliens climb out and look around. The first alien had curly red

hair, three eyes, and long, bony fingers. The second alien had pointy ears

and a round nose that was covered in blue bumps. The third alien had six

short arms and six short legs and the longest tail I have ever seen. After that

day, I stopped eating so many crazy snacks before bed.

1. **Use the word bank to help you describe where the candy () is in each picture.**

between	in	to the left of	on	to the right of	under

a)

The candy is _____ the glass.

b)

The candy is _____ the two balloons.

c)

The candy is _____ the ice cream.

d)

The candy is _____ the candle.

e)

The candy is _____ the teapot.

f)

The candy is _____ the dog.

Language

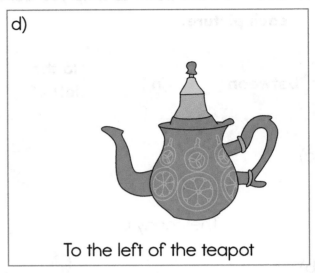

1. Read the directions below, then draw the snail where it belongs.

a)

On the table

d)

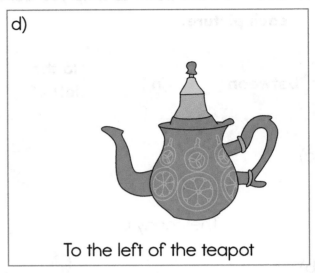

To the left of the teapot

b)

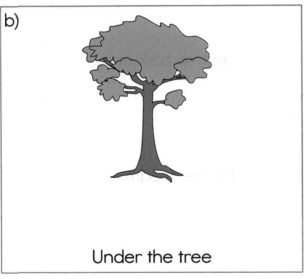

Under the tree

e)

Between the dog
and the boy

c)

In the bathtub

f)

To the right
of the hippopotamus

Exercises

Language

2. Read each sentence and choose the correct preposition from the word bank to complete it.

in	in front of	below	above	under	on

a) The telephone is _____ the table.

b) The floor is _____ the dog.

c) The clouds are _____ the trees.

d) The clothes are _____ the closet.

e) The placemat is _____ the plate.

f) The welcome mat is _____ the door.

3. Look at the map of the school below, and use the clues to label the classrooms.

SCHOOL

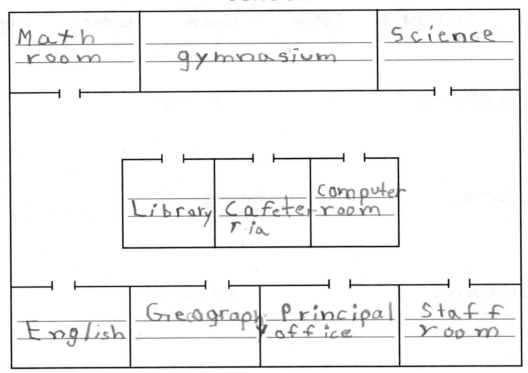

a) The Math Room is to the left of the Gymnasium.

b) The Cafeteria is between the Library and the Computer Room.

c) The English Room is in the bottom left corner.

d) The Science Room is to the right of the gymnasium.

e) The Cafeteria is above the Geography Room and below the Gymnasium.

f) The Principal's Office is beneath the Computer Room.

g) The Staff Room is in the bottom right corner.

h) The Library is in the middle to the left.

TEST 16

1. **Samra is lost. She is in front of the gymnasium and she wants to get to the library. Look at the map below and mark the path she needs to take.**

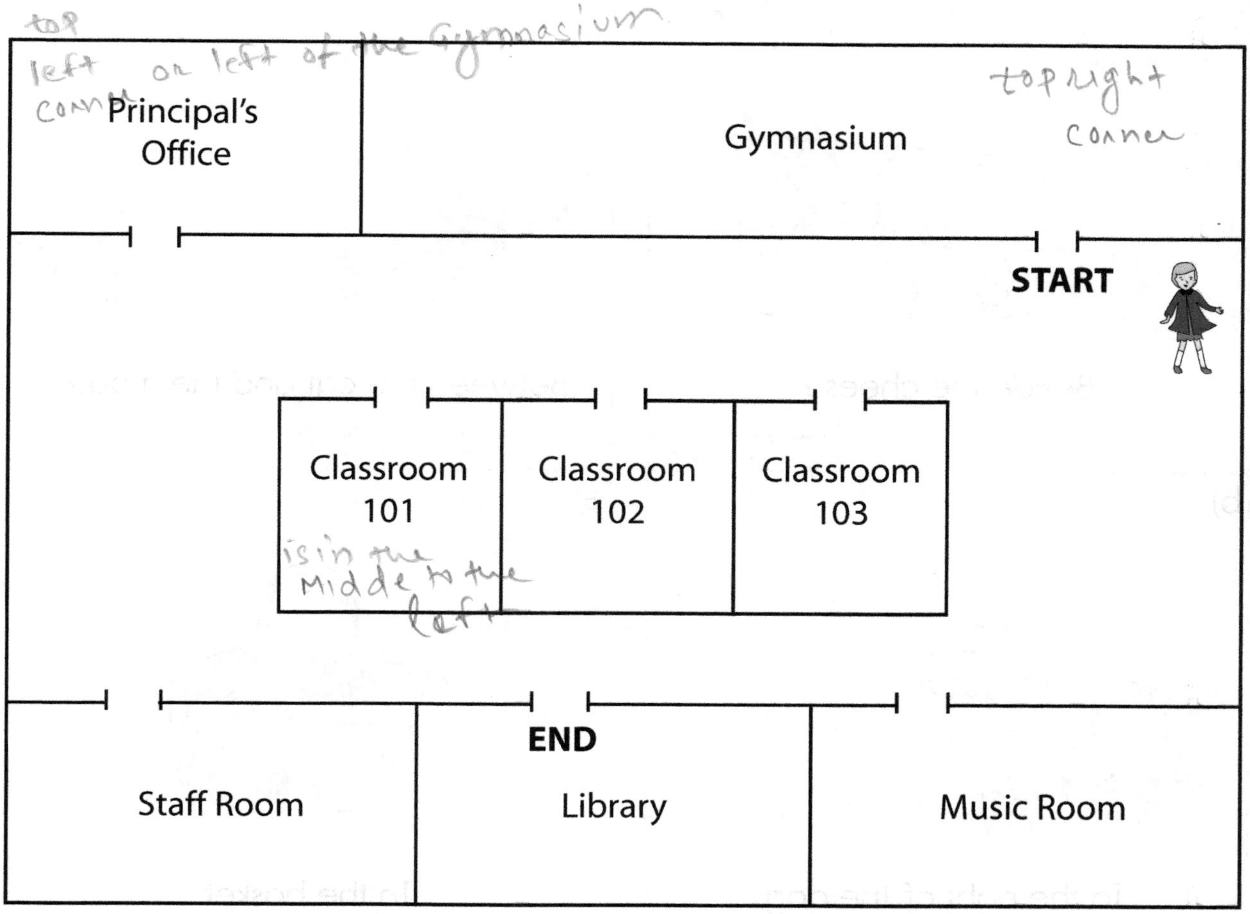
Principal's Office
Gymnasium
START
Classroom 101
Classroom 102
Classroom 103
END
Staff Room
Library
Music Room

2. **Now, write about the path Samra needs to follow, using words like *left, right, back, front, behind, before,* etc.**

____

____

____

____

____

____

____

1. Read the directions. Then, draw the apple where it belongs.

a)

Beside the cheese

d)

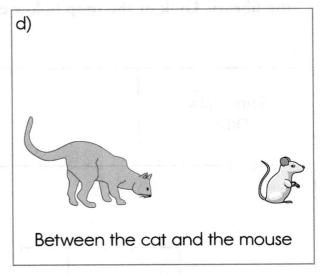

Between the cat and the mouse

b)

To the right of the dog

e)

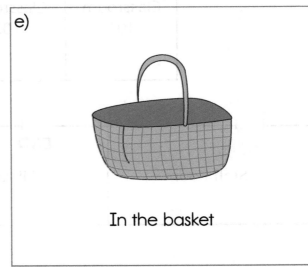

In the basket

c)

On the drum set

f)

Under the horse

2. Use the word bank to help you complete each sentence.

up	right	before	between	on
down	left	after	in	under

a)   I brush my teeth _____ I go to bed.

b)   The driver's seat is on the _____ side of a car.

c)   Look _____ in the sky!

d)   I don't like to go _____ to the basement. It is too dark and scary.

e)   Alexis will be here _____ 4:00 p.m. and 5:00 p.m.

f)   The doors of a school bus are on the_____ side.

g)   Jon is coming to my house _____ school.

h)   Don't forget to put a stamp _____ your envelope.

i)   Every day, my father parks his car _____ the garage.

j)   I am dry _____ my umbrella though it's raining.

3. Read the instructions. Then follow them and draw the objects.

a) An apple is in the middle.

b) A flower is to the right.

c) A banana is to the left.

d) A heart is between the apple and the banana.

e) A glove is beside the flower.

f) A circle is between the apple and the glove.

4. Follow the instructions.

a) Draw a tree.

b) Draw two apples in the tree.

c) Draw four apples under the tree.

d) Draw a girl to the right of the tree.

e) Draw a flower to the left of the tree.

1. Identify all the words that are *not* compound nouns.

pizza   sandpaper

bookcase   handbag

woman   fork

flowerpot   handshake

tradition   bedsheet

2. Use two of the above compound nouns in sentences.

a) _____

_____

b) _____

_____

3. Rewrite these verbs in their contracted form.

For example: They are not. ⟶ They aren't.

a) I am: _____ b) You will not do: _____ c) She did not: _____

4. Write the abbreviations for the following words.

a) Street _____ d) hour _____

b) foot _____ e) Friday _____

c) August _____ f) Mister _____

1. Circle the common part of each pair of compound words below. The first one is done for you.

a) under(ground)   (ground)skeeper

b) supermarket   superman

c) football   basketball

d) school bus   school bag

e) lifeguard   lifelike

f) dining table   table tennis

g) fish tank   water tank

h) toothpaste   toothbrush

i) blackboard   keyboard

j) full moon   moonlight

k) backstreet   streetlight

l) birthday   daylight

m) lamp post   table lamp

2. Separate each of the following compound words into two words. The first one is done for you.

a) backbone back + bone   e) without _____

b) afternoon _____   f) daylight _____

c) hamburger _____   g) hillside _____

d) somewhere _____   h) shoelace _____

A **contraction** is one new word usually made from two words. Some letters are left out and an apostrophe is added. For example: did not ⟶ didn't

3. Change the following words to their contractions. The first one is done for you.

a) we are

we're

b) do not

c) does not

d) you are

e) it is

4. Write the abbreviations for the days of the week. The first one is done for you.

a) Monday Mon.

b) Tuesday

c) Wednesday

d) Thursday

e) Friday

f) Saturday

g) Sunday

5. **Change the following words to their contractions. Be careful: The order of the letters changes for some of them.**

a) we have _____

b) will not _____

c) they are _____

d) I will _____

e) were not _____

An **abbreviation** is the shortened form of a word. For example, **Can.** or **CA** is the abbreviation of **Canada**, and **CDN** of **Canadian**. Remember: If a word begins with a capital letter, the abbreviation must also begin with a capital letter. Most abbreviations end with a period.

6. **Write the abbreviations for the months of the year. The first one is done for you.**

a) January _____ Jan. or JA _____

b) February _____

c) March _____

d) April _____

e) May _____

f) June _____

g) July _____

h) August _____

i) September _____

j) October _____

k) November _____

l) December _____

Exercises

Language

1. Write one compound word for each of the words below.

For example: bed ⇨ <u>bed</u>sheet; ball ⇨ basket<u>ball</u>

a) hand _____   i) sand _____

b) sun _____   j) eye _____

c) sea _____   k) man _____

d) fly _____   l) house _____

e) week _____   m) box _____

f) day _____   n) school _____

g) head _____   o) band _____

h) black _____   p) cross _____

2. Rewrite these verbs in their contracted form.

a) They do not: _____   d) I am not: _____

b) I did not: _____   e) They are: _____

c) She is not: _____   f) They will not: _____

3. Write the correct abbreviation for each word below. Use the word bank for help.

Jr.	Dec.	Sun.	in.

a) Junior _____   c) inch _____

b) Sunday _____   d) December _____

1. Use the words below to make compound words. Cross out the words in the list as you use them. The first one is done for you.

Example: hand+bag ⇨ handbag

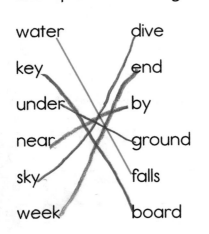
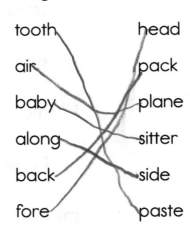
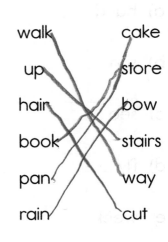

water   dive   tooth   head   walk   cake
key   end   air   pack   up   store
under   by   baby   plane   hair   bow
near   ground   along   sitter   book   stairs
sky   falls   back   side   pan   way
week   board   fore   paste   rain   cut

a) waterfalls

b) Keyboard

c) underground

d) nearby

e) skydive

f) weekend

g) toothpaste

h) airplane

i) babysitter

j) alongside

k) backpacke

l) forehead

m) walkway

n) upstairs

o) haircut

p) bookstore

q) pancake

r) rainbow

Exercises

Language

2. Rewrite these sentences using the contracted form of the underlined words.

Example: <u>I am</u> not your friend.

I'm not your friend.

a) <u>I am</u> not your best friend.

b) They <u>will not</u> see a movie tonight.

c) We <u>have not</u> eaten dinner yet.

d) She <u>has not</u> seen her grandmother in two years.

e) She <u>did not</u> fix her broken bicycle.

f) I <u>have not</u> studied for my test yet.

g) You <u>do not</u> want to share your candy.

h) She <u>is not</u> ready to go out.

i) <u>It is not</u> my turn to speak in front of the class.

j) They <u>do not</u> want to play outside.

3. Write the abbreviations for the province and territory names.

Hint: Think about how they are written in a postal address. The first one is done for you.

a) Newfoundland and Labrador __NL__   h) Saskatchewan _____

b) New Brunswick _____   i) Alberta _____

c) Nova Scotia _____   j) British Columbia _____

d) Prince Edward Island _____   k) Nunavut _____

e) Quebec _____   l) Yukon _____

f) Ontario _____   m) Northwest Territory _____

g) Manitoba _____

4. Match each word below to the correct abbreviation.

March	ON
Doctor	Thu.
Pound	Hwy.
Highway	Mar. or MR
Thursday	lb.
Ontario	Dr.

5. Change the following to their contractions.

a) have not _____   d) has not _____

b) would not _____   e) did not _____

c) is not _____

TEST 19

1. Circle the prefix in the following words, then rewrite each word without the prefix.

a) unhappy _____

b) retell _____

c) impossible _____

d) unkind _____

e) redo _____

f) unafraid _____

g) triangle _____

h) preschool _____

2. Underline the suffix in the following words, then rewrite each word without the suffix.

a) going _____

b) talked _____

c) saying _____

d) teaches _____

e) reading _____

f) doing _____

g) walking _____

h) circles _____

3. Circle the word that is not connected to the common root word. Write the common root word on the line.

a) active, allow, activated, activity _____

b) interests, interested, inside, uninteresting _____

c) running, reaches, reachable, unreached _____

d) obeyer, disobey, obeying, obtuse _____

e) disable, unable, enable, about _____

Language

87

Prefixes are added to the beginning of root words, like do ⟶ redo. When a prefix is added to a root word, the word's meaning is changed. Some common prefixes and their meanings:

re: again   **dis:** not   **pre:** before
un: not, opposite   **mis:** wrong   **under:** below

1. **Circle the prefix in each word below. Then, write the root words (without the prefixes) on the lines. For example:** (un)happy ⟶ **happy**

a) return _____   f) preheat _____

b) dishonest _____   g) untie _____

c) replay _____   h) underwater _____

d) preschool _____   i) unable _____

e) misbehave _____   j) disagree _____

Suffixes are added to the end of root words, like go ⟶ go**ing**. When a suffix is added to a root word, the word's meaning is changed. Some common suffixes and their meanings:

-able: can be done   **-est:** most   **-er:** more
-ful: full of   **-less:** without   **-er:** one who

2. **Circle the suffix in each word below. Then, write the root words (without the suffixes) on the lines. For example: small**(est) ⟶ **small**

a) joyful _____   f) smaller _____

b) youngest _____   g) slower _____

c) worthless _____   h) likeable _____

d) fearless _____   i) singer _____

e) careful _____   j) oldest _____

3. Write the correct word with a prefix on the line to complete each sentence. Use the word bank for help.

preheat	return	unable	unwrap

a) My mother said I had to wait until my birthday to _____ my presents.

b) Did you forget to _____ the oven before you put the cookies in?

c) Maria forgot her passport and had to _____ home to get it.

d) Jack was sad because he was _____ to get tickets for the concert.

4. Add the correct suffix to the end of each root word. Read the meaning of the complete word on the right to help you. The first one is done for you.

a) bound __less__   without limits

b) long _____   the most long

c) care _____   with care, full of care

d) do _____   able to be done, able to do

e) box _____   one who boxes

f) worth _____   without worth

5. Let's play a word-building game! Mix and match to create your own words by adding prefixes and suffixes to the root words below. How many words can you make? Remember that some root words may lose their last letter or change form in some other way when a suffix is added. One is done for you.

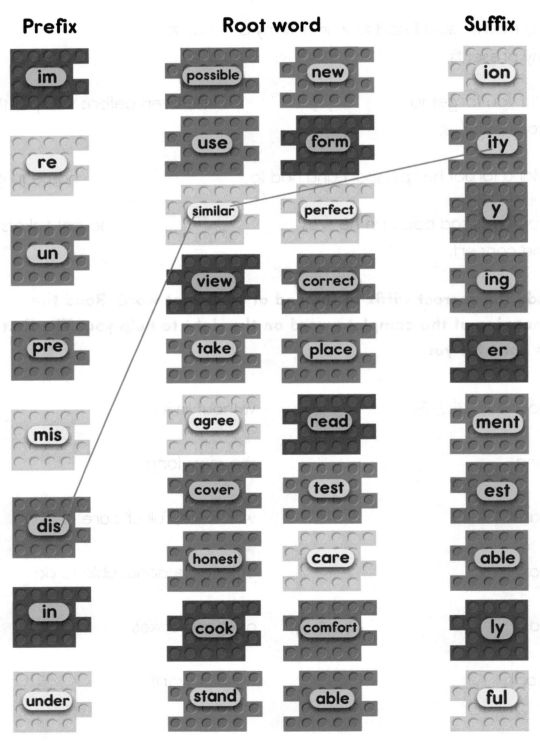

Prefix	Root word		Suffix
im	possible	new	ion
re	use	form	ity
un	similar	perfect	y
pre	view	correct	ing
mis	take	place	er
dis	agree	read	ment
in	cover	test	est
	honest	care	able
	cook	comfort	ly
under	stand	able	ful

TEST 20

1. Write a prefix or suffix in each blank to complete the sentence.

a) We were very _____ happy when the game was cancelled.

b) I had to _____ heat the oven before I could bake the cookies.

c) The firefighter was fear_____ as he ran into the burning house to save the trapped children.

d) Mark watched the fireworks _____ plode in the night sky.

e) Eliza was the young_____ girl in the family.

f) The ground was complete_____ covered with snow after the snowstorm.

2. In each of the words below, identify and circle the root word, then write a sentence using it.

a) tallest: _____

b) misspoke: _____

c) dislike: _____

d) farmer: _____

e) laughing: _____

f) understood: _____

g) joyful: _____

h) indifferent: _____

1. **Write the correct word with a prefix on the line to complete each sentence. Use the word bank for help.**

preview	unlock	mismatched	redo

a) I can't wear those socks — they're _____ .

b) That movie seems so exciting from the _____ , I can't wait for it to be released!

c) I am not able to _____ this door.

d) Shelly had to _____ her project when the cat spilled paint all over it.

2. **Choose any five of these words with suffixes and use them in sentences of your own.**

careless	manageable	carpenter	crying
happiest	sorrowful	reader	shocking
widest	oldest	painter	player

a) _____

b) _____

c) _____

d) _____

e) _____

3. Write a prefix or suffix in each blank to complete the sentence.

a)   Joan had to _____ read the question so she could understand it.

b)   _____ ware of snakes while hiking through the woods.

c)   The desserts added a magic_____ touch to the party.

d)   Betty had to _____ tie her shoes so she could take them off.

e)   My mom told me to be care_____ with the pottery I made.

f)   The orange cat was small_____ than the black cat.

g)   The farm_____ took the cow into the barn.

h)   Don't be _____ honest — I know it was you!

4. Circle the prefix or suffix in each word below. Then, write the root words on the lines.

a) refill _____

b) painter _____

c) refinish _____

d) misbehave _____

e) action _____

f) softness _____

g) moveable _____

h) preschool _____

i) disagree _____

j) neatly _____

k) selection _____

l) rename _____

m) incorrect _____

n) restless _____

o) wooden _____

p) impolite _____

q) unfair _____

r) southern _____

s) sunny _____

t) underground _____

u) musical _____

v) subtraction _____

w) friendship _____

x) nonsense _____

5. **Circle the root word in each of the words below. Then, find the root words in the word search. Remember: A root word can usually stand on its own and you can make a new word by adding a prefix or suffix (or both) to it. The words can be horizontal, vertical or diagonal in the puzzle.**

bottled	watering	disappoint	tallest
roams	underage	precook	builder
lower	nonstop	interschool	unfair
reload	sadness	shopping	childhood
impress	enjoyable	unusual	cheerful
thunderous	gladly	direction	sleepless

```
E A R S E C H I L D S R L T N E L
O S I L E G O U Y T S L E E P D U
R F A I R A S E I J O Y C N E D N
Y S L H A A L U L T R S S L P A C
W T C C L R R D P T O L O A D R C
P O A H A O L U T A G E U S U A L
E P O Y E S H O P A W A T E R A T
R I S I C E M O P P L D T H L S L
N P A A P O R S H R C L E T L I L
P N O F D O B D R E C O O K S O C
B U I L D S P S L S B S B G E O A
S O L E L A D O O S P O U L A D A
H O R L Y W P T W L L R L E K A L
O U L G L A D A P P O I N T T R C
O S T H U N D E R L P R O A M D E
L L D I R E C T R L R E P F H R L
B O T T L E S C H O O L A P L E A
```

TEST 21

1. Find the ten spelling mistakes in the following text. Underline them in red and write the correct spelling of each word on the lines below.

The Ant and the Dove – Adapted from an Aesop's fable

On a hot summer day, an ant went to the river bnk to quench its thirst. It was swept up by the current and was on the verge of drouning. A dove, perched in a three overhanging the water, picked up a leav and let it fall in the water near the ant. The ant clymbed on the leaf and floated safely to the river bank. Shortly after, a bird hunter came near the tree undr which the dove was sitting. He began to place a trap for the dov. The ant, understanding what the huntr was doing, bit his foot. The hunter screamed in paine and dropped his trap to the ground. The dove heard the sound made by the falling trap, flu away and was saved.

a) _____   f) _____

b) _____   g) _____

c) _____   h) _____

d) _____   i) _____

e) _____   j) _____

1. Proofread the text below. Correct the spelling as needed for the twenty errors. Then, write the words correctly on the lines below.

Last sumer, my familee and I went to New York City. We flu on an airplayne. The seets were grate. I sat by the vindow and could see the Statue of Liberty when we flew in.

While we were in New York, we saw a lot in the sity. We went to a big museum, a nise park and eit great food. I had amazing piza and a hot dog one dai.

Anothr day, we took a ferry bote around the island and out to the Statue of Liberty. We vent to the top. I reely liked the view from the top. I took many great pictures. I bot a keychain at a shop on the mane floor.

The day we left for home, I had a hard time repacking my bag. I had too many nu clothes and souvenirs.

What a great tryp we had to the "Big Apple," N.Y.C!

a) _____

b) _____

c) _____

d) _____

e) _____

f) _____

g) _____

h) _____

i) _____

j) _____

k) _____

l) _____

m) _____

n) _____

o) _____

p) _____

q) _____

r) _____

s) _____

t) _____

2. Find the spelling mistakes in the following sentences, correct them and write the correct sentences on the lines. There is only one mistake in each sentence.

a) The children go too school every day.

_____

_____

b) A plane flies acros the sky.

_____

_____

c) The owl hunts at knight.

_____

_____

d) The projet will soon be finished.

_____

_____

e) The princes goes to the ball.

_____

_____

f) I listen to the radio to here my favourite songs.

_____

_____

g) I am goeng to the park.

_____

_____

h) The curtain is blowing in the vind.

_____

_____

i) Matt was dryving too fast.

_____

_____

j) I will be home coon.

_____

_____

3. **Fill in the missing letters to correctly spell the words below. Use the letter bank for help and cross out each letter as you use it.**

k	o	i	a	a	e	o	a	a	e	o	a	a	i	a	n	i	a	s
a	n	i	e	o	o	a	o	e	a	u	u	o	a	o	c	o	a	

a) p____pay____

b) b____ttl____

c) b____c____p____ ____k

d) c____l____nd____r

e) ch____ir

f) ro____f

g) h____us____

h) w____ ____d____w

i) sl____pper

j) v____deo

k) m____tch

l) fl____g

m) p____per

n) p____t ____to

o) pl____ ____t

p) t____ ____sue

q) flo____r

r) l____ ____gh

s) n____t____b____ok

t) gr____ ____nd

Exercises

Language

TEST 22

1. Circle the correctly spelled word in each group below. Then, use it in a sentence of your own.

a) look, looke, loke:

_____

_____

b) sckoolbus, school bus, schoolbuss:

_____

_____

c) marvellous, marvelous, marvelus:

_____

_____

d) blendir, blainder, blender:

_____

_____

2. Underline the spelling mistakes and rewrite the sentences correctly.

a) My cousin has a butiful cat and too dogs.

_____

_____

b) I admire this dancer bcause he dances wery well.

_____

_____

c) I wanted nu skates for my birtday.

_____

_____

d) My sister baked cukies. She made them al day.

_____

_____

1. Circle the correctly spelled word in each list. Then, use it in a sentence of your own.

a) night, knighte, nite:

_____

_____

b) wale, whale, whele:

_____

_____

c) baiggage, bagage, baggage:

_____

_____

d) delicius, dalicious, delicious:

_____

_____

2. The following words are spelled wrong. Correct them. Then, use them in sentences of you own.

a) servar _____

b) outtfit _____

c) boate _____

d) notebok _____

e) ferniture _____

f) adjectif _____

g) computur _____

h) deshes _____

i) magnifficent _____

j) stodent _____

k) speek _____

l) clas _____

Language | Exercises

3. **Find the fifteen mistakes in spelling that are hiding in the story. Correct them and write the correct words on the lines below.**

The Water Fairy and the Woodcutter – Adapted from an Aesop's fable

A woodcutter was cuting a tree by the side of the rivar, when his axe slipped and fell in the water. He was criing over his loss, when a water fairy appeared. She askd him why he was sad. When she herd what happened, she dove down to the riverbed and brought up first an axe made of golde and then one of silver. Each time she asked, "Is this the one that you loost?" "No," said the woodcutter both times. The water fairy dove for a third time and brot back the woodcutter's lost axe. The woodcutter was very happey that he got his axe back. The water fairy, pleased that the woodcutter was honest, gave him the other too axes as a gift. When the woodcutter told this storey to his friend, the greedy friend decided to try his luck. He went to the river and dropd his axe in the water. The water fairy appeared and when she learned that the man's axe had fallen into the water, she dove doun and brought up a golden axe. Without waiting, the woodcutter's friend said: "Yes, that's mine," and he reeched out to grab the axe. The water fairy, angered by the man's dishonesty, refussed to give it to him and he lost his own axe too!

a) _____   f) _____   k) _____

b) _____   g) _____   l) _____

c) _____   h) _____   m) _____

d) _____   i) _____   n) _____

e) _____   j) _____   o) _____

4. Unscramble the following words to spell them correctly. Then, use any five of them in a story of your own on the lines below.

a) toorb: _____

b) cnoatr: _____

c) rsteo: _____

d) rencuot: _____

e) yomen: _____

f) srma: _____

g) sgle: _____

h) eomv: _____

i) erotmh: _____

j) eshuo: _____

_____

_____

_____

_____

_____

_____

_____

_____

_____

_____

_____

1. Write sentences on the lines below as asked.

a) Statements:

1) _____

2) _____

3) _____

4) _____

5) _____

b) Questions:

1) _____

2) _____

3) _____

4) _____

5) _____

c) Exclamations:

1) _____

2) _____

3) _____

4) _____

5) _____

1. **Look at the pictures below. Write a statement sentence for each picture on this page, and a question about each picture on the next page.**

   Remember: A **statement** sentence tells a statement on a subject and ends with a period(.). (For example: It is warm today.)

a)

_____

_____

_____

_____

_____

_____

_____

c)

_____

_____

_____

_____

_____

_____

_____

e)

_____

_____

_____

_____

_____

_____

_____

b)

_____

_____

_____

_____

_____

d)

_____

_____

_____

_____

_____

Exercises

Language

Remember: A **question** asks for information, begins with one of the following – who, what, where, when, why, how – and ends with a question mark(?). (For example: Where are your shoes?)

f)

h)

j)

g)

i)

2. Answer each question with a positive and a negative sentence. The first one is done for you.

a) Do you like watching movies?

Positive sentence: _____Yes, I like watching movies._____

Negative sentence: _____No, I do not like watching movies._____

b) Have you visited Europe?

Positive sentence: _____

Negative sentence: _____

c) Do you have to ask permission to leave the classroom?

Positive sentence: _____

Negative sentence: _____

d) Did you get the cat down from the tree?

Positive sentence: _____

Negative sentence: _____

e) Do we have enough apples for snacks?

Positive sentence: _____

Negative sentence: _____

f) Did they wrap their Christmas presents?

Positive sentence: _____

Negative sentence: _____

1. Change the sentences below into questions.

a) We are reading a very interesting book.

_____

b) My uncle caught a big fish.

_____

c) I am down with the flu.

_____

d) I closed the windows.

_____

e) She passed the ball.

_____

2. Change the sentences below into negative sentences.

a) My sister replaced the tire of her car.

_____

b) We are tired.

_____

c) I like gardening.

_____

d) He gave me the book.

_____

e) Mary goes home tomorrow.

_____

1. Are the following sentences exclamations? Answer yes or no.

Remember: Exclamations show surprise, excitement or some other emotion and end with an exclamation mark.

a) What a beautiful Christmas tree! _____   d) Don't go there. _____

b) I love that book! _____   e) What a night! _____

c) Some holiday this is! _____   f) I am tired. _____

2. Put an X in the correct column to indicate whether the sentence is positive or negative. The first one is done for you.

	Positive	Negative
Do you want dessert?	X	
This medicine is great against colds.		
Fred is not happy.		
Did you find what you were looking for?		
My grandfather does not work anymore.		
My aunt picks rare flowers.		
Do not let the dog inside.		
Martin is not scared of zoo animals.		
Is your mother doing better?		
Are you going on vacation this summer?		

Exercises

Language

3. Change the following sentences from questions to statements. The first one is done for you.

a) Do you play hockey?

You play hockey.

b) Did Stephanie receive her exam?

_____

_____

c) Did your parents give you permission to go to the cinema?

_____

_____

d) Can Felix come play with me?

_____

_____

e) Did Fatima and Omar choose their research subject?

_____

_____

f) Were the students nice during my absence?

_____

_____

g) Did you reserve your airplane tickets?

_____

_____

h) Do you like craftwork?

_____

_____

4. Underline the negative sentences.

a) She does not know my friend's sister.

b) The Inuit hunt and fish to feed themselves.

c) We will not go to the restaurant tonight.

d) Miguel will not be able to participate in the competition.

5. Look at each picture below. Write a statement, a question and an exclamation about each.

a) Statement: _____

_____

Question: _____

_____

Exclamation: _____

_____

b) Statement: _____

_____

Question: _____

_____

Exclamation: _____

_____

1. Rearrange the words to form a sentence that makes sense.

a) all dad apples eats day long. My

_____

_____

b) Mathew played I the and in garden.

_____

_____

c) not I like do strawberry cream. ice

_____

_____

d) cookies. bake mother helped my I

_____

_____

e) match if go not will rains. it I to the

_____

_____

2. Where do you use the following punctuation marks?

a) . _____

b) ? _____

c) ! _____

3. Write one sentence each with the following marks at the end.

a) . _____

b) ? _____

c) ! _____

1. Rearrange the words to form a sentence that makes sense.

a) mother's Suzanne. name first My is

_____

_____

b) Ali lives Oakville. friend My in

_____

_____

c) are animals cats dogs. favourite and My

_____

_____

d) see tomorrow. going movie are to We a

_____

_____

e) friend's I class. checked work my in

_____

_____

2. Place the missing punctuation (. or ? or !) at the end of each sentence below.

a) So good to rest after a hard week

b) Does your mother know you are in detention

c) Such a beautiful moon tonight

d) I went to the store to buy fruits and vegetables

e) He dreams of being on a plane

f) What a beautiful drawing

g) Do you think you will be able to arrive on time

3. Circle and write what helps you to know if each sentence below is a question, statement or exclamation. The first one is done for you.

a) Do you want to dance with me(?) _____question mark_____

b) I do not want to walk with you. _____

c) What a pity! _____

d) It was raining today. _____

e) He is very tall. _____

f) What a day! _____

g) Can you pass the salt? _____

h) I am tired. _____

i) Which school do you go to? _____

j) Watch out! _____

k) Are you coming home now? _____

l) Don't you dare! _____

m) What a long winter this is! _____

n) I finished my homework. _____

o) Can you climb that tree? _____

4. Add the missing punctuation signs in the following sentences. The first two are done for you.

a) The kids, the parents, and their friends are all invited to the end-of-the-year show.

b) Did you find the math textbook?

c) What a marvellous invention

d) He chose a board game for his friend Pedro

e) The baker sells chocolate cakes tarts and croissants

f) All the children want to play with the ball

g) What a great dream I had

h) What is your name

i) Tomorrow I will go to the cinema

j) Where are your shoes

k) I am happy today

l) The pen is blue

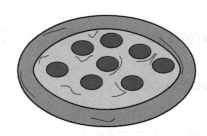

m) The family went on a picnic

n) What a great trip

o) How do you like your pizza

p) Wow that was exciting

q) I like muffins

r) We are moving

s) Is it raining

t) What a game

1. Form a sentence using each group of words below.

Hint: You can change the order of the given words.

a) couch comfortable blue _____

b) water girl pool _____

c) dinner Jason macaroni _____

d) movie tomorrow friends _____

e) kite park Rita _____

f) birthday party fun _____

2. Place the correct punctuation (. or ! or ?) at the end of each sentence below.

Example: Do you want to play with me __?__

a) Why will you not put on your red coat____

b) What an excellent meal____

c) I do not want to lend you my blue crayon____

d) Did you close the window____

3. In the following sentences, underline the nouns in blue, the adjectives in red, and the verbs in green.

a) My brother is very good at hockey.

b) Felix is eating a delicious orange.

c) Marie had a beautiful trip.

d) The school choir put on a great show.

1. The sentences below are incomplete. Can you use the given words to form a complete sentence for each one?

For example: stay at home … raining outside. ⟶ We decided to stay at home because it was raining outside.

a) wade in the river … rescue her dog

   wade in the river + _____

   _____

b) feeling sad … tell him jokes

   _____

   _____

c) broken glass … mother … be careful

   _____

   _____

d) library … story time

   _____

   _____

2. Add the missing punctuation marks for the following sentences (, . ? !).

a) Last night I saw the stars__.__

b) What a beautiful Halloween costume__.__

c) My sister bought socks shoes dresses and skirts__.__

d) Have you been to Italy _?_

e) We need apples oranges bananas and cherries__.__

f) I like my dog__.__

g) Go, Owen__!__

h) What are we eating _?_

3. Unscramble each of the following words and write it correctly. Then write if it's a noun, verb, adjective. Remember: Some words can do more than one duty. The first one is done for you.

a) tihlg: <u>light – noun, adjective, verb</u>

b) slgas: _____

c) reah: _____

d) agme: _____

e) huseo: _____

f) koob: _____

g) eedr: _____

h) ubn: _____

i) wons: _____

j) nelgod: _____

k) gnrtiun: _____

l) yteprt: _____

4. **In the following sentences, underline the nouns in <u>blue</u>, the adjectives in <u>red</u> and the verbs in <u>green</u>.**

a) My neighbour's son is a very good swimmer.

b) Her father felt very proud of her achievement.

c) The police car stopped at the red light.

d) The young boy read his new book.

e) The children eat the green apples.

f) The monkeys climbed up the tall tree.

g) My mother bakes delicious banana cookies.

h) Dark clouds hid the sky.

5. **You are the sentence builder who will rearrange each group of words to build the perfect sentence and add the missing punctuation. The first one is done for you.**

a) [their] [to the] [and Jill] [rode] [park] [Sam] [bikes]

Sam and Jill rode their bikes to the park.

b) [are] [my] [Where] [shoes]

_____

_____

c) [for dinner] [order] [you] [pizza] [tonight] [Can]

_____

_____

d) [in front] [blue car] [parked] [The] [house] [is] [of our]

_____

_____

e) [beautiful] [a] [What] [morning]

_____

_____

1. Use these homophones in sentences of your own.

ate, eight: _____

there, their: _____

write, right: _____

2. Draw lines to the different meanings of each homonym below.

a big furry animal

hit gently

tap   winter, spring, summer or fall

the colour of the sky

work   what a baseball player likes to steal

carry

hit   sad

a job

base   a very popular song

water comes out of it

bear   a piece of art

strike forcefully

season   the bottom part of something

add spices

blue

3. Write three words that rhyme with *light*.

_____

_____

Language

119

1. Draw arrows to connect words that rhyme in the poem below. The first pair is done for you.

Once upon a sunny <u>day</u>,
I skipped along a grassy <u>way</u>.
I sang a song and bounced my ball,
While waiting for that special call.

Then came the yell, I turned to where
The sound had wafted through the air.
Dad gave a wave, and I had a hunch
The message was, "It's time for lunch!"

When I got home, I whispered, "Please,
I hope that Dad has made grilled cheese."
'Cause toast and cheese just can't be beat –
With ketchup, it's the perfect treat!

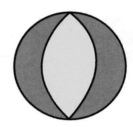

And there it was! My favourite meal!
I took a bite with happy zeal,
Ate every drippy, gooey crumb,
And wiped my plate with my thumb.

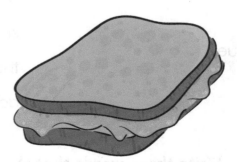

Some day, when I'm as tall as Dad,
I'll make him a meal like that one we had —
A perfect sandwich made with ease,
The most delicious kind, grilled cheese!

Homophones are words that sound the same but have different spellings and meanings. For example: <u>Here, hear</u> or <u>see, sea</u>.

2. Pick the right homophone for each picture. Write it in the box.

a) [ ]

eight   ate

e) [ ]

choose   chews

j) [ ]

piece   peace

b) [ ]

dear   deer

f) [ ]

pair   pear

g) [ ]

heard   herd

k) [ ]

tale   tail

c) [ ]

scent   sent   cent

h) [ ]

they're   there   their

l) [ ]

bear   bare

d) [ ]

hear   here

i) [ ]

aunt   ant

m) [ ]

too   to   two

Exercises

Language

121

Homonyms are words that are spelled the same, but have different meanings. For example: Light (like a lamp) and light (not heavy).

3. **One meaning is written for each of the homonyms below. Write the second meaning. Use a dictionary, if needed.**

a) bat: _flying mammal_

bat: _____

b) cold: _a common illness_

cold: _____

c) bowl: _to throw a ball_

bowl: _____

d) hide: _an animal's skin_

hide: _____

e) bark: _surface of a tree trunk_

bark: _____

f) low: _lacking in height_

low: _____

g) ground: _surface of the earth_

ground: _____

h) box: _a container_

box: _____

i) train: _a type of transportation_

train: _____

TEST 28

1. Find a homophone for each of the following words.

a) hear _____

b) flour _____

c) cell _____

d) waist _____

e) know _____

f) heal _____

g) weak _____

h) son _____

i) won _____

j) dye _____

k) bawl _____

l) brake _____

2. Draw a line to connect each pair of rhyming words.

drive   walk

talk   bun

ten   pen

handle   alive

fun   candle

3. Write two different meanings for each of the homonyms below. Use a dictionary, if needed.

a) bar: _____

   bar: _____

b) address: _____

   address: _____

c) beam: _____

   beam: _____

d) bank: _____

   bank: _____

Language

1. **Find a homophone (word that sounds the same) for each of the following words. The first one is done for you.**

a) rap: _____wrap_____

b) sum: _____

c) wait: _____

d) grate: _____

e) role: _____

f) knight _____

g) meat: _____

h) steel: _____

2. **Draw lines from each homonym (same spelling, different meanings) to its two meanings. Ask an adult or use a dictionary, if you need more help. The first one is done for you.**

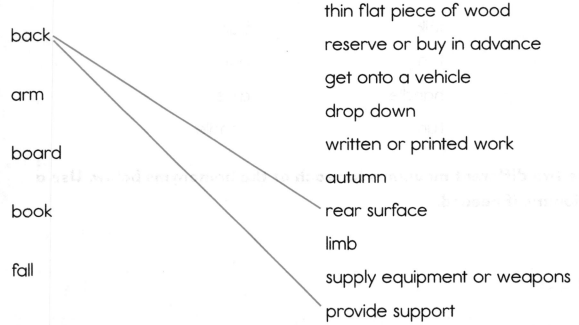

back

arm

board

book

fall

thin flat piece of wood

reserve or buy in advance

get onto a vehicle

drop down

written or printed work

autumn

rear surface

limb

supply equipment or weapons

provide support

3. **Using the word bank, write homphones for the following words. The first one is done for you.**

ant	~~brake~~	buy	bear	board	base

a) break: _____brake_____

b) bye _____

c) bare _____

d) bass _____

e) aunt _____

f) bored _____

4. Find a word that rhymes with (ends with the same sound as) the following words.

Example: great – plate

a) bear _____

b) speed _____

c) sale _____

d) white _____

e) game _____

f) frown _____

g) train _____

h) mother _____

i) fun _____

j) song _____

k) scribble _____

l) flaw _____

5. Write as many words as you can think of that rhyme with each of the following words.

a) ham _____

b) book _____

c) hand _____

d) flower _____

e) house _____

f) light _____

6. Circle the word that does not belong in each group of rhyming words below.

a) mad, happy, sad, dad, pad

b) shut, sheep, beep, creep, sweep

c) best, nest, chest, quest, unless

d) right, light, fight, meat, might

e) girl, hurl, furl, twirl, treat

f) house, heap, mouse, louse, douse

g) pram, dram, gram, gold, tram

7. List three rhyming words for each word below.

a) soap: _____

b) ride: _____

c) tram: _____

d) lap: _____

e) home: _____

f) light: _____

g) throw: _____

8. Match each homophone to its partner.

new   bore

bye   scent

boar   knew

I   buy

cent   eye

TEST 29

1. Write 'fact' or 'opinion' beside each sentence.

a) I make my bed every morning. _____

b) Chocolate chip cookies are the best dessert! _____

c) The province of Ontario is in Canada. _____

d) Ice cream is the worst food. _____

e) You can buy milk at a grocery store. _____

f) There are seven continents in the world. _____

g) My friend John is handsome. _____

h) A blue jay is a type of bird. _____

i) A fish is a great pet to have. _____

j) Every child should read this book. _____

Facts say what is always true about something. They are true statements that can be proved. For example, 'Ottawa is the capital of Canada' is a fact.

Opinions are what the writer thinks or feels about something. They are ideas or thoughts about something and usually cannot be proved. It's hard to say if it is right or wrong. For example, 'Apple pie is delicious' is an opinion.

1. Read each sentence below. Then, write 'fact' or 'opinion' next to it.

a) Soccer is terrible. _____

b) Soccer is the best sport ever. _____

c) Rain helps plants grow. _____

d) Rainy days are the worst. _____

e) My fidget spinner is the best toy. _____

f) A fidget spinner is a toy. _____

g) Green is the colour of grass. _____

h) A pretty colour is green. _____

i) There are seven days in a week. _____

j) Sundays are the best days. _____

2. Write three facts and three opinions of your own on the lines below.

Facts: a) _____

_____

_____

_____

b) _____

_____

_____

_____

c) _____

_____

_____

_____

Opinions: a) _____

_____

_____

_____

b) _____

_____

_____

_____

c) _____

_____

_____

_____

Exercises

Language

3. Decide if the following are fact or opinion. Write *fact* or *opinion* beside each sentence.

a) It is sunny today. _____

b) My brother is tall. _____

c) The children were happy. _____

d) Wednesday is the best day of the week. _____

e) All families like to play games. _____

f) There are seven days in a week. _____

g) This was a boring year. _____

h) Christmas comes once a year. _____

i) I love sunshine. _____

j) My red frock is lovely. _____

k) My new backpack is perfect. _____

l) The fan is on. _____

m) It is a muggy day. _____

n) I am 9 years old. _____

o) It is fun going to the beach. _____

Exercises

Language

1. Think of some facts and opinions and write them on the lines below.

a) Fact: _____

b) Opinion: _____

c) Fact: _____

d) Opinion: _____

e) Fact: _____

f) Opinion: _____

g) Fact: _____

h) Opinion: _____

i) Fact: _____

j) Opinion: _____

k) Fact: _____

l) Opinion: _____

m) Fact: _____

n) Opinion: _____

o) Fact: _____

p) Opinion: _____

q) Fact: _____

r) Opinion: _____

s) Fact: _____

t) Opinion: _____

Language

Read the story and answer the questions below and on the following page.

The Safari

Many people like to go on a safari in Africa. They have a chance to see many animals in their natural environment. Some days, the lions, zebras and hyenas are easy to spot. On other days, the animals almost seem to be hiding from people. The heat of the day makes it hard to hold a camera to take pictures. Many people ask photographers to take pictures for them. It can be exciting to be so close to animals in the wild. Some tourists like to stay in the jeeps or vans and others like to be closer to the animals. What would you do?

1. Write *true* or *false*.

a) This story has both facts and opinions. _____

b) The story talks about going on safari. _____

c) Going on a safari is a great way to see animals in the wild. _____

d) Everyone who goes on safari likes to be close to wild animals. _____

e) Many people think taking photos of animals is exciting. _____

2. Choose the correct option to complete each sentence below.

i.   It is often hard to take pictures on a safari because:

a) the animals try to bite you.

b) the animals chase you.

c) the camera starts to shake.

d) it is too hot to hold a camera properly.

ii.   Going on safari can sometimes be:

a) hot.

b) exciting.

c) scary.

d) all of the above.

iii.   People who go on safari like to:

a) ride a jeep.

b) learn about nature.

c) play cards.

d) eat burgers.

iv.   Sometimes, on safari, you can see people:

a) taking photographs.

b) sleeping.

c) wearing mittens.

d) using skis.

v.   You should go on safari if you:

a) love watching animals.

b) want to take photographs.

c) want to watch TV.

d) like to eat popcorn.

3. **Write a paragraph on any topic of your choice, but make sure to include at least three facts and three opinions.**

_____

_____

_____

_____

_____

_____

_____

_____

_____

_____

_____

_____

_____

_____

_____

_____

_____

_____

Exercises

Language

TEST 31

1. Match each illustration to the correct question (number) below. The first one is done for you.

a) `5`

b) ☐

c) ☐

d) ☐

e) ☐

f) ☐

g) ☐

h) ☐

i) ☐

j) ☐

k) ☐

l) ☐

1. How many snowmen do you see?
2. Is the door open or closed?
3. How many juggling balls are in the air?
4. Who's wearing sunglasses?
5. Where is the bone?
6. When is your birthday?
7. Who's holding the broom?
8. Is the baby sick?
9. What is in the statue's left hand?
10. What are the winning lotto numbers?
11. Is it windy today?
12. What does the Eiffel Tower look like?

1. Match each illustration to the correct question (number) below. The first one is done for you.

a) **3**

e) [ ]

i) [ ]

b) [ ]

f) [ ]

j) [ ]

c) [ ]

g) [ ]

k) [ ]

d) [ ]

h) [ ]

l) [ ]

1. Who bought the ice cream?

2. Hi, how are you on this cold day?

3. Did you have a good night's sleep?

4. Can I have more chicken, please?

5. Where is the lion?

6. What time is it?

7. Who's having a birthday party?

8. Hello, may I speak to Bridget, please?

9. Where is the tools store?

10. Is this bus going to school?

11. Are you sad?

12. Do you love me?

Exercises

Language

2. Underline in <u>blue</u> all the words that are related to the ocean, in <u>red</u> the words that are related to the desert, and in <u>green</u> the words that are related to the forest.

whale	shore	mushroom
trees	seaweed	hot
lizard	starfish	oasis
sand	maple tree	current
thirst	shark	elm
dune	moose	camel
waves	tides	monkey
cactus	bear	snake

3. Cross out the words that are *not* related to school.

principal's office	barn	boys' washroom	computer lab
art room	English room	dentist	cow
ambulance	lamb	blackboard	classroom
janitor	tiger	eraser	squirrel
student	pencil	wave	gymnasium
book	restaurant	chalk	lion

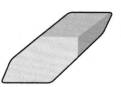

Exercises

Language

4. **Use the word bank to help you complete each question. The first one is done for you.**

Who	What	Where	When	~~Why~~	How

a) "_____Why_____ are you late ?" "Because there was traffic on the road."

b) "_____ are you ?" "I am George."

c) "_____ are you doing in the kitchen ?" "I am cooking."

d) "_____ was your exam?" "I think I passed."

e) "_____ is the ketchup?" "It is in the refrigerator."

f) "_____ is your birthday?" "It is in three months."

TEST 32

1. Cross out the word that does *not* belong in each list.

a) generous, good, helpful, blue

b) sunny, cloudy, dark, windy

c) nine, eleven, fourteen, day

d) august, may, summer, april

e) stars, planets, water, meteor

2. Cross out the words that are *not* connected to food.

house	sandwich	pasta	tomato	orange
baby	school	pool	bread	apple
man	cheese	photo	pizza	hot dog

3. Cross out the words that are *not* connected to a desert, an ocean or a forest.

trees	whales	robber	dunes	oasis
cinema	skyscraper	firs	dolphin	waves
tides	sand	pines	currents	karate

4. Cross out all the words that are *not* related to sports.

swimming	handball	window	skating	track
soccer	net	eyelashes	judo	baseball
golf	galaxy	sandwich	skiing	hurdles

1. Write the missing question word in each sentence. Use the word bank for help. The first one is done for you.

Who	~~Why~~	What	When	Where	How	How much	Which

a) "_____Why_____ is he dressed like that?" "Because it's Halloween!"

b) "_____ did he break his leg?" "He fell down the stairs".

c) "_____ are you going this summer?" "To Europe with my family".

d) "_____ is he going to wash the dishes?" "Right after dinner".

e) "_____ money do you need?" "Five dollars".

f) "_____ broke the window?" "John did".

g) "_____ one do you like the most?" "The one on the left".

h) "_____ are you doing? Building a snowman".

2. Choose the words that are connected to sports.

basketball	court	sunny	eggs	coach
cello	baseball	racket	camera	lake
tennis	golf	net	pie	tree
cheese	computer	baby	score	team
paint	running shoes	rules	badminton	grapes

3. Match each picture with its name.

water bottle

jacket

orange

skates

chess

elephant

kite

4. Find the words related to weather.

donut	thunder	pig	hair	windy
chair	grape	lightning	blueberries	rain
sunny	snow	mudslide	tissue	quilt
fish	three	hail	overcast	deep
clouds	hot	cat	tornado	tsunami

5. Use a dictionary to look up five new words and write each word and its definition on the lines below.

a) _____

_____

_____

b) _____

_____

_____

c) _____

_____

_____

d) _____

_____

_____

e) _____

_____

_____

TEST 33

1. Find these words in the dictionary and write down their meaning.

a) responsible: _____

_____

b) overwhelm: _____

_____

c) absorb: _____

_____

d) privilege: _____

_____

e) elegant: _____

_____

f) predator: _____

_____

2. What do you call the person who writes a book?

_____

_____

3. What do you call a doctor who conducts surgical operations?

_____

_____

1. **Insert the number of the correct definition beside each word. Consult a dictionary if needed.**

a) author_____

b) reviewer _____

c) table of contents _____

d) series _____

e) editor _____

f) dedication _____

g) illustrator _____

h) chapter _____

1) person who edits books.

2) person who writes books.

3) a collection of books on the same subject.

4) list in a book that numbers all the chapters and all the sections of the book and their page numbers.

5) person who illustrates for books.

6) section of a book.

7) inscription at the beginning of the book to someone special.

8) person who gives an opinion about a book.

2. **Place the words about sports from the word bank correctly between the given dictionary guide words (words printed on the top corner of each dictionary page). The first one is done for you.**

Suggestion: Look up the meanings of the guide words as well to learn some interesting new words!

basketball	curling	diving
golf	hockey	karate
lacrosse	ping-pong	soccer
tennis	volleyball	~~water polo~~

a) watergate ___water polo___ water starwort

b) divest _____ divvy

c) Karachai-Cherkessia _____ Kaska

d) hoary _____ Hodgkin

e) basilisk _____ baste

f) voice box _____ Volta River

g) so _____ social

h) gold panner _____ goniometer

i) *curé* _____ curry

j) tenet _____ tentacle

k) lackadaisical _____ Ladakh

l) pinch pleat _____ pink triangle

3. Look up ten new words in the dictionary. Write down the words and their meanings below.

a) _____

_____

_____

b) _____

_____

_____

c) _____

_____

_____

d) _____

_____

_____

e) _____

_____

_____

f) _____

_____

_____

g) _____

_____

_____

h) _____

_____

_____

i) _____

_____

_____

j) _____

_____

TEST 34

1. Research these words in a dictionary and write down their meaning.

a) granular: _____

_____

_____

b) ferocious: _____

_____

_____

c) magnificent: _____

_____

_____

d) spatula: _____

_____

_____

e) surround: _____

_____

_____

f) ridicule: _____

_____

_____

2. What do you call a person who tells the actors in a movie how to act?

_____

_____

1. Write the meanings of the following words. Use a dictionary, if needed.

a) question: _____
_____
_____

b) paragraph: _____
_____
_____

c) sentence: _____
_____
_____

d) title: _____
_____
_____

e) chapter: _____
_____
_____

f) report: _____
_____
_____

g) assignment: _____
_____
_____

Exercises

Language

2. Look at the book cover and label its parts. Use the word bank below for help.

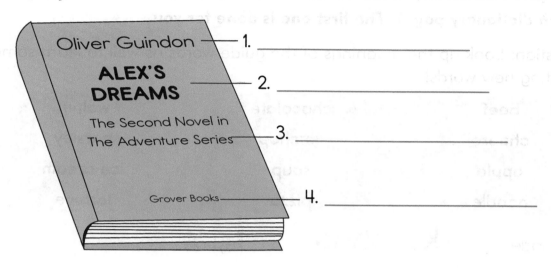

Oliver Guindon — 1. _____

ALEX'S DREAMS — 2. _____

The Second Novel in The Adventure Series — 3. _____

Grover Books — 4. _____

series	author	publisher	title

3. Look again at the book cover above. What do you think the book is about? Use your imagination and write your answer below.

_____

_____

_____

_____

_____

_____

_____

_____

_____

Exercises

Language

4. Place the words about food from the word bank correctly between the given dictionary guide words (words printed on the top corner of each dictionary page). The first one is done for you.

Suggestion: Look up the meanings of the guide words as well to learn some interesting new words!

beef	chocolate	walnut
cheese	~~ketchup~~	parsley
apple	soup	ice cream
noodle	pizza	lettuce

a) kermode _____ketchup_____ keyhole

b) non-surgical _____ Noriega

c) wall hanging _____ Wampanoag

d) checkerberry _____ Cheever

e) sound _____ source code

f) Parry Channel _____ participle

g) bedtime _____ beeswax

h) lettering _____ level

i) ibuprofen _____ iceman

j) chive _____ choir school

k) *appellation contrôlée* _____ Appomattox

l) Pizan _____ plagal

TEST 35

1. Follow the instructions to colour the picture.

1: purple   2: blue   3: red   4: brown   5: dark blue

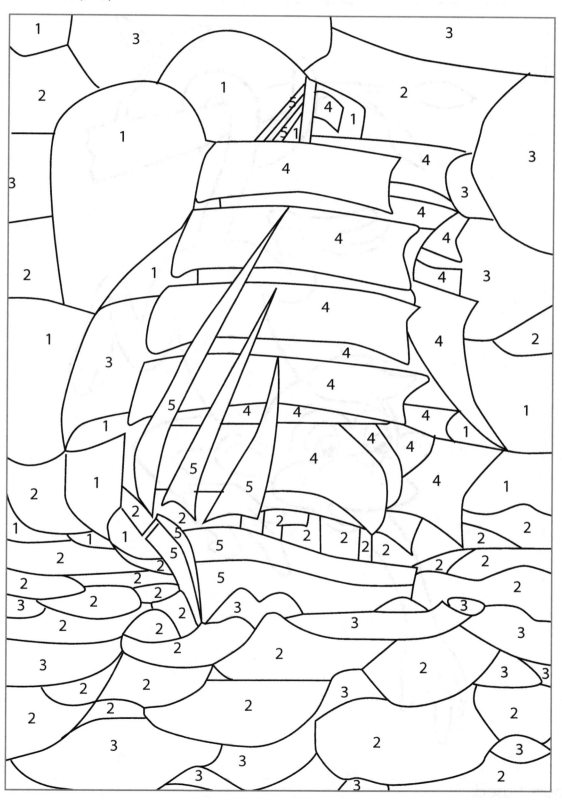

1. **Colour the picture below with the colours of your choice. Then, write on the lines below what colours you used.**

Exercises

Language

Colours I used: _____

2. Look at each word and colour in the letters to match the word.

a)

BLUE

b)

GREEN

c)

YELLOW

d)

RED

e)

ORANGE

3. Match each colour word with the correct picture.

red

orange

yellow

green

blue

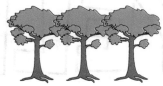

brown

purple

black

1. Colour the flags in the stated colours.

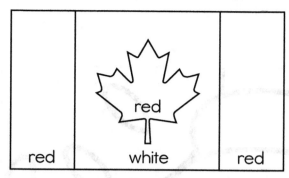

a) Canada

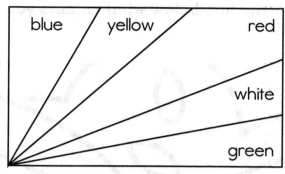

e) Seychelles

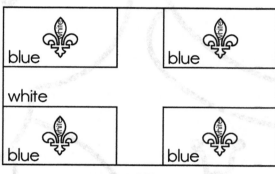

b) Quebec

f) Lebanon

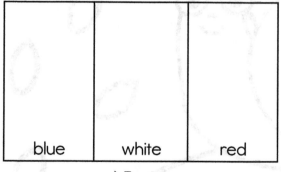

c) France

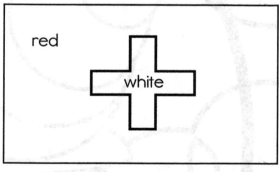

g) Switzerland

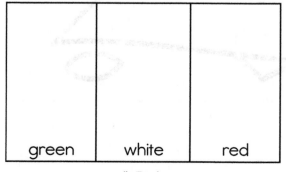

d) Italy

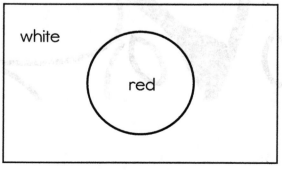

h) Japan

1. **Colour the picture below with the colours of your choice. Then, write on the line below what colours you used.**

Colours I used: _____

Exercises

Language

2. Colour in the rainbow below. Then, name its colours on the line below.

Colours of the rainbow:

_____

_____

3. Read the name of each colour below and write if it is a shade of *blue*, *red* or *green*. Use a dictionary for help, if needed.

a) aquamarine _____

b) shamrock _____

c) azure _____

d) crimson _____

e) teal _____

f) ruby _____

g) periwinkle _____

h) cardinal _____

i) jade _____

j) turquoise _____

k) pine _____

l) navy _____

m) olive _____

n) scarlet _____

TEST 37

1. **These wild animals are found in North America. Use the word bank to help you write the correct name under each picture, and then:**

Colour the mammals in <u>red</u>,
colour the insects in <u>blue</u>, and
colour the birds in <u>green</u>.

Birds:	Mammals:	Insects:
great horned owl	beaver	ladybug
owl	bison	bee
raven	deer	ant
bald eagle	whale	fly

a) _____

b) _____

c) _____

d) _____

e) _____

f) _____

g) _____

h) _____

i) _____

j) _____

k) _____

l) _____

1. Place each animal in the correct column.

Cow

Frog

Deer

Fox

Tiger

Bat

Wolf

Horse

Hedgehog

Zebra

Lion

Cheetah

Moose

Mole

Cougar

Giraffe

Salamander

Herbivore (eats plants)	Carnivore (eats other animals)	Insectivore (eats insects)

Exercises

Language

2. **Look at the picture of the bird below and use the word bank to label each part.**

| eye | wing | beak | leg | tail feathers | talon |

a) _____

b) _____

c) _____

d) _____

e) _____

f) _____

3. Write the name of each insect below its picture. Use the word bank for help.

bee	caterpillar	butterfly	dragonfly	mosquito	fly
worm	grasshopper	ladybug	beetle	moth	ant

a)

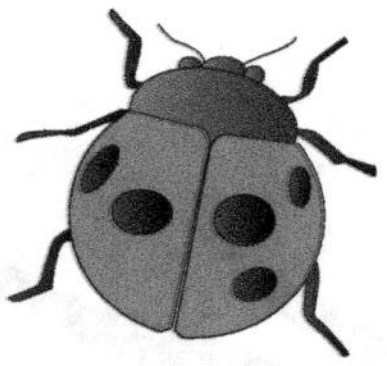

e)

i)

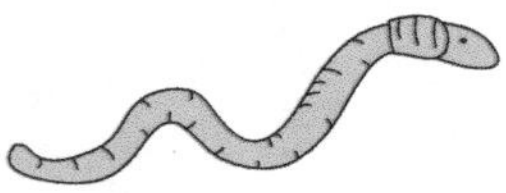

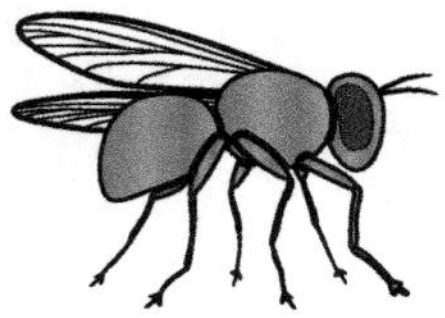

b)

f)

j)

c)

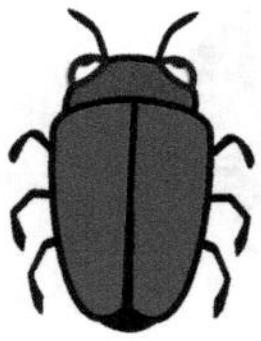

g)

k)

d)

h)

l)

TEST 38

1. Look at the pictures. Complete the crossword puzzle. Use the word bank for help.

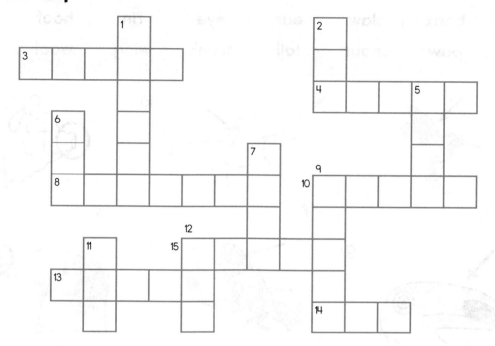

Across

3.

4.

8.

10.

13.

14.

15.

Down

1.

2.

5.

6.

7.

9.

11.

12.

beaver	cow	deer	dog	fox	giraffe	horse	hen
lion	moose	pig	raven	sheep	skunk	whale	

1. Use the word bank to help you label the animal parts correctly.

antler	beak	claw	ear	eye	fin	hoof	
nose	paw	snout	tail	trunk	wing	wool	mane

a)

w_____

b)

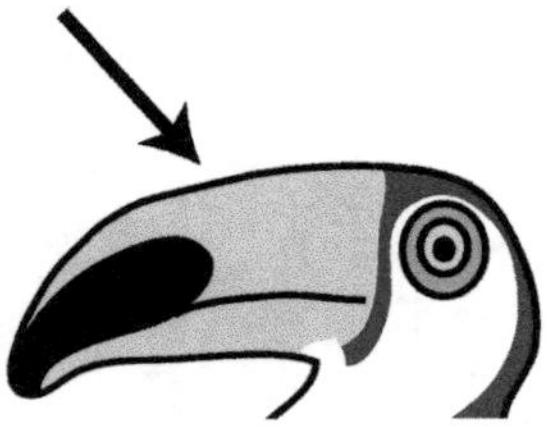

b_____

c)

e_____

d)

a_____

e)

h_____

f)

f_____

g)

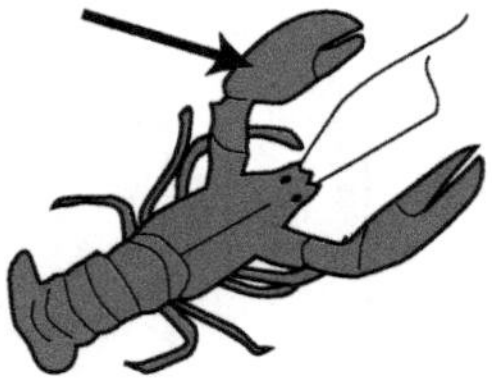

c_____

h)

p_____

i)

e_____

j)

n_____

k)

s_____

l)

t_____

m)

m_____

n)

w_____

o)

t_____

Exercises

Language

2. Complete the table, using words from the list below. Cross out the words as you use them. Ask for an adult's help, if needed. The first row is done for you.

Animals	Male	Female	Young	Sound
bee	drone	queen	fry	buzz
bear				growl
cat			kitten	
chicken		hen		
dog				bark
duck	drake			
elephant		cow		
fox		vixen		
goose				honk
horse		mare		
lion			cub	
ox				bellow/moo
pig		sow		
sheep	ram			

meow/purr	baa/bleat	duckling	~~fry~~	puppy	goose
duck	cackle	boar	tomcat	bark	calf
grunt/squeal	gander	queen	bitch	neigh/whinny	hog
lion	bull	cub	lioness	chick	gosling
quack	calf	dog	foal	cow	piglet
ewe	bull	dog	~~buzz~~	trumpet	sow
lamb	rooster	stallion	~~queen~~	cub	roar

3. Find and circle all the bird names from the list below in the word search puzzle. Remember: The words can be horizontal, vertical or diagonal.

jay	eagle	robin	loon	goose
falcon	chickadee	sparrow	bluebird	owl
hummingbird	parrot	pigeon	crane	hen
penguin	swallow	dove	cuckoo	lark
woodpecker	seagull	duck	ostrich	emu
peacock	crow	flamingo	hawk	wren

```
G U E U O H C U C K O O B G I L N P E H
T U O W L L A M C H I C K A D E E E O Y
N A O G A G F W C R O W R K M D O V E U
E L I B A E R W K D C O S T R I C H L C
E A I E P A R R O T C O O A K F A P D C
H B L O O N H E N G I D F L A M I N G O
O R C R A N E N R O E P S A O I C U C J
C E E S S W A L L O W E F A L C O N L C
L A C A L H R E B S U C D U C K P A N K
U B S R G I U R O E E K G L P B C L R A
U G C S C L E M G G O E E D H V C E N U
A O O L O S E I M L A R K R O B I N R L
M S L K S G E A D I O P E A C O C K N C
H E P E E I J A Y P N K O E M U O C N E
E S E O R S D D G A N G W L E T O H I K
M D N M H G G D J U E O B P R A I B L O
O A G L P I G E O N L R C I E O S G E P
W O U A E I K I K N O L Y O R D K K E N
R P I F C H M D S P A R R O W D N D A R
H R N N R R I G S B L U E B I R D A U U
```

1. **Use the word bank to help you identify the clothes and accessories below.**

Bermuda shorts	T-shirt	earmuffs	glasses	hat	tie
rain coat	pants	shorts	scarf	skirt	sock
winter coat	cap	pyjamas	jacket		

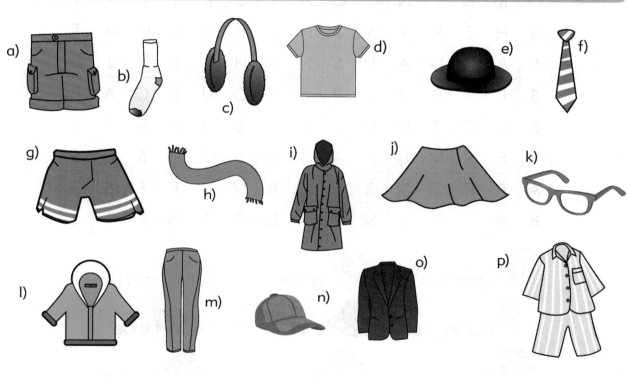

a) B_____

b) s_____

c) e_____

d) T-_____

e) h_____

f) t_____

g) s_____

h) s_____

i) r_____

j) s_____

k) g_____

l) w_____

m) p_____

n) c_____

o) j_____

p) p_____

1. **Read the words related to clothes and accessories below. Then, circle them in the word search and write the remaining letters below to discover the secret word.**

G	L	O	V	E	N	I	G	H	T	G	O	W	N	C
J	A	C	K	E	T	S	L	M	I	T	T	E	N	S
O	R	A	I	N	C	O	A	T	S	K	I	R	T	T
S	H	I	R	T	W	I	N	T	E	R	C	O	A	T
S	A	N	D	A	L	S	H	S	H	O	E	S	I	N
S	L	I	P	P	E	R	T	U	Q	U	E	C	A	P
B	O	O	T	D	R	E	S	S	S	H	O	R	T	S
B	E	R	M	U	D	A	S	B	L	O	U	S	E	S
A	P	R	O	N	S	E	A	R	M	U	F	F	S	G
B	A	T	H	I	N	G	S	U	I	T	H	A	T	S

aprons   glove   shirt

bathing suit   hats   shoes

Bermudas   jackets   shorts

blouses   mittens   skirt

boot   night gown   slipper

dress   raincoat   tuque

earmuffs   sandals   winter coat

cap

Secret word: ___ ___ ___ ___ ___ ___ ___ ___

2. Look at the items of clothing, then draw them on the picture of the boy.

3. Match each sense to its body part.

sight

smell

taste

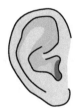

touch

hearing

Exercises

Language

1. Complete the crossword puzzle by looking at the pictures below. Use the word bank if you need more help.

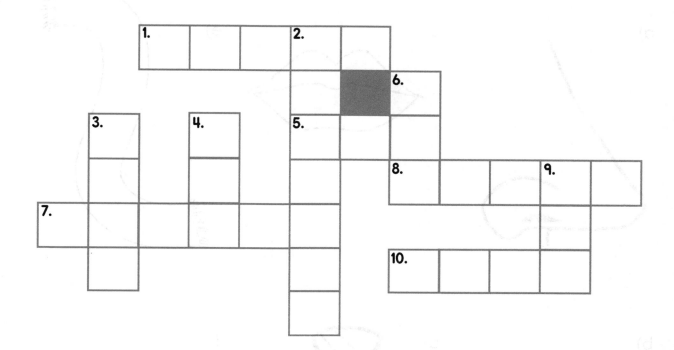

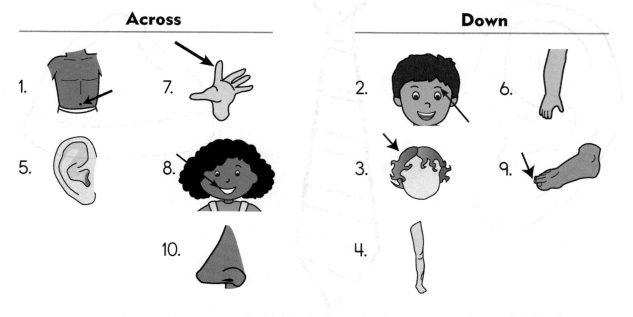

Across			Down	
1.	7.		2.	6.
5.	8.		3.	9.
	10.		4.	

arm	ear	finger	mouth	nose
leg	eyebrow	hair	navel	toe

1. **Colour the pictures below with the colours of your choice. Then, label each body part or clothing item.**

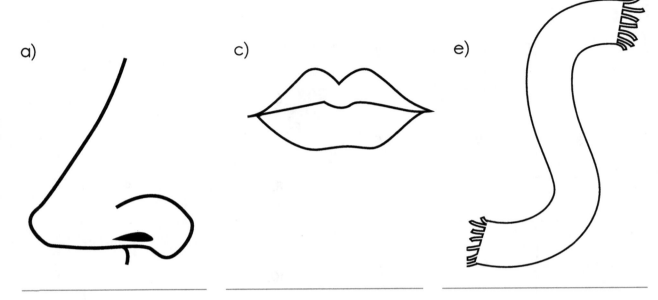

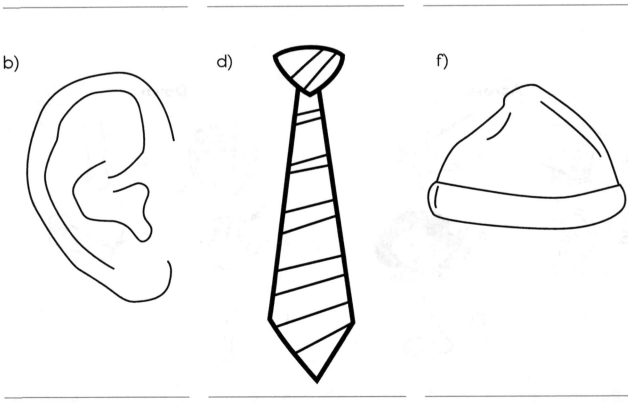

a)

c)

e)

b)

d)

f)

2. Label each item of clothing below with the season you would wear it in.

a)

_____

_____

e)

_____

_____

i)

_____

_____

b)

_____

_____

f)

_____

_____

j)

_____

_____

c)

_____

_____

g)

_____

_____

k)

_____

_____

d)

_____

_____

h)

_____

_____

l)

_____

_____

3. Label each body part.

a) _____

b) _____

d) _____

c) _____

e) _____

f) _____

TEST 41

1. Use the word bank to help you write the names of the school supplies shown below.

backpack	pencil case	blackboard	protractor
scissors	glue	paper clip	sharpener
pen	ruler	eraser	triangle

a)

_____

e)
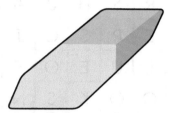
_____

i)
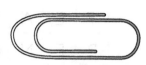
_____

b)

_____

f)
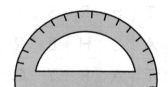
_____

j)

_____

c)

_____

g)

_____

k)

_____

d)
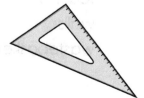
_____

h)

_____

l)

_____

1. Circle the words from the list in the word search, then write the remaining letters below to discover the secret word.

B	A	C	K	P	A	C	K	S	P	E	N	C	I	L
B	L	A	C	K	B	O	A	R	D	C	H	A	I	R
C	S	H	A	R	P	E	N	E	R	R	U	L	E	R
B	I	N	D	E	R	S	H	J	A	N	I	T	O	R
T	E	A	C	H	E	R	S	C	I	S	S	O	R	S
P	E	N	O	G	L	U	E	O	E	R	A	S	E	R
N	O	T	E	B	O	O	K	S	N	U	R	S	E	S
D	E	S	K	S	P	A	P	E	R	C	L	I	P	S
W	A	S	T	E	B	A	S	K	E	T	B	E	L	L
C	O	M	P	U	T	E	R	S	T	U	D	E	N	T
A	R	T	T	E	A	C	H	E	R	C	H	A	L	K
S	E	C	R	E	T	A	R	Y	C	L	O	C	K	S
L	U	N	C	H	B	O	X	E	N	G	L	I	S	H
C	A	L	C	U	L	A	T	O	R	W	A	L	L	S
L	G	Y	M	N	A	S	I	U	M	D	O	O	R	S

art teacher	chair	English	notebooks	scissors
backpack	chalk	eraser	nurses	secretary
bell	clocks	glue	paper clips	sharpener
binders	computer	gymnasium	pen	student
blackboard	desks	janitor	pencil	teacher
calculator	doors	lunch box	ruler	walls
				wastebasket

Secret word: ___ ___ ___ ___ ___ ___

2. Unscramble the words below and write the correct name of each school subject.

a) ygm cssal

_____

b) liEnshg

_____

c) iescne

_____

d) tamh

_____

e) phgeraogy

_____

f) sthiory

_____

g) cisoal udistes

_____

h) enFrch

_____

3. Look at each object and write the name of the class you would use it in.

a)

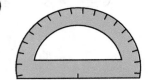

_____

_____

e)

_____

_____

i)

_____

_____

b)

_____

_____

f)

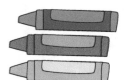

_____

_____

j)

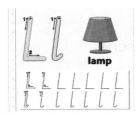

_____

_____

c)

_____

_____

g)

_____

_____

k)

_____

_____

d)

_____

_____

h)

_____

_____

l)

_____

_____

TEST 42

1. **Look at the classroom picture and read the list below. Then, write the correct number in each oval.**

1) window

2) teacher

3) wastebasket

4) clock

5) desk

6) book

1. Look at the pictures and see the map below. Write the room number where you would find each of these school workers. The first one is done for you.

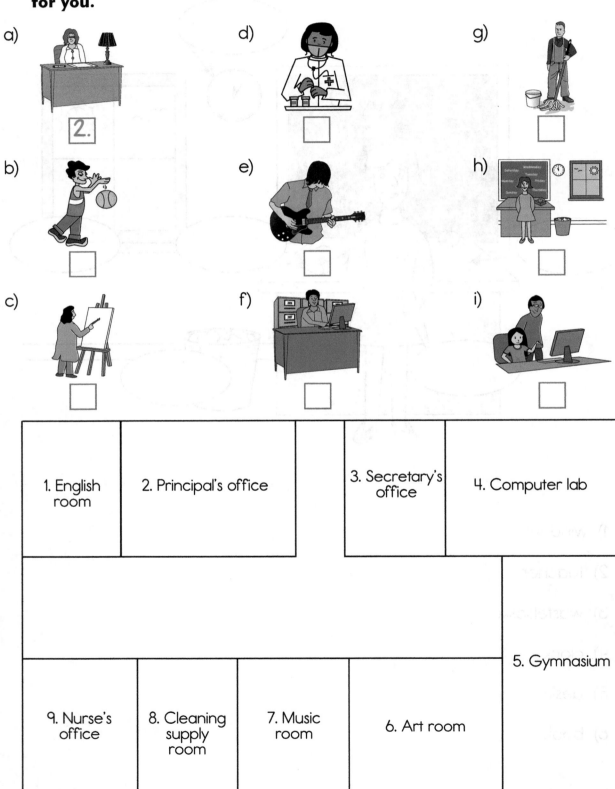

a) `2.`

d) ☐

g) ☐

b) ☐

e) ☐

h) ☐

c) ☐

f) ☐

i) ☐

| 1. English room | 2. Principal's office | | 3. Secretary's office | 4. Computer lab |

| 9. Nurse's office | 8. Cleaning supply room | 7. Music room | 6. Art room | 5. Gymnasium |

2. Fill in the weekly calendar below with your classes. Don't forget to include recess and lunch!

TIME	MONDAY	TUESDAY	WEDNESDAY	THURSDAY	FRIDAY
9:00-10:00					
10:00-11:00					
11:00-12:00					
12:00-1:00					
1:00-2:00					
2:00-3:00					

Exercises

Language

3. Write two sentences about what you are learning in each school subject.

a) English: _____

_____

_____

_____

_____

b) Math: _____

_____

_____

_____

_____

c) Science: _____

_____

_____

_____

_____

d) Gym: _____

_____

_____

_____

_____

Exercises

Language

TEST 43

1. Write the correct picture number next to each chore in the list.

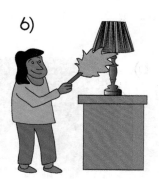

a) Empty the dishwasher. _____

b) Wash the dishes. _____

c) Set the table. _____

d) Dust the furniture. _____

e) Make your bed. _____

f) Clean your room. _____

2. Name any three hobbies.

_____

_____

_____

_____

_____

3. Write a sentence about a sport you like.

_____

_____

Language

1. Write the name of each activity under the correct picture. Use the word bank for help.

acting	cooking	playing the piano
camping	riding a bike	listening to music
playing dominoes	playing a board game	playing snakes and ladders

a)

_____

_____

d)

_____

_____

g)

_____

_____

b)

_____

_____

e)

_____

_____

h)

_____

_____

c)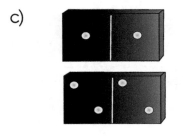

_____

_____

f)

_____

_____

i)

_____

_____

2. Look at each object below, then write the name of the sport it is used in. Use the word bank.

boxing	basketball	skiing	soccer	baseball	golf
tennis	figure skating	diving	running	hockey	badminton

a)

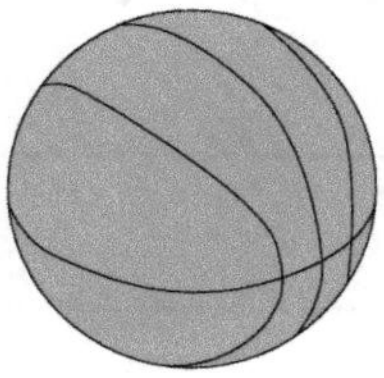

e)

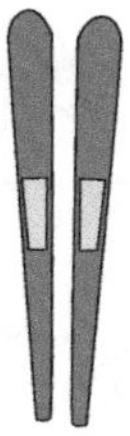

i)

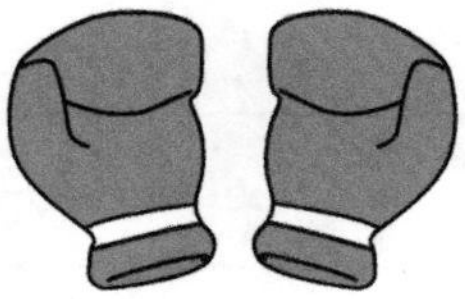

b)

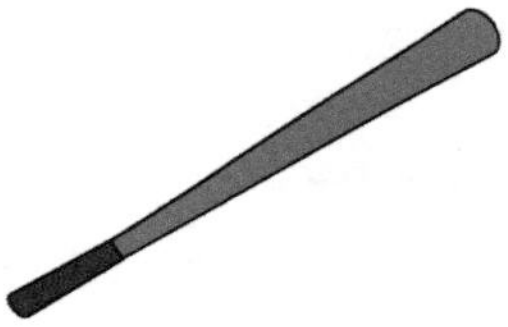

f)

j)

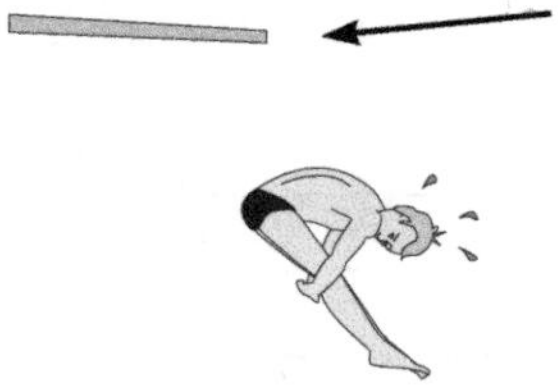

c)

g)

k)

d)

h)

l)

Exercises

Language

3. Write about what chores you do in and around your home. You can draw pictures about them too.

_____

_____

_____

_____

_____

_____

_____

TEST 44

1. Write the name of the activity below each image.

a)

c)

e)

_____
_____

b)

d)

f)

_____
_____

2. Write a sentence about a chore you do at home.

_____
_____

3. Name any three sports.

_____
_____
_____
_____
_____

1. Draw a line from each sport to the object it is played with.

skating	bicycle
downhill skiing	stick
tennis	skates
weight lifting	club
chess	ball
bobsled	skis
football	chessboard
cycling	racket
golf	sled
hockey	weights

2. Write the name of each activity under the correct picture. Use the word bank for help.

collecting hockey cards	reading a book	playing card game
collecting stamps	singing	watching TV

a)

_____
_____

c)

_____
_____

e)

_____
_____

b)

_____
_____

d)

_____
_____

f)

_____
_____

3. **Danica is making a chore chart for herself and her siblings. Each of them does only three chores. Read the clues below, and then write each chore from the word bank in its correct place in the chart.**

wash the dishes	take out the recycling	fold the laundry
dry the dishes	take out the garbage	put away the dishes
shovel snow	put away the laundry	sweep the floor

Exercises

Language

Danica	Melanie	Peter

Only Melanie and Peter do the dishes.

Danica folds the laundry.

Peter shovels snow.

Melanie and Peter don't take out the garbage, but one of them takes out the recycling.

Danica doesn't put the laundry away.

Melanie only washes the dishes.

Only Danica and Melanie do the laundry.

VOCABULARY: SPORTS, CHORES AND HOBBIES

4. Look at the pictures below, and then write a story about what happens.

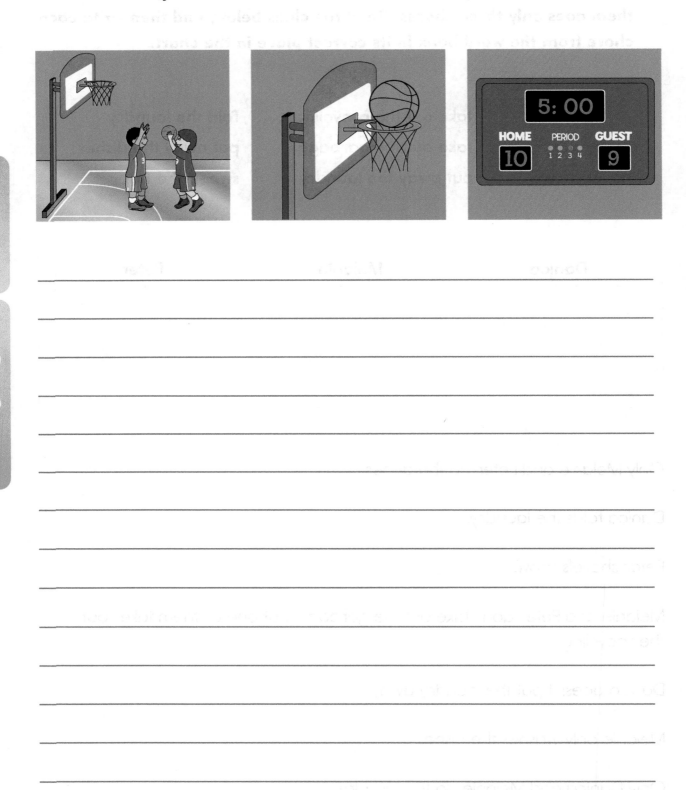

_____

_____

_____

_____

_____

_____

_____

_____

_____

_____

_____

_____

_____

_____

1. **Read the following story and write a brief summary of it on the lines below.**

   Hint: First, identify the main idea, then ask: Who did what, when, why and what happened?

The Boy Who Cried Wolf

Once upon a time, there was a boy whose father sent him to the field to watch over their sheep. If he saw a wolf, he had to yell as loud as possible: "Wolf! Wolf!"

One day, the boy felt bored. He started yelling: "Wolf! Wolf!" His dad, his brothers and sisters and his neighbour ran to the field to chase away the wolf. When they got there, they saw the boy laughing and saying, "There's no wolf!"

The next afternoon, he again started yelling: "Wolf! Wolf!" Everyone ran over to chase it away. When they arrived, the boy was rolling on the ground laughing, "No wolf!". This time, the people were very angry and his dad told him: "Lying is not good. One day, the wolf will come and you will need help, but nobody will believe you because you have lied too often." His dad, brothers, sisters, and neighbours decided to teach him a lesson.

A couple of days later, one of his brothers got disguised as a wolf and hid behind a bush in the farm. The boy yelled: "Wolf! Wolf!" He continued yelling, but no one came to help him. The boy was certain the wolf would come and eat him. He left the field and ran towards the house. His brother laughed, then went home and told him the truth. But the boy had learned his lesson — he would never tell another lie, ever! And he never did lie again.

Summary:

_____

_____

_____

_____

_____

The **main idea** is the most important meaning of something you read. It does not include less important details.

1. Read these passages. Answer the questions.

Ken is very active. He gets up early every morning and goes for a jog before school. Ken rides his bike to school instead of taking the bus.

a) What is the main idea?
   i) Ken likes school.
   ii) Ken is fit.
   iii) Ken likes to ride his bike.

Lisa developed a business plan. She decided to walk dogs for people in the neighbourhood. She created posters and went door to door looking for customers. Lisa got so many customers that she had to hire her friend Elaine to help.

b) What is the main idea?
   i) Lisa is friendly.
   ii) Lisa likes dogs.
   iii) Lisa worked hard to make her plan work.

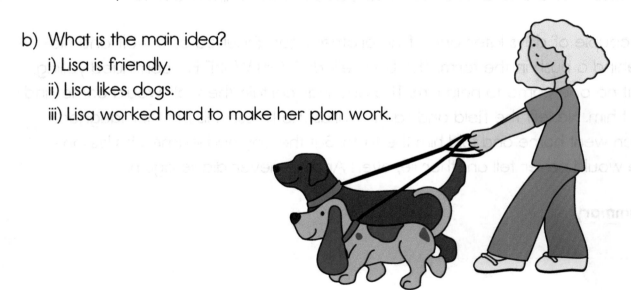

2. Read the story below. Then, answer the questions on the next page.

The Hare and the Tortoise

One day, a hare was mocking a tortoise. "You are a slow poke!" said the hare. "You cannot run even if you try." "You are laughing at me," said the tortoise. "But I think I can beat you in a race." "You will not be able to!" cried the hare. "Oh yes," said the tortoise. "No way!" said the hare. "I will race you and I will win, even with my eyes closed." They asked a fox to be the referee.

"Ready, set, go!" said the fox. The hare left at a fast pace. He travelled so far in such little time that he decided to take a little nap. But his nap turned into a deep sleep! The tortoise continued on his way, one steady step after another, and did not stop. When the hare woke up, he saw the tortoise far ahead of him. He ran as fast as possible to the finish line. But he arrived too late, because the tortoise had already won the race!

a) What is the main idea of this story? Answer in complete sentences.

_____

_____

_____

_____

_____

_____

_____

_____

_____

_____

b) Answer True or False:

i) The hare was mocking the tortoise. _____

ii) The tortoise said he cannot beat the hare in a race. _____

iii) They asked a horse to be the referee. _____

iv) The hare ran very fast and then napped. _____

v) The tortoise stopped often. _____

vi) The hare won the race. _____

1. Read the paragraph. Then, answer the questions below.

Almost everyone likes to eat pizza. In fact, pizza is eaten all over the world. Many different toppings can be put on pizza. The most popular one in Canada is pepperoni. Pizza has ingredients from all four food groups. The crust is a grain product, the cheese is a milk product, the tomato sauce is a vegetable, and the pepperoni is meat. It can be a very healthy dinner if you add a salad on the side and a cold glass of milk.

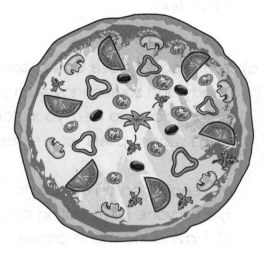

a) What is the main idea of the paragraph? Answer in complete sentences.

_____

_____

_____

_____

b) Which of the following statements is <u>not</u> true? Circle 1, 2, 3 or 4.
  (1) Pizza is a healthy dinner.
  (2) Pizza is only sold in Canada.
  (3) Pizza has ingredients from all four food groups.
  (4) There are many different toppings that can be put on pizza.

c) What do you think should be the title of the paragraph above? Why?

_____

_____

_____

Language

1. Read each text below. Then, choose what you think is the main idea of each text.

a) You probably love eating candy of all sorts: chocolates and gum, sugar candy and sour candy, yum yum! But if you eat too much candy, especially before going to bed, your stomach is likely to feel sick. That's because all the extra sugar upsets your digestion.

   i) Sleeping on an empty stomach is best.
   ii) Everyone loves eating candy.
   iii) Having too much candy can upset the stomach.

b) It is good to try different things yourself before believing them, but some experiments are unnecessary, if not dangerous. Placing your hand in fire is not the best way to learn that fire burns. Believing your parents may be a better option – safety first!

   i) Fire burns.
   ii) Some things are safer to accept than prove through experience.
   iii) Always believe everything your parents say.

c) If you work hard on an assignment, you are likely to not just get a good mark, but may also learn something you didn't know – maybe some new information, maybe a new skill. You are also more likely to remember that information or skill for a long time.

   i) Hard work on assignments leads to good marks, new learning and better recall.
   ii) If you don't work hard, you will fail.
   iii) Working hard is the only way to remember anything.

2. Read each paragraph. Then, write its main idea below in complete sentences.

a) Big Brother

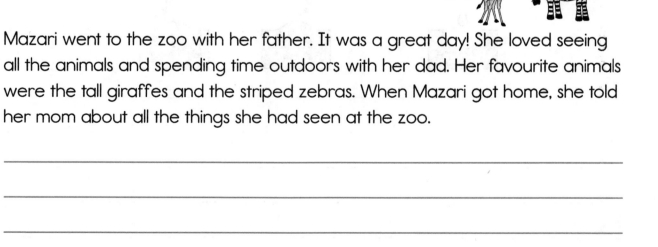

Darren walks his little brother to school every day. They never run, even if they are late for school. They walk only on the sidewalk, except when crossing a street at a pedestrian crosswalk. Darren holds his brother's hand and helps him safely cross the street. He walks his brother to the lineup outside his class door, then goes to his own class.

_____

_____

_____

_____

_____

b) The Zoo

Mazari went to the zoo with her father. It was a great day! She loved seeing all the animals and spending time outdoors with her dad. Her favourite animals were the tall giraffes and the striped zebras. When Mazari got home, she told her mom about all the things she had seen at the zoo.

_____

_____

_____

_____

_____

3. Read the text. Then, answer the question.

Roshawn has never made a school team before. He used to be one of the shortest boys in his class, but this year he has grown so much that now he is the tallest. Every Saturday morning, Roshawn plays basketball at the community centre. He has learned how to dribble and shoot very well.

What is the main idea of this text? Answer in complete sentences.

_____

_____

_____

_____

_____

4. Look at the pictures to get the main idea. Then write a paragraph using the main idea.

_____

_____

_____

_____

_____

_____

_____

Exercises

Language

1. **Read the sentences below about brushing your teeth. Number them in the correct order from 1 to 7 in the boxes.**

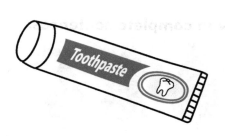  

Spit out the toothpaste. ☐

Put the toothbrush and toothpaste away. ☐

Move the brush all over your teeth. ☐

Wet the toothbrush and toothpaste with a little water. ☐

Get out your toothbrush and the toothpaste. ☐

Rinse off the toothbrush. ☐

Squeeze toothpaste onto your toothbrush. ☐

Sequencing means putting things in correct order. It is the order in which the events take place. To understand the order in which things happen in a story, look for time order words like *first*, *next*, and *finally*.

1. Read the story. Then answer the questions below in complete sentences.

The Campfire

Samantha helped her father start a campfire. First, she cleared the fire pit. Next, she set up lots of kindling that would burn quickly and then added two big logs that would burn more slowly. After striking the match and lighting the fire, she waited a few minutes to see if the wood had caught fire. Finally, Samantha put a hot dog on a long stick and held it just above the fire until it was cooked.

a) What did Samantha do first?

_____

_____

_____

_____

b) What did Samantha do next to start the camp fire?

_____

_____

_____

c) What did Samantha do last?

_____

_____

_____

2. **Look at the following pictures on this page and the next. What is happening in them? Write a sentence below each picture to tell the story. Use words like *first, then, afterwards, later, however, finally*, to show the sequence in your story.**

a)

_____

_____

b)

_____

_____

c)

_____

_____

d)

_____

_____

e)

_____

_____

f)

_____

_____

g)

_____

_____

h)

_____

_____

1. **Read the following sentences. Write them in the correct order on the lines provided.**

Carving a Pumpkin

Carve a face into the pumpkin.

Bring the pumpkin home.

Put a candle in the pumpkin.

Get out a sharp knife.

Cut off the top and scoop out the seeds.

Pick a pumpkin from the patch.

Light the candle and set the pumpkin outside when dark.

a) _____

b) _____

c) _____

d) _____

e) _____

f) _____

g) _____

Exercises

Language

1. **Look at the pictures on this page and the next. What is happening in them? Write a line below each picture to tell the story. Use words like *first*, *then*, *afterwards*, *later*, *however*, *finally*, to show the sequence in your story.**

a)

_____

_____

b)

_____

_____

c)

_____

_____

d)

_____

_____

e)

_____

_____

f)

_____

_____

2. Your friend gave you a recipe but it is all mixed up. Read it, then write the recipe steps in the correct order on the lines below.

Banana cookies

Ingredients:

125 ml of flour
2 ml of baking soda
1 pinch of nutmeg
2 ml of cinnamon powder
250 ml of sugar

450 ml of oats
250 ml of mashed bananas
125 ml of cocoa flakes
450 ml of melted butter
1 egg

Method:

Secondly, add oats, mashed bananas and cocoa flakes.

Finally, cook in the oven at 180° Celsius for 12 to 15 minutes.

First, mix together the flour, baking soda, nutmeg, cinnamon powder and sugar.

Fourthly, mix well. Make little balls and place them on a baking sheet.

Thirdly, melt the butter and add it to the rest of the ingredients. Beat an egg lightly and add to the mix.

_____

_____

_____

_____

_____

_____

_____

_____

Exercises

Language

1. **Before reading the following story, look at the list of categories below.**
   As you read, circle the words that fit in any of the four categories.
   Then fill in the categories with the words you've circled.
   ***Bonus – Which category has four items in it?**

Jeffery, Samantha, and Kevin are talking about where they hope to travel some day. "I want to go on a plane to Germany." Samantha says. "My mom says they make delicious pretzels and sausages!"

"I can't wait to drive to the United States and spend time in Florida. My dad bought me a new bathing suit," says Jeffery. "Oh yes," says Kevin. "You would love Florida. They have lots of ice cream stands and you might get to drive a golf cart."

"I'm going to take a train to France to buy some new shoes and a pretty dress," says Samantha. "I've been saving up since last summer!"

"It sounds like everyone will have a wonderful trip some day!" says Jeff.

Countries

1. _____
2. _____
3. _____
   _____

Clothing and Accessories

1. _____
2. _____
3. _____
   _____

Ways to travel

1. _____
2. _____
3. _____
   _____

Food

1. _____
2. _____
3. _____
   _____

1. Read the story. Answer the questions on the next page.

Summer Camp Story

Rob was nervous. In less than one week, he was leaving to go to camp for the first time. Rob had read about camp, and his older brother Jeff had gone for the last two summers, but he still couldn't help being afraid. Rob was always scared when he tried new things.

On Saturday morning, his mom and dad woke him at 8 o'clock so he could have a good breakfast before leaving for camp. Rob's stomach flipped when he saw his bags beside the front door. He calmed himself down during breakfast by pretending he wasn't going, but that didn't last long. Before he knew it, the car was packed and the family was on their way.

As they drove, Rob's family told him funny stories about when they had been at camp. Jeff talked about a time when he fell out of a canoe and got soaked. Rob's mom talked about meeting lots of friends and the funny pranks they played on each other.

When they arrived at camp, Rob met his counsellor and the rest of the boys in his cabin. He said a tearful goodbye to his family and then set up his sleeping bag and gear. That night, Rob found it really hard to get to sleep. All he could think about was his family.

The next morning finally came. After breakfast, it was time for a canoe lesson. Rob found out he liked something called "gunwale bobbing" and that the other boys in his cabin were really nice. Before he knew it, the day was over and it was time to go to sleep. The rest of the week flew by. Rob tried many new things. He went canoeing and kayaking. He went hiking in the woods with a map and compass. Rob even slept outdoors on the last night!

Rob was sad when he woke up on the last morning. He couldn't believe how much fun camp had been. When his mom and dad arrived, Rob gave them both a big hug. He told them he was counting down the days until next summer when he would be going to camp again!

Answer these questions about "Summer Camp Story". Write your answers in complete sentences.

a) Why was Rob so nervous?

_____

_____

_____

_____

b) What were some of the things his family did to help Rob feel better?

_____

_____

_____

_____

c) Was there a time when you were nervous about something? Why?

_____

_____

_____

_____

d) What did Rob learn about himself while he was at camp?

_____

_____

_____

_____

2. Read the story and answer the questions on the next two pages. Write in complete sentences.

Jack and Ol' Mossyfoot – A Folk Tale

Jack was 10 years old. He was getting bored of playing in his yard. He told himself he was old enough to explore a bit, so he went out. Jack was fascinated by everything he saw. However, exploring is tiring work and Jack fell asleep under a tree. He slept for a long time. When he woke up, the sun was setting.

When it began to get dark, Jack followed a path and found himself in a big forest. To stay warm, he made a fire. Then, he heard something like: whoomity whop, whoomity whop! Right away, Jack knew it was Ol' Mossyfoot and he was very scared!

He grabbed a stick from the fire and threw it in the direction of the sound. The stick fell and sparked, which scared the monster away. Jack thought maybe he should leave, when he heard it again: whoomity whop, whoomity whop! He grabbed another stick and waited for Ol' Mossyfoot. Jack threw the stick as hard as he could.

The stick landed directly on the mossy, sticky feet of the monster. The creature ran away again into the forest. Jack knew it would be better if he left. However, before he could leave, he heard again, whoomity whop, whoomity whop!

Jack began to run as fast as he could. Behind him, he heard the loud steps of the monster. Jack climbed up a tree. The monster was so sticky that it could not climb up the tree. Then, Jack heard the munching of big teeth. The monster was eating the tree! The tree began to bend more and more and more. Finally, there was a big rumble and the tree began to fall. Jack was falling towards Ol' Mossyfoot. Right before the tree hit the ground... Jack woke up!

a)   How old is Jack?

_____

_____

b)   Where did Jack sleep?

_____

_____

c)   What did Jack do to stay warm?

_____

_____

d)   What did Jack throw at the monster twice?

_____

_____

e)   Where did Jack take shelter?

_____

_____

f)   What words did Jack use to describe the steps of the monster?

_____

_____

g)   Why couldn't the monster climb the tree?

_____

_____

h)   Why was the monster eating the tree?

_____

_____

i)   What happened before Jack touched the ground?

_____

_____

j) What is the setting for this story? Where does the story take place? Draw Jack, Ol' Mossyfoot and the setting for this story.

TEST 50

1. Read the text, then answer the questions.

Bender

Bender is a large black cat. He loves to _____ around the neighbourhood looking for things to do. Sometimes neighbours find him far from his home and need to contact his owners. Bender's favourite thing to do is sleep in the sun, either inside or outside, depending on the time of year. He has a really loud purr that gives instant gratification to the person who is patting him. Hearing Bender purr always makes people smile.

1. Circle the best word for the blank in this paragraph.
   a) skip
   b) roam
   c) hop
   d) dance

2. Circle the word that means the same as *gratification*.
   a) shock
   b) headache
   c) pleasure
   d) dismay

3. Underline the words in the paragraph that helped you answer #2.

4. Write a sentence of your own using the word *gratification*.

_____

_____

_____

_____

_____

1. Read the letter. Then, answer the questions on the next page in complete sentences.

Dear Julie,

Thank you for having our class visit your farm near Orangeville last week. I loved feeding the goats and chickens. Your little dog Bailey made me laugh when he trotted down the lane beside your tall horse, Thunder.

On the bus trip back to Barrie, I told my teacher, Mrs. Chen, how much I loved taking care of the animals. She told me that if I study hard at school, maybe I could become a vet one day.

All the pupils at Pine Lane School are looking forward to visiting your farm again when the baby chicks hatch!

Yours truly,

Anika

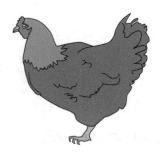

a) Who is writing this letter?

Anika is writing the letter.

b) Which school does the letter writer go to? In which town?

The letter writter goes to pine lane school which is in orangeville.

c) Where did the students go on a class visit? What did they do there?

They went to farm near orangeville. They took care of some of the animals.

d) What made the letter writer laugh?

There was a dog called bailey at the farm made her laugh when he trotted beside Julie's tall horse

e) What did the letter writer tell her teacher? What was the reply?

She told her teacher how much she loved taking care of the pets and the teacher replied if you study hard you can be a vet.

f) Where would you like to go on a class visit? Why?

I want to go to a war museum on a school trip so that i can Learn about historical events that happened in the past.

2. Read the story. Then, answer the questions on the next page.

A Trip to the Park — by Ahsan Rahim-Zada

Daniel and I stood with my dad at the entrance to the park. "Race you to the swings!" yelled Daniel. I ran so hard I felt my legs were going to fall off.

"Hey Dad, can you come and push us, pretty please?" My dad came over and pushed both of us at once! I went so high I felt like I could reach up and grab a piece of the clouds and bring it down. When we jumped off, I felt a little dizzy. "Let's go down the slide now," I said to Daniel. "Mr. Morra, could you please push us down the slide?" asked Daniel. Then, we went down zippy fast to the bottom.

"Let's go on the monkey bars now," Daniel said. Uh, oh, I thought. You see, the thing is Daniel is in Grade 4 and I am in Grade 3 and the monkey bars wobble. My dad says they are at least five feet high so you have to jump to get on them.

"Hurry up, Matthew!" yelled Daniel. So I walked slowly over, thinking, I can do this! Daniel had already done it, so he was waiting on the other side.
I jumped up and, yes, I grabbed the first bar! Only nine more.

"Just think: one hand, two hand," said Daniel.

"Okay, so one and two, one and two, one and two, one and two, one and two, one and two, one and two, one and two, one and two!"

"Matthew, you did it!" yelled Daniel.
"Way to go, Sport!" said my dad.
"Wow, I did it."
"Okay, guys, time to go," my dad said.
"Hey, Dad? Can we come back tomorrow?"
"Sure thing, Matthew, and Daniel can come too."
So that was my most favourite trip to the park.

After reading "A Trip to the Park", answer these questions. Write your answers in complete sentences.

a) Why was Matthew so nervous?

_____

_____

_____

_____

_____

b) Why did Matthew start counting to himself?

_____

_____

_____

_____

_____

_____

c) Have you ever felt this way before trying something new? What did you do?

_____

_____

_____

_____

_____

d) Do you think that having Daniel there helped Matthew complete the monkey bars? Why or why not?

_____

_____

_____

_____

_____

_____

Setting

e) Where is "A Trip to the Park" set? Draw the setting for the story.

1. **Create a story about your favourite hero or heroine. You can use the words in parentheses below or add your own. Do not forget that your story must have a beginning, a middle and an end.**

(firstly, primarily, once upon a time, one day, at the beginning, etc.)

The pals was a big group channel it contains Corl, Denis, Sketch, Alex and Sub. The main person who gave the pals alot of fans was Denis.

(secondly, afterwards, however, later, etc.)

Earlier The pals was in drama kind of about stealing small youtubers thumbnail. Then the group deleted those videos. So then the pals were not being talked about, until 2019.

(finally, to conclude, lastly, then, etc.)

Then Corl was being rude to a fan. That got so popular that the pals had to take action about so they removed Corl from the pals. Then stoped uploading on the pals because they didn't feel like uploading anymore

1. **Get ready to write a letter to your friends inviting them over for a sleepover. You need to tell them what time to come, what they need to bring, what fun things you will do together, and what time their parents need to pick them up the next day.**

a) Use the space below to plan your letter and write a rough draft. Then, edit it yourself or ask for the help of a friend or parent.

Remember that a letter needs to include your address, the date, greeting words ("Dear" or "Hi" and your friend's name), closing words ("Goodbye", "Thanks", "Take care", "See you soon", etc.) and your name as signature at the bottom.

_____

_____

_____

_____

_____

_____

_____

_____

_____

_____

_____

_____

_____

_____

_____

_____

_____

b) Now that you have planned out your letter, write out its final draft below.

_____

_____

_____

_____

_____

_____

_____

_____

_____

_____

_____

_____

_____

_____

_____

_____

_____

_____

_____

_____

_____

_____

_____

_____

_____

_____

2. Read the story. Answer the questions on the next page.

The School Trip

Berner Trail's Grade 3 class was going on a trip to the sugar bush to learn all about maple syrup. They had been studying about the early pioneers in class. They knew that the pioneers had learned from the First Nations people how to make maple syrup and use it as a sweetener. The class had worked hard, and their teacher, Mrs. Shroff, had arranged the trip as a reward for all their hard work.

Mr. Hoby, the school bus driver, parked the bus in front of the school and the students all boarded. They were off! After about 30 minutes, the bus pulled into a Conservation Area. It was beautiful! A guide named Sue met them as the students all filed out of the bus. She led them along a path towards the sugar shack, pointing out the sap buckets along the way. Soon the group arrived at an area that had a big fire going and a large black pot hanging over it. Sue explained to the students that the sap they had seen being collected along the way was boiling in the pot over the fire. She explained the steps needed to turn the sap into syrup.

Sue told the students to take a seat on the logs around the fire. Next, she went into the sugar shack and came out with plates piled high with pancakes for each of them. Mrs. Shroff was given a jug of maple syrup to pour over the pancakes. The students loved the treat. They all agreed that Canadian maple syrup was one of the best things that the early pioneers learned to make from the First Nations people. It was a great day!

a) Prepare to rewrite the Grade 3 school trip from the point of view of Sue, the tour guide, or of Mr. Hoby, the bus driver. Make a plan for the beginning, middle and end of your story. Brainstorm some new vocabulary. Use the lines below to jot down points that will help you write your story of the Grade 3 trip from a different point of view on the next page.

Bus Driver or Tour Guide? Choose: _____

Plot: _____

Beginning: _____
_____
_____
_____
_____

Middle: _____
_____
_____
_____
_____

End: _____
_____
_____
_____
_____

New vocabulary: _____
_____
_____
_____
_____
_____

New story title: _____

b) Now, write your new story about the Grade 3 school trip below.
    Remember to use connecting words like *first, then, next, finally*, etc.

A **haiku** is a poem of three lines. The first line has five syllables, the second has seven, and the last has five.

For example: Happy, sunny day, (5)
Swimming, hiking, playing ball, (7)
Warm, no shoes, ice cream. (5)

1. a) **Get ready to write a haiku. Choose a topic that you know well – for example, friends, family, seasons, sports, etc. Use the brainstorm bubbles below to jot down words about that topic.**

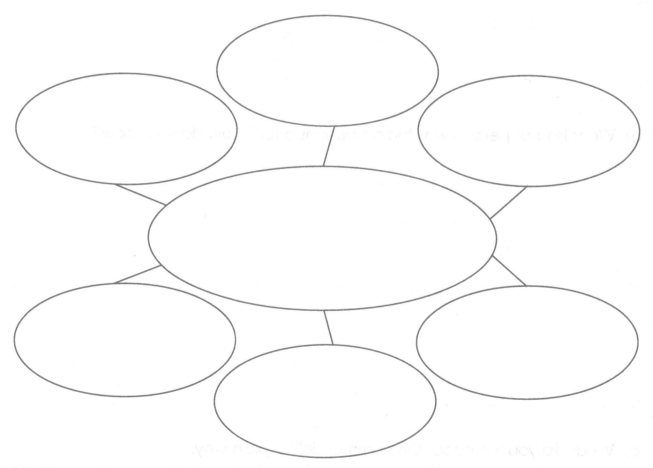

b) **Now write your haiku on the lines. Remember to count the number of syllables.**

_____ (5)

_____ (7)

_____ (5)

Media Literacy: TV Commercial and Magazine Ad

1. **Watch a commercial on TV. Pay close attention to the people shown and the words and colours used. Make sure you know what the ad is for. Complete the following questions about what you saw. Remember to use what you've already learned about fact vs. opinion.**

a) Describe what was being sold. (Use your senses to help you.)

_____

_____

_____

_____

_____

_____

b) What kind of person was this ad designed for? How do you know?

_____

_____

_____

_____

_____

_____

_____

_____

_____

_____

_____

c) What did you like about this commercial? Explain why.

_____

_____

_____

_____

_____

d) Design your own magazine ad for the same product. Remember to use a memorable catchphrase, strong selling words and colourful images.

e) Explain how your magazine ad is different from the TV commercial for the same product. Hints: Think about the different formats (sound and video words and images) and their effects on the audience, (Who watches TV around the time you saw the commercial? Who reads the type of magazine in which your ad will appear?).

Fables are stories that teach a lesson or moral. There are many famous fables that you have probably heard about. Fables usually use animals as the main characters.

2. Read the fable called "The Man and the Crow".

One day, a man was walking in a park. He sat on a bench to eat his lunch. A crow flew by and tried to eat his sandwich. The man told the crow, "Fly away!" Then, the man thought the crow must be hungry and told the crow he would leave him some crumbs to eat. The crow ate the crumbs and was very thankful.

The man started to leave the park. The wind became very strong and blew his hat off. The crow caught the hat in his beak and brought it back to the man. The man thanked the crow.

The moral of the story is: Help others as you want to be helped.

a) Now get ready to write your own fable. Use the space below to help you build your ideas about the following:

Main characters: If your main character is sly, you might choose a fox. If it is wise, you could choose an owl. Setting: Where does your story take place? Plot: Beginning: What happens in the beginning? How will you introduce your characters? Middle: What problem arises? End: How is the problem solved? What lesson is taught in this fable?

b) Now that you have planned out your fable, write it out.

_____

_____

_____

_____

_____

_____

_____

_____

_____

_____

_____

_____

_____

_____

_____

_____

_____

_____

_____

_____

_____

_____

Exercises

Language

TEST 53

1. **Plan and write a big paragraph about your favourite food. Remember to have a topic sentence (beginning), supporting details (middle) and a closing sentence (end). Jot down your points on a different sheet of paper, organize them, write a rough draft and edit it, and then write your final paragraph here.**

   Hints: Think about what your favourite food is and since when, what it is made of, where you eat it or who makes it, when and how often you eat it, what makes it your favourite food, and anything else you can think of.

My favorite food is chili panneer. It became my favorite since 2020. Sometimes my mom makes it but ussually i order it from resturants. We eat it if theres party. Ussually i eat it at a resturant called avani and they one of the best chili panneers. So a chili paneer taste kind of like a momo or a dumpling but a tiny bit spicear. So a chili paneer is like a cheese cube with hot and sour sause.

A **paragraph** is a piece of writing that usually has just one main point or idea.

1. a) Choose a topic from the following list:

i) Your pet
ii) A summer day
iii) Your favourite sport
iv) Your favourite subject at school

b) Once you've chosen the topic, use the bubbles below to brainstorm ideas and words you will use to write a paragraph.

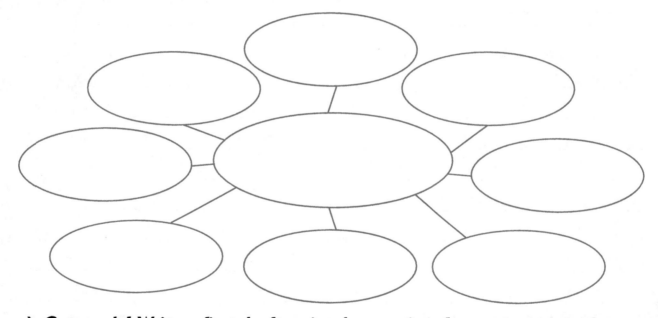

c) Get ready! Write a first draft or jot down points for your paragraph using your ideas and vocabulary. Then, organize your points (one way is to number them in the order you will write them). Have someone help you edit your work for spelling and punctuation.

_____

_____

_____

_____

_____

Exercises

Language

d) Ready? Write your final paragraph here. Remember to have a beginning, middle and end, and to use connecting words like *first*, *then*, *next*, *finally*, etc.

_____

_____

_____

_____

_____

_____

_____

_____

_____

_____

_____

_____

_____

_____

_____

_____

_____

_____

_____

_____

_____

2. a) You need to prepare to write one big paragraph about your favourite animal. To help you, first write a few words on each topic below that will help you organize your paragraph.

Name of the animal: _____

Habitat (where it usually lives): _____

Its physical appearance (weight, size, colour, height, and other important characteristics):

_____

_____

_____

_____

_____

_____

Its normal lifespan (how long it lives): _____

What it eats: _____

Other facts:

_____

_____

_____

_____

_____

_____

_____

_____

_____

Exercises

Language

b) Draw this animal and its habitat.

c) **Now write one big paragraph about your favourite animal, using your points from the previous page to organize it properly.**

_____

_____

_____

_____

_____

_____

_____

_____

_____

_____

_____

_____

_____

_____

_____

_____

_____

_____

_____

_____

_____

_____

_____

_____

Exercises

Language

TEST 54

1. **Plan and write a paragraph about your home. Remember to have a topic sentence (beginning), supporting details (middle) and a closing sentence (end). Jot down your points on a different sheet of paper, organize them, write a rough draft and edit it, and then write your final paragraph here.**

Hints: Think about what kind of home you live in, its size, the number and type of rooms, the colours of the walls, what kind of floors it has, who lives in it, what you like and don't like about it, and anything else you can think of.

1. a) Think about your last vacation. Prepare to write a paragraph about it on the next page. To help you, use the space below to make notes and organize the order of the events in your story.

When did you go on vacation?: _____

Who did you go with?: _____

_____

Where did you go?: _____

How did you travel? (airplane. train, bus, car, etc): _____
Places where you slept (hotel, camp, cottage, etc):

_____
_____
_____

Interesting places that you visited:

_____
_____
_____

Interesting activities that you did:

_____
_____
_____

People you met:

_____
_____
_____

The best part of the vacation:

_____
_____
_____

The worst part of the vacation:

_____
_____

b) **Using your notes from the previous page, write a big paragraph about your vacation.**

_____

_____

_____

_____

_____

_____

_____

_____

_____

_____

_____

_____

_____

_____

_____

_____

_____

_____

_____

_____

_____

2. Your sailing ship has just been shipwrecked on a deserted island. There are mysterious lizards on the island. It is your job to write a report about them. Answer the following questions using describing words about the lizards.

a) What do the lizards' heads look like? Describe their eyes, ears, nose and mouth.

_____

_____

_____

b) What do the lizards' bodies look like? What is the size, shape and colour of their bodies?

_____

_____

_____

c) How do the lizards move around? How do they communicate?

_____

_____

_____

d) Use your imagination to get ready to write a big paragraph about what the lizards look like and what they do. Use the space below or a separate sheet of paper to organize your points.

e) Write a big paragraph about the lizards using all your points from the previous page. Make sure to include a topic sentence and to use describing words.

_____

_____

_____

_____

_____

_____

_____

_____

_____

_____

_____

_____

_____

_____

_____

_____

f) Draw one of the lizards that you saw on the island.

g) Draw the deserted island.

MATHEMATICS

Numbers to 1000 and Place Value

Addition, Subtraction, Multiplication, Division

Fractions, Decimals, Money

Shapes and Measurement

Location, Symmetry and Patterns

Data Management and Probability

CANADIAN CURRICULUM PRESS

Forward Learning

1. Circle the number that correctly matches the words.

a) one hundred and seventy-five

    75   (175)   425

b) one hundred and twenty-one

    (121)   321   431

c) three hundred

    400   500   (300)

d) one hundred

    200   300   (100)

e) two hundred and eighty

    347   (280)   184

2. Round the following numbers to the closest ten.

a) 311 _____310_____

c) 138 _____140_____

b) 274 _____270_____

d) 481 _____480_____

3. Answer the following questions.

a) How many ones are there in 463? _____3_____

b) How many hundreds are there in 367? _____3_____

c) What number is in the tens place in 384? _____8_____

4. Write the following numbers in expanded form.

a) 301 _____

c) 424 _____

b) 238 _____

d) 158 _____

1. Write the numbers that follow on the number line. The first one is started for you.

a) 174 175 176 177 178 179 180 181 182 183

b) 321 322

c) 253 254

d) 79 80

e) 353 354

f) 160 161

g) 256 257

h) 287 288

2. Write the following numbers in expanded form.

Here is an example: 157 = 100 + 50 + 7

a) 454 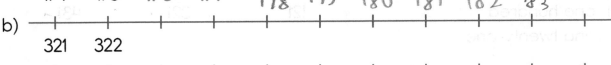 400 + 50 + 7

g) 438 _____

b) 365  300 + 60 + 5

h) 399 _____

c) 187 = 100 + 80 + 7

i) 452 _____

d) 215 _____

j) 277 _____

e) 471 _____

k) 402 _____

f) 458 400 + 50 + 8

l) 379 _____

Exercises

Mathematics

3. **What is the place value of the underlined digit in each number?**
The first one is done for you.

a) 5<u>9</u>3   90   e) <u>2</u>58   200   i) 47<u>9</u>   9

b) 1<u>7</u>4   70   f) <u>3</u>94   300   j) 1<u>3</u>   3

c) <u>4</u>58   400   g) <u>8</u>7   80   k) 3<u>3</u>3   30

d) <u>2</u>1   20   h) <u>1</u>85   100   l) 3<u>3</u>0   30

4. **Write each digit in the correct place value column for the following**
numbers. The first one is done for you.

		Hundreds	Tens	Ones
a)	489	4	8	9
b)	323	3	2	3
c)	474	4	7	4
d)	166	1	6	6
e)	225	2	2	5

5. **Place the following numbers on the number line at the correct places and in the**
correct order. Then, add the missing numbers to complete each number line.

a) 120, 122, 124, 125

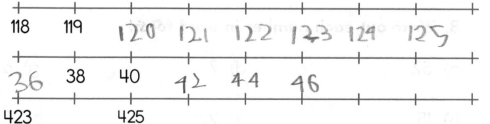

118   119   120   121   122   123   124   125

b) 52, 42, 46, 36

36   38   40   42   44   46

c) 424, 427, 430, 429

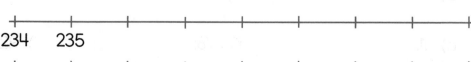

423   425

d) 236, 239, 238, 241

234   235

e) 195, 190, 210, 200

175   180

6. Complete the maze table with the missing numbers.

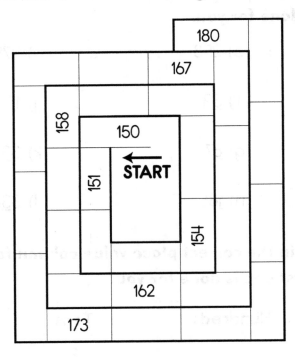

7. Complete the table.

	Standard Form	Expanded Form
a)	212	200 + 10 + 2
b)	464	400 + 60 + 4
c)	395	300 + 90 + 5
d)	498	400 + 90 + 8
e)	196	100 + 90 + 6

8. Write out each number in word form.

a) 52: _____

b) 15: _____

c) 11: _____

d) 7: _____

e) 22: _____

f) 78: _____

g) 66: _____

h) 100: _____

i) 92: _____

9. Write each number in word form. The first one is done for you.

i) **11** eleven	viii) **6** six	xv) **25**	xxii) **34**
ii) **30**	ix) **40** forty	xvi) **37**	xxiii) **7**
iii) **5**	x) **19**	xvii) **26**	xxiv) **70**
iv) **55**	xi) **15**	xviii) **67**	xxv) **2**
v) **9**	xii) **21**	xix) **31**	xxvi) **60**
vi) **29**	xiii) **33**	xx) **1**	xxvii) **27**
vii) **14**	xiv) **100**	xxi) **17**	xxviii) **22**

10. Read each number in word form and write it in digits. The first one is
   done for you.

i) eighteen 18	viii) thirty-five	xv) thirteen	xxii) nineteen
ii) fifty	ix) twenty-four	xvi) thirty-nine	xxiii) fourteen
iii) thirty-six	x) three	xvii) eighty	xxiv) sixty
iv) twenty-eight	xi) seventy-one	xviii) eight	xxv) one hundred
v) twelve	xii) twenty	xix) twenty-six	xxvi) forty-two
vi) thirty-eight	xiii) ten	xx) sixteen	xxvii) thirty-seven
vii) ninety	xiv) four	xxi) thirty-two	xxviii) one

TEST 56

1. Find the pattern for each series below and continue it for the next six numbers.

a) 115, 120, 125, __130 135 140 145 150 155 160__

b) 246, 271, 296, __321 346 371 396 421 446__

c) 350, 340, 330, __320 310 300 290 280 270 260 250__

d) 100, 150, 200, _____

e) 215, 224, 233, __242 251 260 269 166 155__

2. Circle the number in digits that corresponds to the one in words.

a) one hundred and eighty   389   (180)   125

b) three hundred   (300)   339   309

c) four hundred and one   400   (401)   444

d) two hundred and twelve   (212)   301   294

e) one hundred and ninety-four   151   127   (194)

3. Complete the place value table.

		Hundreds	Tens	Ones
a)	389	3 00	8 0	9
b)	236	2 00	3 0	6
c)	495			
d)	152			
e)	358			

Mathematics

1. Write the following numbers in digits.

a) three hundred and ten: _____

b) four hundred and twenty: _____

c) two hundred and thirty-one: _____

d) four hundred and thirteen: _____

e) one hundred and twelve: _____

f) three hundred and seven: _____

g) two hundred and twenty-one: _____

h) four hundred and seventy-three: _____

i) one hundred and thirty-nine: _____

j) three hundred and nine: _____

2. Write the missing numbers to complete the table.

424	425	426	427	428	429	430	431	932
				437				
	443							
						457		
		462						
							476	
				482				
	488							
				500				

3. Find the pattern and continue it for 3 more numbers.

a) 225, 230, 235, __240__ , __245__ , __250__

b) 237, 247, 257, __267__ , __272__ , __287__

c) 213, 215, 217, __219__ , __221__ , __224__

d) 215, 224, 233, __242__ , __251__ , __260__

e) 192, 292, 392, __492__ , __592__ , __692__

4. **Write each numeral in its correct place value spot for the following numbers. The first one is done for you.**

		Hundreds	Tens	Ones
a)	158	1	5	8
b)	387			
c)	148			
d)	432			
e)	246			

5. **What is the place value of the underlined digit in each number?**

a) 1̲25 _____

c) 45̲8 _____

e) 18̲9 _____

b) 352̲ _____

d) 2̲41 _____

f) 2̲94 _____

6. **Using the numbers 1, 3, 9 in any order, write as many numbers as you can think of that fit these patterns.**

a) A one-digit number: _____

b) A two-digit number: _____

c) A three-digit number: _____

7. **Write the following numerals in words.**

a) 447 _____

b) 381 _____

c) 201 _____

8. Find the number of ones, tens, and hundreds in the following numbers. The first one is done for you.

a) **389**

How many ones? _____9_____

How many tens? _____8_____

How many hundreds? _____3_____

b) **478**

How many ones? _____

How many tens? _____

How many hundreds? _____

c) **199**

How many ones? _____

How many tens? _____

How many hundreds? _____

d) **241**

How many ones? _____

How many tens? _____

How many hundreds? _____

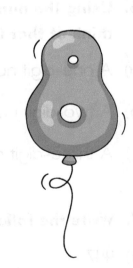

e) **369**

How many ones? _____

How many tens? _____

How many hundreds? _____

TEST 57

1. Find the pattern and continue it for 5 more numbers.

a) 258, 259, 260, _____

b) 455, 410, 365, ⟨10⟩ ⟨45⟩ 315 260 200 _____

c) 129, 249, 369, 389 409 429 449 469 489 509 529

2. Write the following numerals in words.

a) 123 _____

b) 871 _____

c) 325 _____

d) 258 _____

3. Continue the number pattern for 4 more numbers.

a) 441, 440, 439, _____ , _____ , _____ , _____

b) 125, 126, 127, _____ , _____ , _____ , _____

c) 550, 555, 560, 565 , 470 , 975 , 480

4. Indicate the place value of the underlined digit in each number.

a) 8̲74 _____   c) 7̲20 _____

b) 74̲1 _____   d) 81̲5 _____

Mathematics

Exercises

Mathematics

1. Complete the maze table by adding the missing numbers.

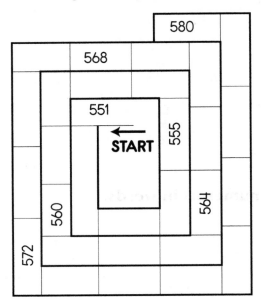

2. Write the following numbers in the place value chart.

		Hundreds	Tens	Ones
a)	589			
b)	785			
c)	148			
d)	777			
e)	333			
f)	978			

3. Answer the questions.

a) How many ones are there in 524? _____

b) How many hundreds are there in 426? _____

c) What number is at the ones place in 899? _____

d) What number is at the tens place in 125? _____

4. Round to the closest ten.

a) 789 _____

b) 123 _____

c) 336 _____

d) 458 _____

e) 999 _____

f) 551 _____

5. Round to the closest hundred.

a) 326 _300_

b) 223 _200_

c) 178 _200_

d) 496 _500_

e) 843 _800_

f) 721 _700_

6. Write the following numbers in standard form. The first one is done for you.

a) 300 + 80 + 4 _384_

b) 700 + 10 + 2 _712_

c) 700 + 60 + 3 _763_

d) 600 + 50 + 5 _____

e) 500 + 30 + 2 _532_

f) 100 + 90 + 7 _197_

7. Write the following numbers as digits.

a) two hundred and twenty-eight: _____

b) nine hundred and sixty-one: _____

c) three hundred and fifty-five: _____

d) one hundred and seventy: _____

e) three hundred and twenty-three: _____

8. Write the following numbers in expanded form.

a) 750 _____

b) 896 _____

c) 478 _____

d) 783 _____

e) 111 _____

f) 555 _____

9. Write the hundreds, tens and ones for the following numbers in the place value chart. The first one is done for you.

		Hundreds	Tens	Ones
a)	587	5	8	7
b)	369			
c)	581			
d)	416			
e)	236			
f)	547			
g)	123			
h)	475			
i)	347			
j)	148			
k)	563			

Exercises

Mathematics

TEST 58

1. Write the number that comes…

before	after	between

a) _____ 785   e) 239 _____   i) 258 _____ 260

b) _____ 992   f) 523 _____   j) 361 _____ 363

c) _____ 563   g) 247 _____   k) 840 _____ 842

d) _____ 785   h) 239 _____   l) 239 _____ 241

2. Place each digit from these numbers in its place value spot.

a) 159

Hundreds: _____

Tens: _____

Ones: _____

b) 741

Hundreds: _____

Tens: _____

Ones: _____

c) 362

Hundreds: _____

Tens: _____

Ones: _____

3. Answer the questions.

a) How many ones are there in 442? _____

b) How many hundreds are there in 631? _____

c) What number is at the ones place in 745? _____

d) What number is at the tens place in 588? _____

1. Complete the table.

221						227		
				234				
	240							
						254		
		259						
							273	
				279				
	285							
				297				

2. Write the numbers that follow on the number line. The first one is started for you.

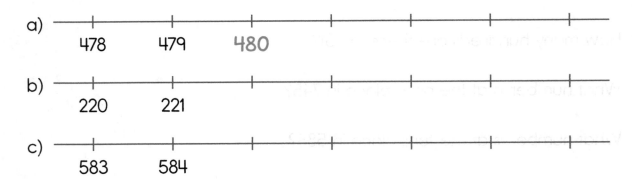

a) 478 479 480

b) 220 221

c) 583 584

3. Write the number of ones, tens, and hundreds for the following numbers. The first one is done for you.

a) **589**

How many ones? _____ 9 _____

How many tens? _____ 8 _____

How many hundreds? _____ 5 _____

b) **121**

How many ones? _____

How many tens? _____

How many hundreds? _____

c) **256**

How many ones? _____

How many tens? _____

How many hundreds? _____

d) **788**

How many ones? _____

How many tens? _____

How many hundreds? _____

e) **367**

How many ones? _____

How many tens? _____

How many hundreds? _____

4. Write each numeral in its correct place value spot for the following numbers.

a) 478

Hundreds: _____

Tens: _____

Ones: _____

b) 823

Hundreds: _____

Tens: _____

Ones: _____

c) 661

Hundreds: _____

Tens: _____

Ones: _____

5. Write the place value of the underlined digit in each number.

a) 169 _____

b) 815 _____

6. Round each number to the nearest hundred.

a) 963 _____

b) 457 _____

c) 146 _____

d) 412 _____

e) 284 _____

f) 121 _____

7. Complete the table.

326					332			
				339				
	345							
					359			
		364						
						378		
				384				
	390							
				402				

1. Compare the numbers using the symbols >, < or =.

a) 445 ◯ 357

b) 254 ◯ 254

c) 452 ◯ 371

d) 354 ◯ 247

e) 187 ◯ 279

f) 237 ◯ 157

2. Circle the largest number in each group.

a) 452	147	129	458
b) 730	739	147	458
c) 321	415	236	129

3. Place the numbers in order from least to greatest.

a) 627   215   125   28   129

b) 236   124   897   128   139

c) 947   949   846   752   738

Mathematics

263

1. Place the following numbers in order from least to greatest.

a) 258, 358, 474, 478, 198 _____

b) 136, 125, 378, 224, 111 _____

c) 174, 247, 421, 321, 219 _____

d) 321, 231, 497, 114, 386 _____

2. Compare the following numbers using the symbols <,>.

a) 179 (<) 258

b) 258 (<) 487

c) 158 (<) 345

d) 389 ( ) 478

e) 258 (>) 189

f) 358 ( ) 436

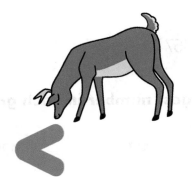

3. Write the following numbers in greatest to least order.

a) 412, 995, 539, 933 ___995___933___539___412___

b) 533, 645, 834, 649 _834_649___645___533___

c) 369, 721, 848, 439 ___848___721___439___369___

4. Circle the biggest number in each group.

a) 950   235   429   521

b) 458   256   631   458

c) 932   163   325   899

d) 789   258   127   522

5. Circle the number where 7 has the greatest value.

237   750   978   367

6. Circle the number where 7 has the least value.

473   750   927   376

7. Place the numbers in order from least to greatest.

a) 236   101   369   623   478

_____

b) 896   789   269   741   125

_____

c) 539   878   731   632   769

_____

d) 421   632   593   718   943

_____

e) 602   376   894   538   749

_____

8. Place the numbers in order from greatest to least.

a) 691   966   411   933   716

_____

b) 737   800   291   444   799

_____

c) 942   732   298   563   137

_____

d) 312   245   720   800   432

_____

e) 940   635   512   789   133

_____

f) 781   439   264   873   949

_____

g) 115   878   519   435   973

_____

h) 328   466   178   944   718

_____

i) 158   309   748   533   890

_____

Mathematics   Exercises

1. Compare the numbers by using the symbols < or >.

a) 879 ◯ 258

b) 258 ◯ 587

c) 158 ◯ 745

d) 789 ◯ 578

e) 258 ◯ 789

f) 458 ◯ 236

g) 139 ◯ 472

h) 320 ◯ 321

2. Compare the numbers by using the symbols <, > or =.

a) 587 ◯ 789

b) 125 ◯ 369

c) 587 ◯ 587

d) 375 ◯ 376

e) 135 ◯ 421

f) 99 ◯ 199

g) 531 ◯ 208

h) 399 ◯ 399

i) 398 ◯ 399

j) 400 ◯ 401

1. Compare the numbers using the symbols <, > or =.

a) 952 ◯ 950

b) 102 ◯ 478

c) 458 ◯ 458

d) 139 ◯ 148

e) 726 ◯ 258

f) 410 ◯ 236

g) 539 ◯ 538

h) 416 ◯ 329

i) 632 ◯ 519

j) 806 ◯ 383

Exercises

Mathematics

2. Write the following numbers in order from least to greatest.

a) 523   125   256 _____

b) 125   458   521 _____

c) 254   214   125 _____

d) 256   129   133 _____

e) 135   710   645 _____

f) 933   728   115 _____

g) 834   699   100 _____

h) 128   909   830 _____

i) 413   208   577 _____

j) 302   769   383 _____

3. **Compare the following numbers using the symbols <,> or =.**

a) 411 ◯ 412

b) 347 ◯ 254

c) 123 ◯ 147

d) 654 ◯ 547

e) 885 ◯ 411

f) 521 ◯ 171

g) 306 ◯ 306

h) 817 ◯ 139

i) 239 ◯ 700

j) 573 ◯ 573

TEST 61

1. Solve the following addition problems.

a) $5 + 7 = 12$

b) $10 + 5 =$

c) $9 + 6 =$

d) $11 + 7 = 18$

e) $15 + 8 = 23$

f) $10 + 12 = 22$

g) $13 + 14 = 27$

h) $17 + 9 = 26$

i) $14 + 12 = 26$

j) $18 + 13 = 21$

k) $28 + 11 = 39$

l) $46 + 53 = 99$

m) $60 + 17 = 77$

n) $137 + 185 = 322$

o) $433 + 108 = 541$

p) $714 + 197 = 901$

q) $296 + 385 = 681$

r) $602 + 299 = 701$

s) $524 + 186 = 710$

t) $389 + 252 = 631$

u) $322 + 148 = 470$

v) $195 + 625 =$

w) $39 + 27 = 66$

x) $173 + 58 = 231$

2. Solve the following word problems using addition.

a) Marina picked 500 carrots. Sophie picked 125 more. How many carrots did Sophie pick?

Show your work: $500 + 125 = 625$

Answer: _____

b) Mary bought twenty-three stickers on Monday. On Tuesday, she bought thirty-one, and on Wednesday, she bought twenty-six. How many stickers did she buy in total?

Show your work: $23 + 31 + 26$

Answer: _____

c) Martin has 119 little cars. His friend Peter has 187. How many do they both have in total?

Show your work: $119 + 187 = 306$

Answer: _____

1. Complete the addition table below. Two have been done for you.

+	1	5	9	8	4	6	7
6							
5							
9							
4							
8							
3							
7							

(6 + 1 = 7)   (4 + 8 = 12)

2. Solve the following addition problems.

a) 2 + 3 + __6__ = 11

b) 4 + __7__ + 3 = 14

c) 6 + __6__ = 12

d) 7 + 8 = __15__

e) __6__ + 3 = 9

f) __5__ + 6 + 3 = 14

g) 7 + 2 + __5__ = 14

h) 4 + __7__ + 4 = 15

i) 8 + 2 + __6__ = 16

3. Complete the magic squares. Note: The sum is the same for all horizontal, vertical and diagonal lines in each square.

a)
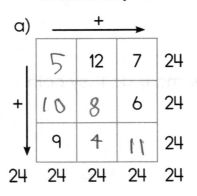

	+ →		
5	12	7	24
10	8	6	24
9	4	11	24
24	24	24	24 · 24

b)

	+ →		
6	20	10	36
16	12	8	36
14	14	18	36
36	36	36	36 · 36

c)

	+ →		
		8	27
	9		27
	10	12	27
27	27	27	27 · 27

4. Solve the following addition problems.

a)
```
    44
+   20
+   16
```

d)
```
   536
+  153
```

g)
```
   228
+  334
```

j)
```
   104
+  150
```

b)
```
   621
+  147
```

e)
```
   194
+  621
```

h)
```
   240
+  423
```

k)
```
   170
+   70
```

c)
```
   224
+   37
+  175
```

f)
```
   181
+  276
+  136
```

i)
```
   271
+   97
```

l)
```
   157
+   56
```

5. Find the missing number. The number at the centre is the sum of the four numbers around it. The first one is done for you.

a)

```
        127
117  794  399
        151
```

```
    127            677
+   399    or  +  ____
    151
  ____         = 794
  = 794
```

So ____ = 794 - 677 = 117

c)

```
        141
251  755  222
```

b)

```
        346
151      272
        186
```

d)

```
        222
178      301
        155
```

6. Solve the following word problems using addition.

a) Raj picked up 127 empty bottles for a school fundraiser. His friend Ira picked up 284. How many bottles did the two friends pick up?

Show your work: _____ $127 + 284 = 411$ _____

Answer: _____

b) There are a lot of ants in my backyard. I counted 215 ants in one part, 256 in a second part, and there were the same amount in the third part as in the second. How many ants did I count in my yard?

Show your work: _____ $215 + 256 = 471 + 256 = 727$ _____

Answer: _____

c) Aliya travelled 136 km on her bike on Monday. On Tuesday, she biked 127 km and on Wednesday, 58 km. How many kilometres did Aliya travel in three days?

Show your work: _____ $136 + 127 = 263 + 58 = 321$ _____

Answer: _____

d) Ivana works at the ticket counter for the House of Horrors. At nine o'clock, a group of 174 children entered. At noon, 458 visitors entered. Finally, at three o'clock, a group of 158 children entered. How many people visited the House of Horrors during this day?

Show your work: _____ $174 + 458 = 632 + 158 = 790$ _____

Answer: _____

Exercises

Mathematics

1. Solve the following addition problems.

a) 4 + 9 =   e) 10 + 6 =   i) 344 + 125 =   m) 141 + 110 =

b) 6 + 7 =   f) 11 + 4 =   j) 224 + 175 =   n) 175 + 175 =

c) 3 + 10 =   g) 8 + 5 =   k) 628 + 183 =   o) 276 + 236 =

d) 9 + 7 =   h) 9 + 4 =   l) 344 + 227 =   p) 526 + 253 =

2. Find the missing numbers.

a) 342 + _____ = 526   d) 180 + 449 = _____

b) 218 + _____ = 449   e) _____ + 325 = 758

c) 435 + _____ = 821   f) _____ + 283 = 498

3. Solve the following addition problems.

a) 246 + 438   c) 358 + 195   e) 598 + 258   g) 478 + 223

b) 525 + 258   d) 258 + 196   f) 541 + 369   h) 369 + 236

4. A farmer counts the animals on his farm. He has 258 cows, 712 sheep, 12 chickens and 3 dogs. How many animals does the farmer have in total?

Show your work: _____

Answer: _____

1. Complete the following table. Two have been done for you.

+	5	9	7	10	8
3	8				
6					
4					
2					
5				15	
7					
9					

2. Solve the following addition problems.

a) 7 + 8 = _____   h) 2 + 5 = _____   o) 4 + 9 = _____   v) 8 + 4 = _____

b) 4 + 8 = _____   i) 6 + 7 = _____   p) 2 + 9 = _____   w) 4 + 5 = _____

c) 4 + 5 = _____   j) 2 + 3 = _____   q) 3 + 4 = _____   x) 9 + 8 = _____

d) 8 + 9 = _____   k) 6 + 3 = _____   r) 3 + 9 = _____   y) 4 + 7 = _____

e) 3 + 8 = _____   l) 5 + 8 = _____   s) 2 + 4 = _____   z) 3 + 5 = _____

f) 6 + 8 = _____   m) 5 + 9 = _____   t) 3 + 7 = _____

g) 7 + 9 = _____   n) 2 + 7 = _____   u) 7 + 8 = _____

Exercises

Mathematics

3. Find each pair of numbers whose sum is 150. Write them on the lines below the table, crossing off each pair as you use it. The first one is done for you.

~~75~~	61	89	25
10	100	62	138
125	98	12	140
88	50	52	~~75~~

75 + 75,

4. Add up the numbers in each column and write the answer below.

148	140	184	137
163	158	175	179
142	155	156	166
165	173	146	185

a) _____ b) _____ c) _____ d) _____

ADDITION

5. Solve the following addition problems.

a)   126
     + 326

g)   785
     + 197

m)   115
     + 125

s)   444
     +   99

b)   147
     + 659

h)   689
     + 289

n)   411
     + 103

t)   409
     + 178

c)   311
     + 258

i)   876
     + 108

o)   328
     + 302

u)   686
     +   94

d)   400
     + 589

j)   601
     + 253

p)   623
     + 213

v)   599
     + 132

e)   589
     + 196

k)   223
     + 549

q)   715
     + 199

w)   657
     + 294

f)   557
     + 284

l)   658
     + 339

r)   601
     + 107

x)   319
     + 228

6. Add 45 to each number. Write your answers on the lines.

a) 414 _____

b) 500 _____

c) 397 _____

d) 251 _____

e) 495 _____

f) 150 _____

TEST 63

1. Solve the following subtraction problems.

a) $20 - 4 =$ d) $17 - 8 =$ g) $6 - 3 =$ j) $12 - 6 =$

b) $16 - 3 =$ e) $11 - 7 =$ h) $20 - 5 =$ k) $13 - 7 =$

c) $17 - 4 =$ f) $15 - 8 =$ i) $9 - 8 =$ l) $16 - 4 =$

2. Solve the following subtraction problems.

a) 826
    $-\ \ 14$

e) 720
    $-\ 220$

i) 844
    $-\ 325$

m) 957
    $-\ 392$

b) 272
    $-\ 145$

f) 946
    $-\ 273$

j) 958
    $-\ 100$

n) 545
    $-\ 438$

c) 988
    $-\ 655$

g) 520
    $-\ 250$

k) 445
    $-\ 213$

o) 832
    $-\ 155$

d) 376
    $-\ 125$

h) 843
    $-\ 226$

l) 375
    $-\ 125$

p) 431
    $-\ 118$

3. Solve the following word problems using subtraction.

a) Mathew needs twenty-three points to beat the high score in his game. He already has fifteen points. How many points is he missing?

Show your work: _____

Answer: _____

b) Julie dropped the ball fifty-eight times. Nolan dropped it twelve fewer times. How many times did Nolan drop the ball?

Show your work: _____

Answer: _____

1. Solve the following subtraction problems.

a) 15 – 8 =

b) 17 – 13 =

c) 15 – 12 =

d) 18 – 9 =

e) 17 – 10 =

f) 22 – 3 =

g) 5 – 2 =

h) 16 – 4 =

i) 9 – 7 =

j) 19 – 6 =

k) 11 – 6 =

l) 21 – 8 =

m) 14 – 6 =

n) 20 – 7 =

o) 18 – 5 =

p) 63 - 12 =

2. Play a subtraction game! Start from the number in the yellow circle at the centre, then subtract a number in the blue circle from it and write your answer in the orange circle. Each has been started for you.

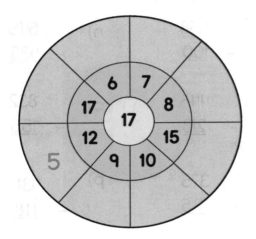 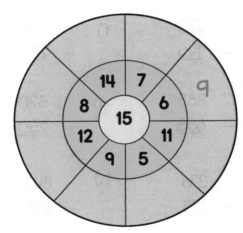

3. Complete the following chart. Two have been done for you.

–	12	3	8	6	4	7	9	5	11
17	5								
15									
13									
16					12				
12									
14									

4. Solve the following subtraction problems.

a) 40
   − 12

d) 546
   − 284

g) 630
   − 125

j) 515
   − 432

b) 88
   − 25

e) 631
   − 125

h) 988
   − 657

k) 868
   − 427

c) 56
   − 26

f) 720
   − 320

i) 547
   − 283

l) 386
   − 231

5. Find the missing numbers.

a) 735 - _____ = 387

d) 626 - _____ = 314

g) 283 - _____ = 150

b) _____ - 425 = 534

e) _____ - 237 = 419

h) 663 - _____ = 258

c) 857 - _____ = 326

f) 952 - _____ = 425

i) _____ - 369 = 145

6. Solve the following word problems using subtraction.

a) Roger, Tony and Jay cut 600 Christmas trees in total. Tony cut 259 trees and Jay cut 27. How many trees did Roger cut?

Show your work: _____

Answer: _____

b) My grandma baked 125 donuts for Christmas. She gave 48 to her daughter and 68 to her son. How many donuts did she have left?

Show your work: _____

Answer: _____

7. Solve the following subtraction problems.

a) 325
  − 214

c) 546
  − 283

e) 528
  − 263

g) 200
  − 124

b) 364
  − 157

d) 947
  − 523

f) 389
  − 154

h) 876
  − 562

8. Subtract 345 from each number. Write your answers on the lines.

a) 814 _____

c) 479 _____

e) 495 _____

b) 500 _____

d) 751 _____

f) 950 _____

9. Solve the following subtraction problems.

a) 815 – 258 =

e) 259 – 258 =

i) 104 – 51 =

m) 601 – 147 =

b) 633 – 258 =

f) 858 – 551 =

j) 799 – 551 =

n) 444 – 147 =

c) 700 – 258 =

g) 621 – 558 =

k) 300 – 147 =

o) 125 – 47 =

d) 490 – 258 =

h) 219 – 151 =

l) 193 – 147 =

p) 737 - 263 =

10. Solve the following subtraction problems.

a) 643
  − 353

c) 189
  − 81

e) 178
  − 93

g) 863
  − 478

b) 134
  − 71

d) 294
  − 173

f) 526
  − 139

h) 500
  − 378

TEST 64

1. Complete the following table.

–	12	3	8	6	4	7	9	5	11
18	–								
20									
24									
19									
25									
23									

2. Solve the following subtraction problems.

a) $\begin{array}{r} 143 \\ -\ 121 \end{array}$

f) $\begin{array}{r} 486 \\ -\ 323 \end{array}$

k) $\begin{array}{r} 289 \\ -\ 256 \end{array}$

p) $\begin{array}{r} 449 \\ -\ 315 \end{array}$

b) $\begin{array}{r} 237 \\ -\ \ \ 6 \end{array}$

g) $\begin{array}{r} 77 \\ -\ 26 \end{array}$

l) $\begin{array}{r} 444 \\ -\ 424 \end{array}$

q) $\begin{array}{r} 568 \\ -\ 525 \end{array}$

c) $\begin{array}{r} 379 \\ -\ 142 \end{array}$

h) $\begin{array}{r} 699 \\ -\ 510 \end{array}$

m) $\begin{array}{r} 155 \\ -\ \ \ 2 \end{array}$

r) $\begin{array}{r} 266 \\ -\ 141 \end{array}$

d) $\begin{array}{r} 78 \\ -\ 43 \end{array}$

i) $\begin{array}{r} 295 \\ -\ 125 \end{array}$

n) $\begin{array}{r} 768 \\ -\ 625 \end{array}$

s) $\begin{array}{r} 266 \\ -\ 134 \end{array}$

e) $\begin{array}{r} 489 \\ -\ 152 \end{array}$

j) $\begin{array}{r} 679 \\ -\ 541 \end{array}$

o) $\begin{array}{r} 297 \\ -\ 242 \end{array}$

t) $\begin{array}{r} 651 \\ -\ 511 \end{array}$

SUBTRACTION

1. **Choose any five numbers from the table and subtract 45 from each. Use the lines below the table to make your calculations and write the answers.**

50	76	70	69
49	233	68	132
77	48	251	316
58	320	240	59

_____

_____

_____

_____

_____

2. **Solve the subtraction problems. Then, use the key and write the letter below each answer to solve the mystery message. The first one is done for you.**

Key:

9	18	6	15	13	12	16	11	8	14	17
r	u	c	f	o	t	s	b	a	n	i

24	28	20	18	16	15	18	23
− 8	− 10	− 9	− 6	− 7	− 7	− 12	− 11
= 16	=	=	=	=	=	=	=
s							

23	15	20	25	30	24	20	18
− 6	− 2	− 6	− 8	− 14	− 9	− 2	− 4
=	=	=	=	=	=	=	=

3. **Solve the subtraction problems. Check your answer by adding.**

a) 52 − 37 _____ b) 80 − 26 _____

284

4. Solve the following word problems using subtraction.

a) There are twenty-five students in Nadia's class. Thirteen students leave. How many students are left in the class?

Show your work: _____

Answer: _____

b) Jason has 144 blue marbles. He gives 72 to Jack. How many marbles does he have left?

Show your work: _____

Answer: _____

c) Sheila collects erasers. She has 274. She gives 14 to Laura and 36 to Brenda. How many does she have left?

Show your work: No. Of erasers Sheila has =274
No. of erasers given to Laura =14
No. of erasers given to brenda = 36
Answer: She has =274-14-36=224 erasers left

d) In the Botanical Gardens, there are 568 roses. A hailstorm destroyed 321 roses. How many roses are left?

Show your work: _____

Answer: _____

e) Robert raised $289 from his garage sale. He gives $125 to the children's hospital foundation. How much money does he have left?

Show your work: _____

Answer: _____

$$\begin{array}{r} 425 \\ -178 \\ \hline 247 \end{array}$$

f) There are 425 people who live in the condo building down the road. Soon, 178 will move away. How many people will be left?

Show your work: No. of people in condo =425
No. of people soon moving away =178
Answer: total number of people left = 425-178 =247

Exercises

Mathematics

5. Subtract 175 from each number. Write your answers on the lines.

a) 250 _____

b) 790 _____

c) 805 _____

d) 352 _____

e) 236 _____

f) 478 _____

g) 415 _____

h) 423 _____

i) 698 _____

j) 932 _____

k) 193 _____

l) 214 _____

m) 313 _____

n) 427 _____

o) 914 _____

6. Calculate the following. Write your answers on the lines.

a) Remove 7 hundreds from 952. _____

b) Remove 147 ones from 782. _____

c) Remove 5 hundreds from 789. _____

d) Remove 3 tens from 478. _____

e) Remove 5 ones from 760. _____

f) Remove 6 tens from 587. _____

g) Remove 18 ones from 421. _____

h) Remove 3 hundreds from 897. _____

i) Remove 2 tens from 632. _____

Mathematics | Exercises

TEST 65

1. Change the addition problems to multiplication sentences.

a) $2 + 2 + 2 + 2$ _____

b) $5 + 5 + 5 + 5 + 5$ ___ $5 \times 5 = 25$

c) $3 + 3$ ___ $3 \times 2 = 6$

d) $9 + 9 + 9$ _____

e) $7 + 7 + 7 + 7 + 7 + 7 + 7 + 7 + 7$
___ $7 \times 9 = 63$

2. Find the product.

a) $3 \times 4 =$ _____

b) $5 \times 7 =$ _____

c) $3 \times 8 =$ _____

d) $4 \times 4 =$ _____

e) $7 \times 3 =$ _____

f) $2 \times 4 =$ _____

g) $9 \times 2 =$ _____

h) $1 \times 6 =$ _____

i) $6 \times 5 =$ _____

3. Complete the multiplication table.

x	0	1	2	3	4	5	6
0							
4							
2							
5							
3							
6							
7							
9							

Mathematics

MULTIPLICATION

1. Find the product for the following:

Table of 1	Table of 2	Table of 3
1 x 0 = _____	2 x 0 = _____	3 x 0 = _____
1 x 1 = _____	2 x 1 = _____	3 x 1 = _____
1 x 2 = _____	2 x 2 = _____	3 x 2 = _____
1 x 3 = _____	2 x 3 = _____	3 x 3 = _____
1 x 4 = _____	2 x 4 = _____	3 x 4 = _____
1 x 5 = _____	2 x 5 = _____	3 x 5 = _____
1 x 6 = _____	2 x 6 = _____	3 x 6 = _____
1 x 7 = _____	2 x 7 = _____	3 x 7 = _____
1 x 8 = _____	2 x 8 = _____	3 x 8 = _____
1 x 9 = _____	2 x 9 = _____	3 x 9 = _____
1 x 10 = _____	2 x 10 = _____	3 x 10 = _____

2. Fill in the multiplication table.

x	1	5	8	4	3	9	6	10	2	7
4										
5										

3. Match each illustration with the multiplication problem that represents it. One is done for you.

a) 7 x 2

b) 5 x 3

c) 4 x 4

d) 3 x 3

e) 6 x 3

1. ★ ★ ★ ★ ★   ★ ★ ★ ★ ★   ★ ★ ★ ★ ★

2. ★ ★ ★   ★ ★ ★   ★ ★ ★

3. ★ ★ ★ ★ ★ ★   ★ ★ ★ ★ ★ ★   ★ ★ ★ ★ ★ ★

4. ★ ★ ★ ★   ★ ★ ★ ★   ★ ★ ★ ★   ★ ★ ★ ★

5. ★ ★ ★ ★ ★ ★ ★   ★ ★ ★ ★ ★ ★ ★

4. Write a multiplication sentence to represent each of the following illustrations.

a) ⊂⊂⊂ ⊂⊂⊂ ⊂⊂⊂ ⊂⊂⊂

4 X 3

d) ⊂⊂⊂⊂ ⊂⊂⊂⊂ ⊂⊂⊂⊂
⊂⊂⊂⊂ ⊂⊂⊂⊂ ⊂⊂⊂⊂

6 X 4

b) ⊂⊂ ⊂⊂ ⊂⊂ ⊂⊂ ⊂⊂
⊂⊂ ⊂⊂ ⊂⊂ ⊂⊂

9 X 2

e) ⊂⊂⊂ ⊂⊂⊂ ⊂⊂⊂ ⊂⊂⊂
⊂⊂⊂ ⊂⊂⊂ ⊂⊂⊂

c) ⊂⊂⊂⊂⊂ ⊂⊂⊂⊂⊂ ⊂⊂⊂⊂⊂
⊂⊂⊂⊂⊂ ⊂⊂⊂⊂⊂

f) ⊂⊂⊂⊂ ⊂⊂⊂⊂ ⊂⊂⊂⊂ ⊂⊂⊂⊂
⊂⊂⊂⊂ ⊂⊂⊂⊂ ⊂⊂⊂⊂ ⊂⊂⊂⊂
⊂⊂⊂⊂

5. Solve the following word problems using multiplication.

a) Three teams made up of seven people each decide to help renovate a school. How many people are working on the renovations of the school?

Show your work: no of teams = 3
each team has 7 people

Answer: no of people working = 7×3 = 21

b) A secret adventurers' club is organizing a recruitment night and eight people bring two desserts each. How many desserts will be served in total?

Show your work: no of people = 8
each person brings 2 dessert each

Answer: no of desserst = 8×2 = 16

c) The students of a school sell chocolates for a fundraiser. Each student is asked to sell nine chocolate bars at the price of three dollars each. How much money will each student raise?

Show your work: Each student asked to sell 9 chocolate bar
Each bar = $3

Answer: Students will raise = 9×3 = 27

d) There are three classes of Grade Three at a school and eight students from each class have prepared a magic show for the end-of-the-year show. How many student magicians will be in the show?

Show your work: Number of Grade 3 classes = 3
No. of students from each class = 8

Answer: Total no. of student magicians = 8×3 = 24

e) Justin decides to pick strawberries to make some money. He picks nine cartons with eight big strawberries in each of them. How many strawberries did he pick in total?

Show your work: No. of cartons = 9
No. of strawberries in each carton = 8

Answer: Justin picked = 9×8 = 72 strawberries

No.

TEST 66

1. Find the product of the following multiplication problems.

a) 5 x 6 = _____

b) 1 x 8 = _____

c) 4 x 8 = 32

d) 3 x 8 = 24

e) 4 x 9 = _____

f) 3 x 6 = _____

g) 6 x 6 = _____

h) 2 x 8 = _____

i) 5 x 9 = _____

j) 2 x 7 = _____

k) 3 x 9 = _____

l) 4 x 7 = _____

2. Complete the following multiplication sentences.

Table of 4	Table of 5	Table of 6
4 x 0 = 0	5 x 0 = 0	6 x 0 = 0
4 x 1 = _____	5 x 1 = _____	6 x 1 = _____
4 x 2 = _____	5 x 2 = _____	6 x 2 = _____
4 x 3 = _____	5 x 3 = _____	6 x 3 = _____
4 x 4 = _____	5 x 4 = _____	6 x 4 = _____
4 x 5 = _____	5 x 5 = _____	6 x 5 = _____
4 x 6 = 24	5 x 6 = _____	6 x 6 = _____
4 x 7 = _____	5 x 7 = _____	6 x 7 = _____
4 x 8 = 32	5 x 8 = _____	6 x 8 = _____
4 x 9 = _____	5 x 9 = _____	6 x 9 = 54
4 x 10 = 40	5 x 10 = _____	6 x 10 = _____

Mathematics

291

1. Colour the picture based on the following clues:

Red: for the products less than or equal to 9.
Blue: for the products between 9 and 25.
Yellow: for the products greater than 35 and less than 50.
Green: for the products equal to or greater than 50.

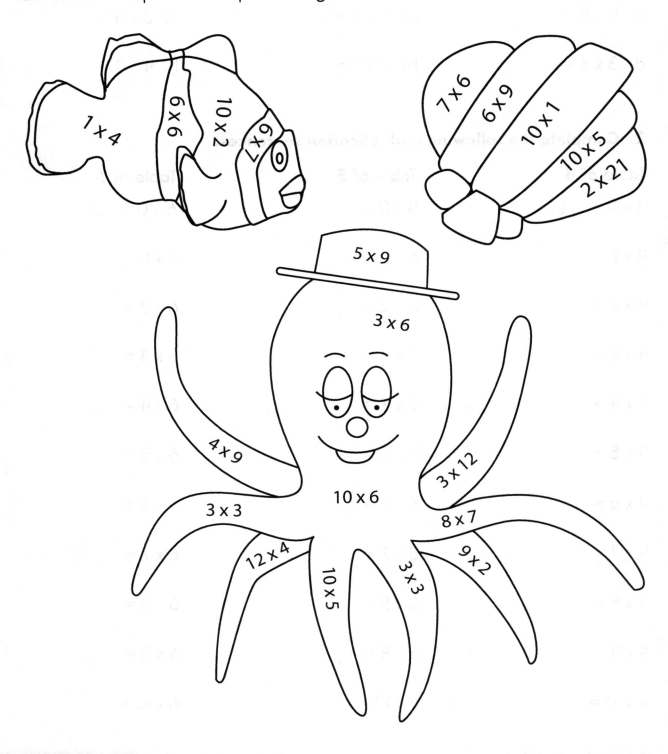

2. Complete the following multiplication sentences.

a) 4 x 8 = _____ e) 5 x 1 = _____

b) 5 x 7 = _____ f) 8 x 4 = _____

c) 7 x 3 = _____ g) 3 x 2 = _____

d) 9 x 2 = _____ h) 6 x 7 = _____

3. Complete the following multiplication tables. The first one has been started for you.

a)

x	3	5	8	6	4
7	21	35	56	42	28
3	9	15	24	18	12
4	12	20	32	24	16
6	18	30	48	36	24
5	15	25	40	30	20

b)

x	5	7	9	4	8
2					
6					
9					
8					

MULTIPLICATION

4. Solve the following:

a)
$$5 \times 8$$

d)
$$4 \times 4$$

g)
$$2 \times 3$$

j)
$$5 \times 2$$

b)
$$7 \times 4$$

e)
$$6 \times 2$$

h)
$$3 \times 3$$

k)
$$3 \times 5$$

c)
$$8 \times 3$$

f)
$$2 \times 5$$

i)
$$7 \times 2$$

l)
$$4 \times 2$$

5. Complete the following:

a) ___7___ x 10 = 70

b) 10 x ___6___ = 60

c) 4 x ___8___ = 32

d) 2 x ___9___ = 18

e) 9 x ___3___ = 27

f) 4 x 6 = ___24___

g) 9 x ___5___ = 45

h) 3 x ___5___ = 15

i) 6 x 7 = ___42___

j) 5 x ___7___ = 35

k) 7 x ___7___ = 49

l) 3 x 7 = ___21___

m) 8 x ___6___ = 48

n) 6 x 9 = ___54___

o) 2 x ___8___ = 16

6. Find the product.

a) 6 x 8 = _____

b) 3 x 3 = _____

c) 5 x 4 = _____

d) 6 x 9 = _____

e) 4 x 7 = _____

f) 7 x 5 = _____

g) 9 x 8 = _____

h) 7 x 6 = _____

i) 4 x 4 = _____

j) 6 x 4 = _____

k) 8 x 3 = _____

l) 3 x 9 = _____

TEST 67

1. Draw lines to split the symbols in each oval into three equal groups.

a)
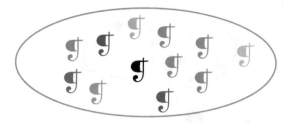

c)
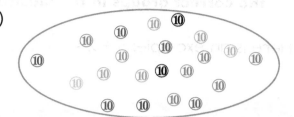

b)
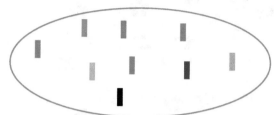

d)

2. Draw lines to split the symbols in each oval into four equal groups.

a)
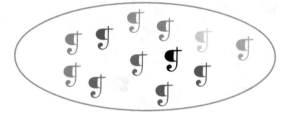

c)
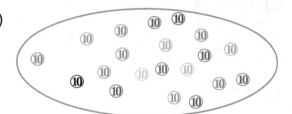

b)
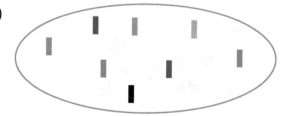

d)

3. Anita shared thirty-six marbles between four children equally.

Each child will have _____ marbles.

Show your work: _____

4. Solve the following division problems.

a) $8 \div 2 =$ _____

b) $6 \div 2 =$ _____

c) $10 \div 5 =$ _____

d) $9 \div 3 =$ _____

e) $8 \div 4 =$ _____

f) $16 \div 4 =$ _____

g) $20 \div 2 =$ _____

h) $20 \div 5 =$ _____

i) $12 \div 3 =$ _____

1. Solve each division problem. Write the answer on the line. Then, circle the correct groups in the illustration.

Here is an example: 8 ÷ 2 = __4__

a) 12 ÷ 6 = _____

b) 10 ÷ 2 = _____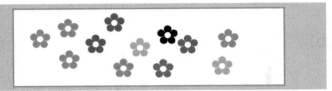

c) 12 ÷ 4 = _____

d) 9 ÷ 3 = _____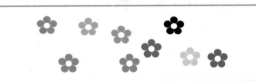

e) 15 ÷ 5 = _____

f) 20 ÷ 4 = _____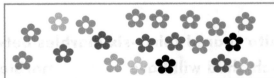

g) 24 ÷ 6 = _____

h) 18 ÷ 9 = _____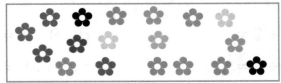

Exercises

Mathematics

2. Share twenty apples equally between five students. Circle the correct groups in the illustration.

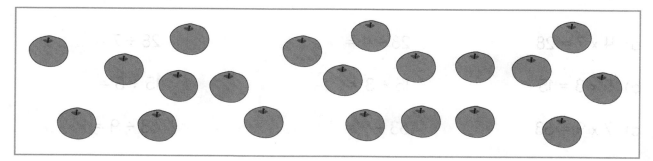

3. Share twelve apples equally between four people. Circle the correct groups in the illustration.

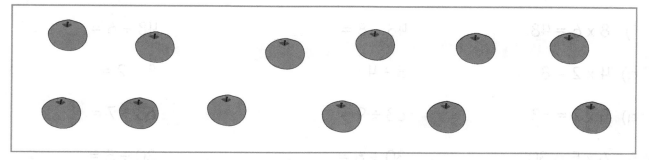

4. Share eighteen candies equally between six students. Circle the correct groups in the illustration.

5. Share twenty-five candies equally between five students. Circle the correct groups in the illustration.

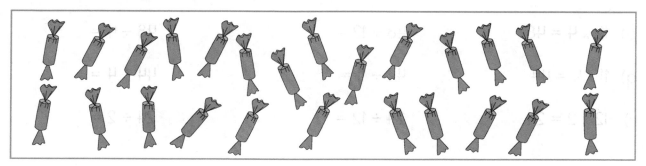

6. Use the multiplication statements on the left to help you solve the division problems.

a) $4 \times 7 = 28$ $28 \div 4 =$ _____ $28 \div 7 =$ _____

b) $5 \times 3 = 15$ $15 \div 3 =$ _____ $15 \div 5 =$ _____

c) $7 \times 9 = 63$ $63 \div 7 =$ _____ $63 \div 9 =$ _____

d) $6 \times 4 = 24$ $24 \div 6 =$ _____ $24 \div 4 =$ _____

e) $10 \times 5 = 50$ $50 \div 10 =$ _____ $50 \div 5 =$ _____

f) $8 \times 6 = 48$ $48 \div 8 =$ _____ $48 \div 6 =$ _____

g) $4 \times 2 = 8$ $8 \div 4 =$ _____ $8 \div 2 =$ _____

h) $9 \times 7 = 63$ $63 \div 9 =$ _____ $63 \div 7 =$ _____

i) $6 \times 5 = 30$ $30 \div 6 =$ _____ $30 \div 5 =$ _____

j) $7 \times 3 = 21$ $21 \div 7 =$ _____ $21 \div 3 =$ _____

k) $5 \times 9 = 45$ $45 \div 5 =$ _____ $45 \div 9 =$ _____

l) $10 \times 6 = 60$ $60 \div 10 =$ _____ $60 \div 6 =$ _____

m) $9 \times 2 = 18$ $18 \div 9 =$ _____ $18 \div 2 =$ _____

n) $6 \times 7 = 42$ $42 \div 6 =$ _____ $42 \div 7 =$ _____

o) $10 \times 9 = 90$ $90 \div 10 =$ _____ $90 \div 9 =$ _____

p) $12 \times 4 = 48$ $48 \div 12 =$ _____ $48 \div 4 =$ _____

q) $11 \times 4 = 44$ $44 \div 11 =$ _____ $44 \div 4 =$ _____

r) $12 \times 2 = 24$ $24 \div 12 =$ _____ $24 \div 2 =$ _____

1. **Show two ways to divide the shapes into the required number of equal parts.**

   a) 2 equal parts

   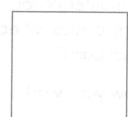

   b) 2 equal parts

   c) 3 equal parts

2. **My parents served forty-eight mini-donuts for dessert to the six people who came to my house last night. If each of them had the same number of mini-donuts, how many did each person eat?**

   Show your work: _____

   Answer: _____

3. **A class of thirty-six students are leaving on a field trip in four school buses. If the number of students in each bus is the same, how many students are there in each bus?**

   Show your work: _____

   Answer: _____

1. Solve the following word problems using division.

a) My mother prepared a cake to share equally among six people. How many pieces will each person receive if the cake is cut into twenty-four equal parts?

Show your work: Pieces of cake = 24
number of people = 6

Answer: Each person will recieve = 24 ÷ 6 = 4 pieces of cake

b) There are eight students in Amy's class. She has forty crayons to give out. How many crayons will each student receive if she splits them equally?

Show your work: No of students in Amy's class = 8
No of crayons = 40

Answer: Each student gets = 40 ÷ 8 = 5 crayons

c) There are six members in George's scout group. The chief brought twelve marshmallows for the campfire. How many marshmallows will each scout receive if the chief divides them equally?

Show your work: Members in George's scout group = 6
no of marshmallows chief bought = 12

Answer: Each member will get = 12 ÷ 6 = 2 marshmallows

d) Richard wants to get rid of his stamp collection. He divides thirty-six stamps between three of his friends equally. How many stamps will each of Richard's friends receive?

Show your work: no of Friends = 3
no of stamp = 36

Answer: no of stamps each of richards freind gets = 36 ÷ 3 = 12

e) Zora feeds the birds in her yard. She gives thirty worms to two birds. How many worms will each bird get if Zora splits them equally?

Show your work: no of worms = 30
no of birds = 2

Answer: Each bird will get = 30 ÷ 20 = 15 worms

2. Use the groups of stars to write a division statement.

Here is an example: ★★★★ ★★★★   16 ÷ 2 = 8

a) ★★★★ ★★★★ ★★★★   _____ ÷ _____ = _____

b) ★★★ ★★★ ★★★ ★★★   _____ ÷ _____ = _____

c) ★★★★★ ★★★★★ ★★★★★   _____ ÷ _____ = _____
   ★★★★★ ★★★★★ ★★★★★

d) ★★★★★★ ★★★★★★   _____ ÷ _____ = _____

e) ★★★★★ ★★★★★ ★★★★★   _____ ÷ _____ = _____

f) ★★★★★ ★★★★★ ★★★★★   _____ ÷ _____ = _____
   ★★★★★ ★★★★★

g) ★ ★ ★ ★ ★ ★ ★ ★ ★   _____ ÷ _____ = _____

h) ★★★★ ★★★★   _____ ÷ _____ = _____

i) ★★★★★ ★★★★★   _____ ÷ _____ = _____
   ★★★★★ ★★★★★

j) ★★★ ★★★ ★★★ ★★★   _____ ÷ _____ = _____
   ★★★ ★★★ ★★★ ★★★

k) ★★★★★ ★★★★★   _____ ÷ _____ = _____

l) ★★ ★★ ★★ ★★   _____ ÷ _____ = _____

m) ★★★★ ★★★★   _____ ÷ _____ = _____
   ★★★ ★★★

3. Solve the following division problems.

1) $1 \div 1 =$ _____

2) $2 \div 2 =$ _____

3) $3 \div 3 =$ _____

4) $4 \div 4 =$ _____

5) $2 \div 1 =$ _____

6) $4 \div 2 =$ _____

7) $6 \div 3 =$ _____

8) $8 \div 4 =$ _____

9) $3 \div 1 =$ _____

10) $6 \div 2 =$ _____

11) $9 \div 3 =$ _____

12) $12 \div 4 =$ _____

13) $4 \div 1 =$ _____

14) $8 \div 2 =$ _____

15) $12 \div 3 =$ _____

16) $16 \div 4 =$ _____

17) $5 \div 1 =$ _____

18) $10 \div 2 =$ _____

19) $15 \div 3 =$ _____

20) $20 \div 4 =$ _____

21) $6 \div 1 =$ _____

22) $12 \div 2 =$ _____

23) $18 \div 3 =$ _____

24) $24 \div 4 =$ _____

25) $7 \div 1 =$ _____

26) $14 \div 2 =$ _____

27) $21 \div 3 =$ _____

28) $28 \div 4 =$ _____

29) $8 \div 1 =$ _____

30) $16 \div 2 =$ _____

31) $24 \div 3 =$ _____

32) $32 \div 4 =$ _____

33) $9 \div 1 =$ _____

34) $18 \div 2 =$ _____

35) $27 \div 3 =$ _____

36) $36 \div 4 =$ _____

37) $10 \div 1 =$ _____

38) $20 \div 2 =$ _____

39) $30 \div 3 =$ _____

40) $40 \div 4 =$ _____

41) $11 \div 1 =$ _____

42) $22 \div 2 =$ _____

43) $33 \div 3 =$ _____

44) $44 \div 4 =$ _____

45) $12 \div 1 =$ _____

46) $24 \div 2 =$ _____

47) $36 \div 3 =$ _____

48) $48 \div 4 =$ _____

TEST 69

1. **Count the shaded parts in each figure. Then, count the total number of parts. Write a fraction for each shaded part of the whole.**

a)

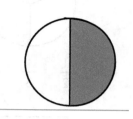

_____

_____

c)

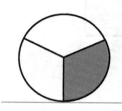

_____

_____

b)

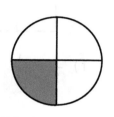

_____

_____

d)

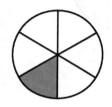

_____

_____

2. **Colour part of each shape according to the fraction.**

a) $\frac{1}{3}$

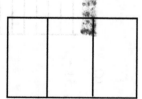

c) $\frac{1}{4}$

b) $\frac{1}{2}$

d) $\frac{3}{8}$

3. **Colour $\frac{2}{3}$ of the following illustration. To help you, first count how many circles there are.**

Exercises

Mathematics

1. Circle the fraction that is represented by the shaded area in each shape.

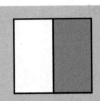

a) $\left(\dfrac{1}{2}\right)$ $\dfrac{1}{4}$ $\dfrac{1}{3}$

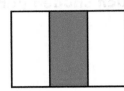

c) $\dfrac{1}{2}$ $\left(\dfrac{1}{3}\right)$ $\dfrac{1}{4}$

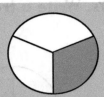

e) $\dfrac{1}{2}$ $\left(\dfrac{1}{3}\right)$ $\dfrac{1}{4}$

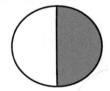

b) $\left(\dfrac{1}{2}\right)$ $\dfrac{1}{4}$ $\dfrac{1}{3}$

d) $\dfrac{1}{2}$ $\dfrac{1}{3}$ $\left(\dfrac{1}{4}\right)$

f) $\dfrac{1}{2}$ $\dfrac{1}{3}$ $\left(\dfrac{1}{4}\right)$

2. Colour the parts in each shape according to the fraction.

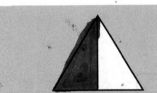

a) $\dfrac{1}{2}$

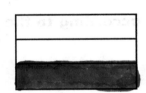

d) $\dfrac{1}{3}$

g) $\dfrac{1}{10}$

b) $\dfrac{1}{4}$

e) $\dfrac{3}{10}$

h) $\dfrac{2}{5}$

c) $\dfrac{4}{12}$

f) $\dfrac{1}{3}$

i) $\dfrac{1}{2}$

3. Colour the number of birds in each picture based on the fraction.

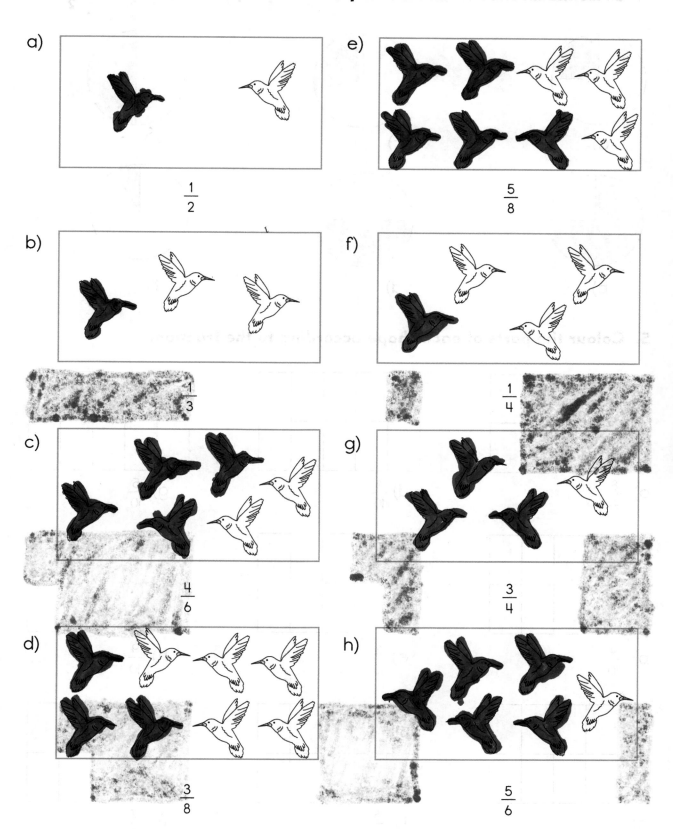

a)

$\dfrac{1}{2}$

b)

$\dfrac{1}{3}$

c)

$\dfrac{4}{6}$

d)

$\dfrac{3}{8}$

e)

$\dfrac{5}{8}$

f)

$\dfrac{1}{4}$

g)

$\dfrac{3}{4}$

h)

$\dfrac{5}{6}$

4. Circle the illustration where the shaded area represents more than $\frac{1}{2}$.

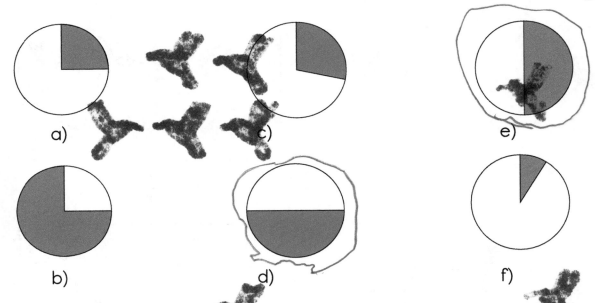

a)

b)

c)

d)

e)

f)

5. Colour the parts of each shape according to the fraction.

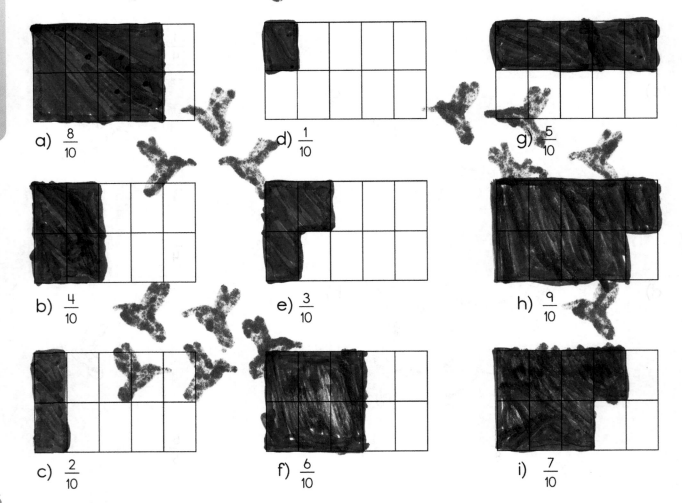

a) $\frac{8}{10}$

b) $\frac{4}{10}$

c) $\frac{2}{10}$

d) $\frac{1}{10}$

e) $\frac{3}{10}$

f) $\frac{6}{10}$

g) $\frac{5}{10}$

h) $\frac{9}{10}$

i) $\frac{7}{10}$

TEST 70

1. Shade the parts according to the fraction.

a) $\frac{9}{10}$

b) $\frac{1}{8}$

c) $\frac{2}{9}$

d) $\frac{4}{8}$

2. Circle the illustration where the shaded area represents less than $\frac{1}{4}$.

a)

b)

c)

3. Show two ways to separate the rectangle into three equal parts.

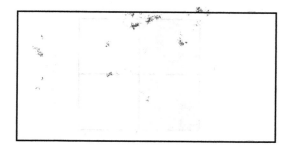 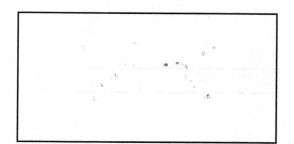

4. Divide the circles into equal parts.

a) 4 parts: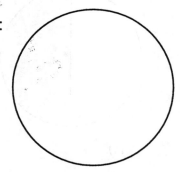

b) 8 parts: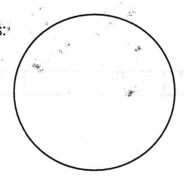

1. Write the fraction represented by the shaded area of each figure below.

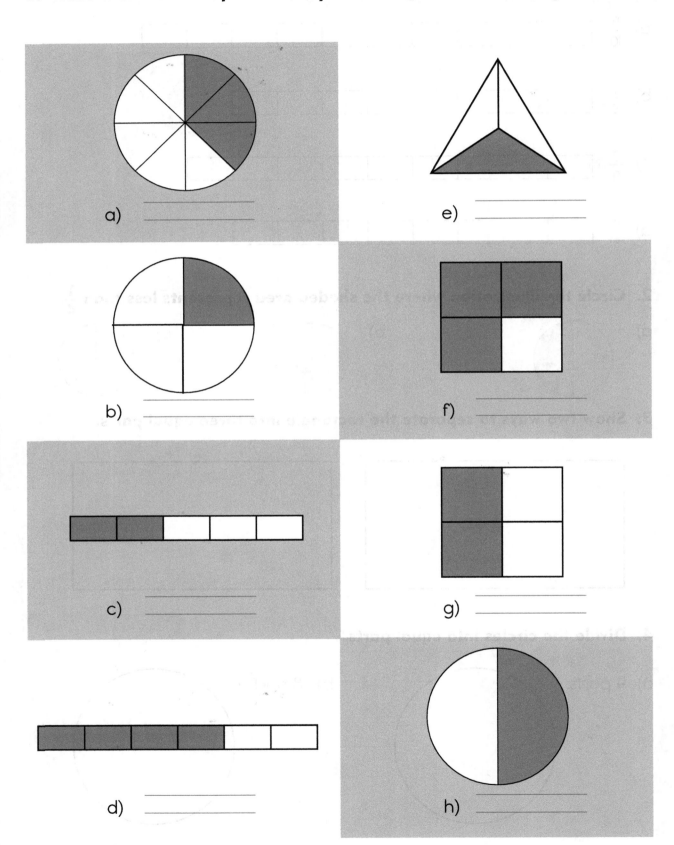

a) _____

b) _____

c) _____

d) _____

e) _____

f) _____

g) _____

h) _____

2. Colour the parts according to the fraction.

a) $\frac{1}{2}$

b) $\frac{1}{4}$

c) $\frac{1}{3}$

d) $\frac{3}{4}$

e) $\frac{1}{10}$

f) $\frac{7}{10}$

g) $\frac{9}{10}$

h) $\frac{6}{10}$

i) $\frac{3}{10}$

3. **Divide each illustration into two equal parts.**

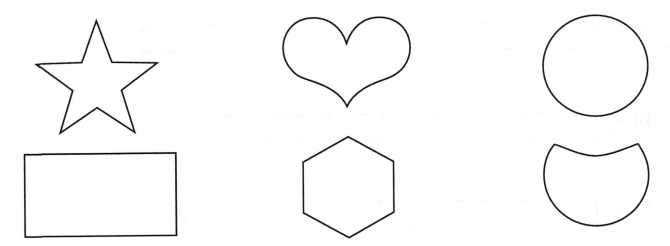

4. **Circle the illustration in each row where the shaded areas correctly represent the fraction.**

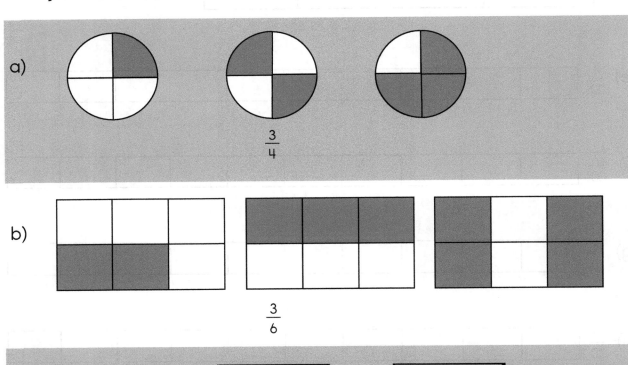

TEST 71

1. Add the following decimal numbers to find the sum.

a) 5.6 + 1.3 =

e)
```
   7.2
 + 1.8
_____
```

b) 3.2 + 7.4 =

f)
```
   5.3
 + 6.1
_____
```

c)
```
   9.1
 + 8.8
_____
```

g) 3.2 + 5.1 =

d)
```
   3.8
 + 3.7
_____
```

h) 2.1 + 1.3 =

2. Find the difference:

a) 7.8 - 6.3 =

e)
```
   9.8
 - 3.9
_____
```

b) 9.6 - 2.5 =

f)
```
   6.2
 - 4.8
_____
```

c)
```
   7.6
 - 1.3
_____
```

g) 9.9 - 7.3 =

d)
```
   8.3
 - 4.9
_____
```

h) 3.7 - 1.2 =

Mathematics

1. Add the following decimal numbers and find the sum.

a) 1.3 + 3.6 =

b) 7.2 + 1.4 =

c) 6.1 + 4.8 =

d) 5.1 + 3.4 =

e) $\begin{array}{r} 6.4 \\ +\ 3.6 \\ \hline \end{array}$

f) $\begin{array}{r} 4.8 \\ +\ 5.7 \\ \hline \end{array}$

g) 2.1 + 3.2 =

h) 5.4 + 3.3 =

i) 4.7 + 1.1 =

j) 3.6 + 1.2 =

k) $\begin{array}{r} 8.7 \\ +\ 2.5 \\ \hline \end{array}$

l) $\begin{array}{r} 8.9 \\ +\ 1.6 \\ \hline \end{array}$

2. Find the difference:

a) $\begin{array}{r} 8.4 \\ -\ 3.5 \\ \hline \end{array}$

b) $\begin{array}{r} 9.6 \\ -\ 4.9 \\ \hline \end{array}$

c) $\begin{array}{r} 4.3 \\ -\ 1.5 \\ \hline \end{array}$

d) $\begin{array}{r} 7.6 \\ -\ 3.9 \\ \hline \end{array}$

e) 3.6 - 2.1 =

f) 9.8 - 4.3 =

g) 6.9 - 5.4 =

h) 8.6 - 3.6 =

i) $\begin{array}{r} 5.8 \\ -\ 3.6 \\ \hline \end{array}$

j) $\begin{array}{r} 6.9 \\ -\ 3.7 \\ \hline \end{array}$

k) 8.7 - 3.4 =

l) 6.7 - 2.2 =

3. Circle the name of the tallest person and underline the name of the shortest person.

Anne: 1.65 m   Ram: 1.25 m   Justin: 1.80 m

Jenny: 1.55 m   Laura: 1.79 m   Michelle: 1.78 m

4. Add the following amounts of money. Use the illustrations to help you calculate the sum.

Here is an example:
$$\begin{array}{r} \$1.25 \\ + \ \$1.00 \\ \hline \$2.25 \end{array}$$

a)
$$\begin{array}{r} \$1.35 \\ + \ \$0.65 \\ \hline \end{array}$$

b)
$$\begin{array}{r} \$2.25 \\ + \ \$1.15 \\ \hline \end{array}$$

c)
$$\begin{array}{r} \$0.55 \\ + \ \$0.10 \\ \hline \end{array}$$

d)
$$\begin{array}{r} \$2.75 \\ + \ \$1.10 \\ \hline \end{array}$$

e)
$$\begin{array}{r} \$3.35 \\ + \ \$1.65 \\ \hline \end{array}$$

f)
$$\begin{array}{r} \$2.45 \\ + \ \$0.25 \\ \hline \end{array}$$

g)
$$\begin{array}{r} \$2.75 \\ + \ \$2.25 \\ \hline \end{array}$$

5. Write the amount of money in each group. Show your work.

a)

_____

_____

b)

_____

_____

c)

_____

_____

d)

_____

_____

e)

_____

_____

f)

_____

_____

g)

_____

_____

h)

_____

_____

Exercises

Mathematics

6. **Tony, Ben, Anna and Zoe are buying food at the grocery store. Each has a different amount of money in his or her wallet. Calculate how much money each person has. Next, find out what each of them has bought. Remember: They can't spend more than what they have!**

Tony has: 2 five-dollar bills, 2 loonies, 2 dimes and 1 nickel.
Ben has: 1 ten-dollar bill, 1 toonie, 2 loonies, 4 dimes and 2 nickels.
Anna has: 4 toonies, 2 loonies, 4 quarters, 3 dimes and 1 nickel.
Zoe has: 1 five-dollar bill, 7 loonies, 4 quarters, 2 dimes and 7 nickels.

a)

$4.20 $3.10
$4.15 $3.05

Total: _____
Who bought these items?
_____

b)

$2.23 $2.00
$3.00 $4.12

Total: _____
Who bought these items?
_____

c)

$2.17 $3.10
$3.28 $5.00

Total: _____
Who bought these items?
_____

d)

$3.05 $1.50
$2.50 $5.20

Total: _____
Who bought these items?
_____

7. **How much money is there in each group? Use the images to help you.**

a) 1 twenty-dollar bill and 2 five-dollar bills: _____

b) 2 loonies and 1 toonie: _____

c) 2 nickels, 3 dimes and 4 quarters: _____

d) 2 ten-dollar bills, 1 loonie and 4 toonies: _____

e) 2 ten-dollar bills, 2 five-dollar bills and 1 twenty-dollar bill: _____

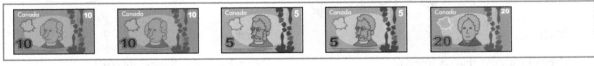

f) 1 fifty-dollar bill and 3 ten-dollar bils: _____

g) 1 toonie, 3 loonies and 4 quarters: _____

h) 2 nickels, 5 dimes and 7 quarters: _____

TEST 72

1. How much money is in each group? Show your work.

a)

_____

b)

_____

c)

_____

d)

_____

e)

_____

f)

_____

g)

_____

h)

_____

1. Add the following:

a)
$$3.7$$
$$+ 5.3$$

e) $3.6 + 2.1 =$

i)
$$1.6$$
$$+ 1.3$$

m) $4.3 + 3.1 =$

b)
$$9.2$$
$$+ 4.5$$

f) $4.4 + 3.3 =$

j)
$$4.9$$
$$+ 2.2$$

n) $8.1 + 1.6 =$

c)
$$5.6$$
$$+ 3.4$$

g) $5.3 + 2.2 =$

k)
$$6.7$$
$$+ 3.2$$

d)
$$1.9$$
$$+ 1.7$$

h)
$$8.4$$
$$+ 2.2$$

l) $7.3 + 2.6 =$

2. Find the difference:

a) $8.2 - 3.1 =$

e)
$$7.6$$
$$- 4.9$$

i) $4.3 - 2.1 =$

m)
$$7.5$$
$$- 2.3$$

b) $6.9 - 3.6 =$

f)
$$8.2$$
$$- 3.6$$

j) $8.6 - 5.3 =$

n)
$$4.1$$
$$- 3.2$$

c) $5.3 - 2.1 =$

g)
$$5.8$$
$$- 3.9$$

k)
$$7.8$$
$$- 6.3$$

d)
$$9.4$$
$$- 3.8$$

h) $9.9 - 7.2 =$

l)
$$9.8$$
$$- 5.3$$

Exercises

Mathematics

3. **Add the following amounts of money. Use the illustrations to help you calculate.**

a) $5.40
   + $1.25

b) $4.20
   + $1.00

c) $7.10
   + $0.25

d) $3.35
   + $1.10

e) $9.00
   + $0.75

f) $5.25
   + $0.25

g) $1.75
   + $1.20

h) $4.15
   + $4.25

4. Add the following:

a) 7.9
    + 2.1

b) 8.3
    + 6.9

c) 5.4
    + 3.9

d) 7.3
    + 5.6

e) 5.3 + 3.3 =

f) 3.1 + 2.7 =

g) 5.4 + 2.1 =

h) 6.3
    + 2.7

i) 7.9
    + 1.1

j) 5.4
    + 2.2

k) 1.8
    + 7.9

l) 3.1
    + 2.9

m) 6.4
    + 3.7

n) 3.9
    + 2.1

o) 6.7
    + 4.7

5. Find the difference:

a) 7.9 - 6.3 =

b) 8.4 - 2.2 =

c) 7.5 - 2.3 =

d) 9.3
    - 7.6

e) 8.4
    - 6.3

f) 7.4
    - 3.7

g) 3.4
    - 1.9

h) 8.9 - 2.7 =

i) 9.8 - 4.3 =

j) 8.6 - 4.3 =

k) 7.7
    - 3.3

l) 8.6
    - 3.9

m) 9.3
    - 6.8

n) 4.2
    - 3.9

Exercises

Mathematics

6. How much money is there in each group? Use the images to help you.

a) 2 quarters, 3 dimes and 5 nickels: _____

b) 1 toonie, 3 quarters, 3 dimes and 2 nickels: _____

c) 1 five-dollar bill, 2 loonies and 3 nickels: _____

d) 1 five-dollar bill and 4 quarters: _____

e) 2 toonies, 1 loonie, and 3 dimes: _____

f) 1 toonie, 3 quarters, and 5 nickels: _____

g) 1 five-dollar bill, 4 quarters and 3 dimes: _____

h) 5 quarters, 6 dimes and 4 nickels: _____

Exercises

Mathematics

7. Write these sums of money as shown in the example below.

1 toonie ($2), 1 loonie ($1), 1 quarter (25¢), 1 dime (10¢), and 1 nickel (5¢)

a)  _____

b)  _____

c)  _____

d)   _____

e)  _____

f)   _____

g)     _____

h)   _____

i) _____

j) _____

TEST 73

1. Colour the four-sided shapes.

a)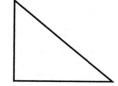

c)

b)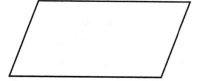

d)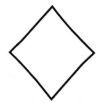

2. Which of the following angles is bigger than a right angle?

a)

c)

b)

d)

3. Write the number of sides each polygon has.

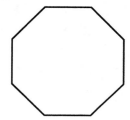   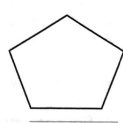

a) _____ b) _____ c) _____ d) _____

1. Trace dots to form the shapes described below.

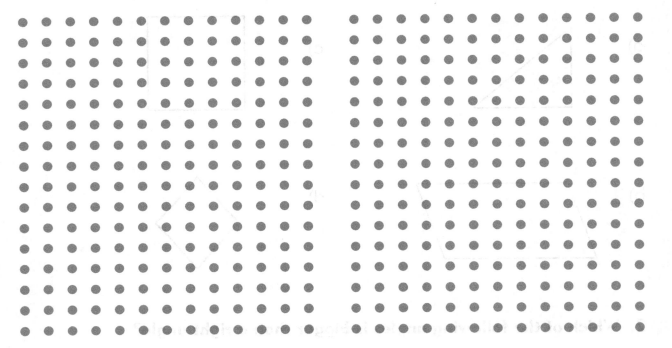

a) 2 figures with 3 sides

c) 2 figures with 4 angles

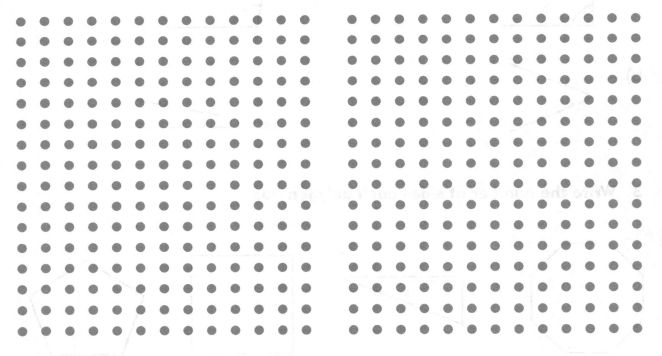

b) 2 figures with 4 sides

d) 2 figures with 5 sides

2. Colour in blue the figures with one or more right angles.

a)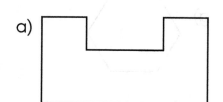

d)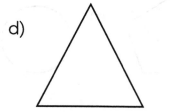

g)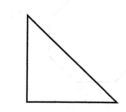

b)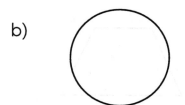

e)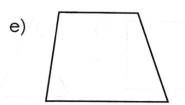

h)

c)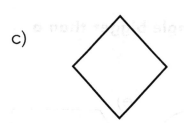

f)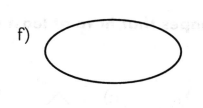

i)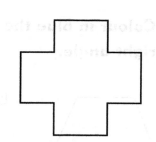

3. How many of each shape are in this picture?

squares: _____

diamonds: _____

triangles: _____

rectangles: _____

circles: _____

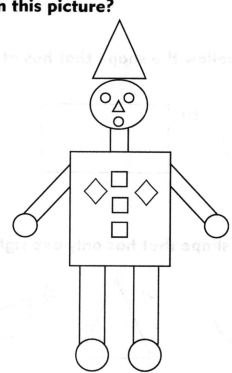

Exercises Mathematics

4. Identify the polygons. Colour them green.

a)
c)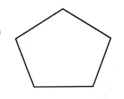
e)
g)

b)
d)
f)
h)

5. Colour in blue the shapes that have at least one angle bigger than a right angle.

a)
b)
c)
d)
e)

6. Colour in yellow the shape that has at least two right angles.

a)
b)
c)
d)

7. Circle the shape that has only one right angle.

a)
b)
c)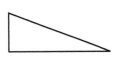
d)

TEST 74

1. Write the number of sides for each shape.

a) Number of
   sides: _____

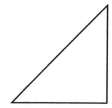

c) Number of
   sides: _____

e) Number of
   sides: _____

b) Number of
   sides: _____

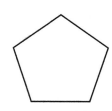

d) Number of
   sides: _____

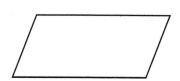

f) Number of
   sides: _____

2. Join dots in the grid to form a diamond, a parallelogram, a triangle and a rectangle.

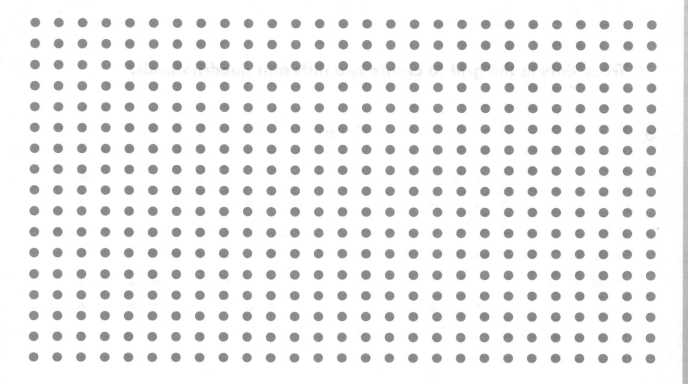

1. **Draw a clown, using the following – at least two circles, three triangles and four rectangles.**

2. **Trace dots in the grid to create two different quadrilaterals.**

a)

b)

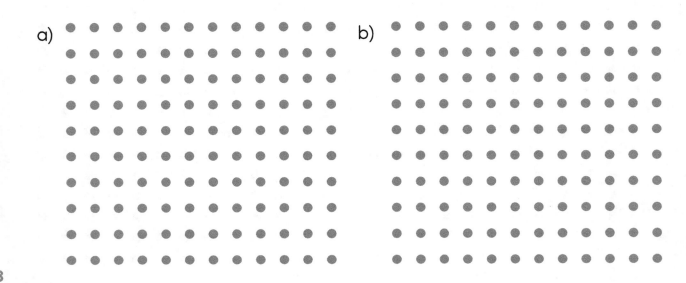

3. Colour the shapes that have at least one right angle.

a)

c)

e)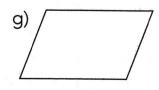

g)

b)

d)

f)

4. Draw a house, using the following shapes – four rectangles, two circles, four squares and three triangles.

5. Draw 3 different triangles.

  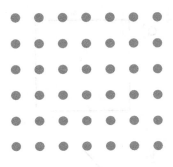

6. Draw 3 rectangles of different sizes.

7. Draw 3 different quadrilaterals.

 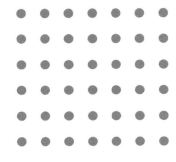 

8. Draw 3 different polygons.

Exercises

Mathematics

9. Write your own colour code, then colour the picture.

triangles: _____   rectangles: _____

circles: _____   squares: _____

10. Follow these steps to draw a robot.

Draw one square for its body and another one for its head.

Draw two rectangles for its eyes.

Draw one triangle for its nose.

Draw an oval for its mouth.

Draw a rectangle for its neck.

Draw rectangles for its legs and arms with a circle at the end of each for hands and feet.

Draw other geometric shapes to complete your robot.

TEST 75

1. **Using words from the word bank, write the names of the 3-D shapes below.**

| rectangular prism | triangular prism | cube | square pyramid | rectangular pyramid | triangular pyramid |

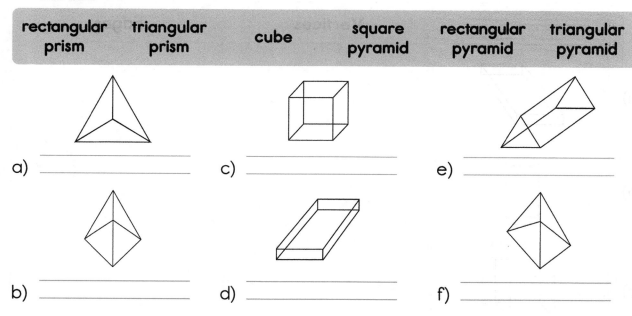

a) _____

c) _____

e) _____

b) _____

d) _____

f) _____

2. **Write the number of faces and edges for the following 3-D shapes.**

a)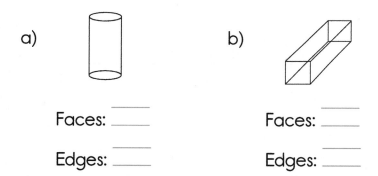

     Faces: _____

     Edges: _____

b)

     Faces: _____

     Edges: _____

3. **Write the name of a 3-D shape that can roll.**

_____

_____

4. **Write the name of a 3-D shape with a square base.**

_____

_____

1. Write how many vertices and edges each 3-D shape below has.

		Vertices	Edges
a)			
b)			
c)			
d)			
e)			
f)			
g)			

2. Circle the 2-D parts that make the net of each 3-D shape on the left. The first one is done for you.

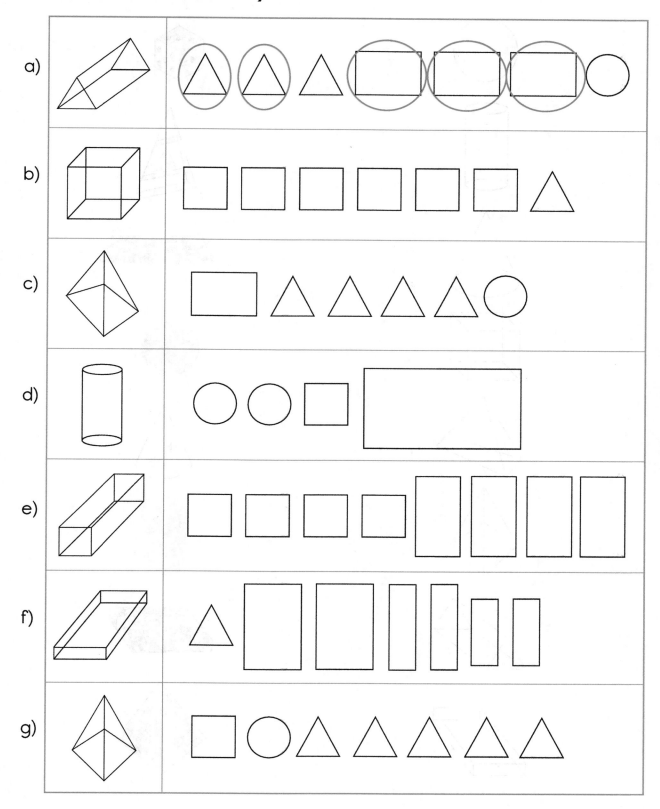

3. Connect each 3-D shape to the object it is similar to.

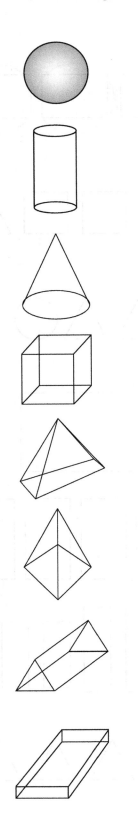

Exercises

Mathematics

TEST 76

1. **Write the number of faces and vertices for each 3-D shape.**

a)

Faces: _____

Vertices: _____

c)

Faces: _____

Vertices: _____

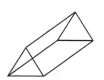

e)

Faces: _____

Vertices: _____

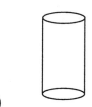

b)

Faces: _____

Vertices: _____

d)

Faces: _____

Vertices: _____

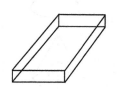

f)

Faces: _____

Vertices: _____

2. **Read the description of each 3-D shape and then circle the correct one.**

a) It has two flat sides and one curved side. (cylinder, cube, sphere)

b) It does not have any square sides. (cube, square prism, rectangular pyramid)

3. **Which net matches the shape shown on the left?**

a)

b)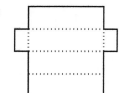

c)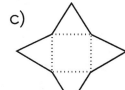

d)

1. **Write the number of faces, edges and vertices for each of the following 3-D shapes.**

		Faces	Edges	Vertices
a)				
b)				
c)				
d)				
e)				
f)				
g)				
h)				
i)				

2. Complete the table by putting an X in the correct column for each shape.

	Flat faces	Curved faces	Flat and curved faces
a)			
b)			
c)			
d)			
e)			
f)			
g)			
h)			
i)			

3. Write the number of 2-D shapes that form the net of each 3-D shape. The first one is done for you.

	Triangles △	Squares □	Circles ○	Rectangles ▭
a)		6		
b)				
c)				
d)				
e)				
f)				
g)				
h)				
i)				

1. **Draw the other half of the illustrations. Use the grid to create a mirror image of the left half.**

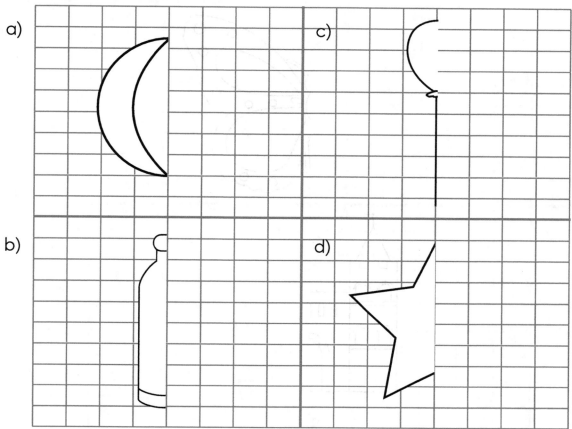

a) b) c) d)

2. **If I walked four miles north, then turned east and walked for three miles, then turned south and walked for two miles, and then six miles west, and finally two miles south, how far am I from where I started? In which direction? Draw and explain.**

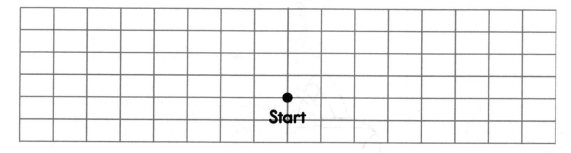

Start

3. **Colour this pattern with four different colours.**

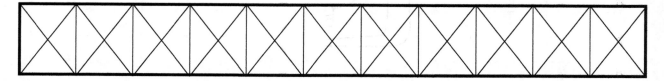

1. Complete each drawing using the grid.

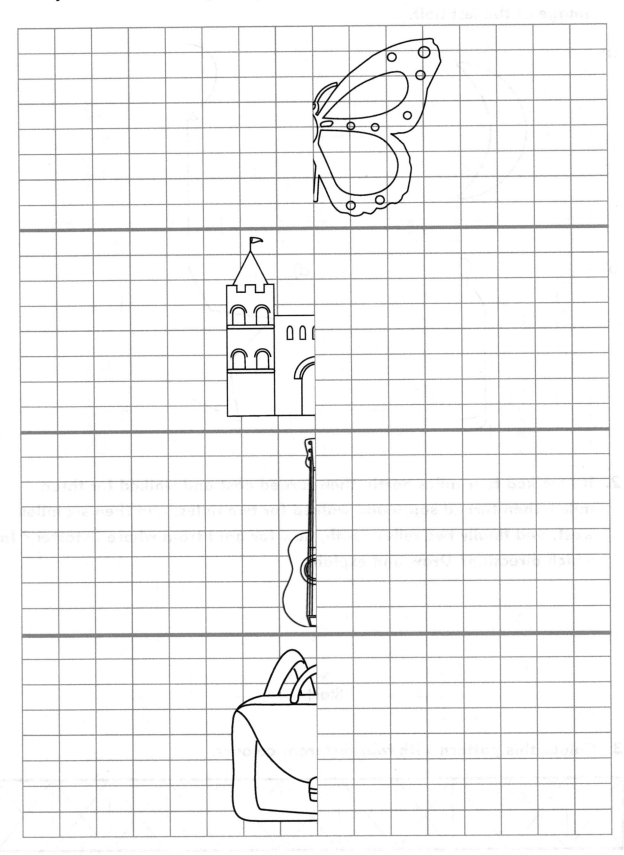

2. Draw one line of symmetry for each illustration.

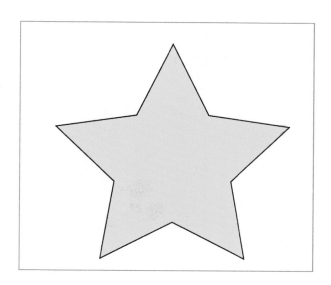

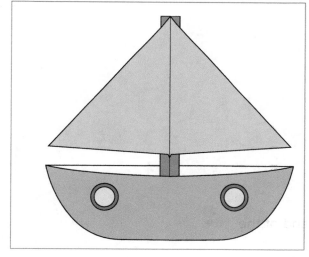

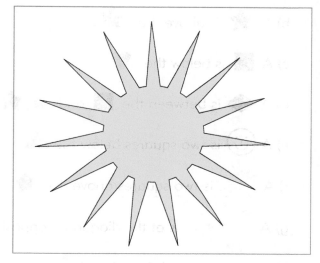

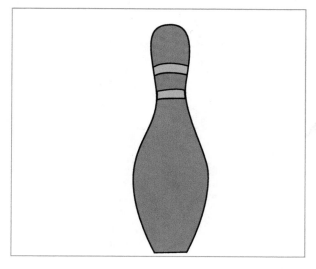

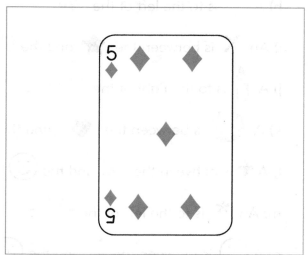

3. Read the clues, then draw each object in the correct area of the grid.

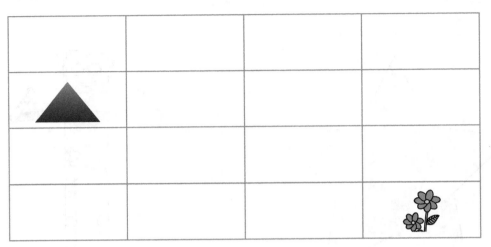

a) A ♡ is to the right of the ▲ .

b) A ★ is above the 🌸 .

c) A ■ is below the ♡ .

d) A ◆ is between the ■ and the ★ .

e) A ☺ is two squares below the ▲ .

f) A ☀ is two squares above the ★ .

g) A ✏ is at the diagonally opposite end of the 🌸 .

h) A 🎈 is to the left of the 🌸 .

i) An **X** is between the ★ and the ☀ .

j) A 🕯 is to the right of the ✏ .

k) A ◖ is between the ♡ and the **X** .

l) A ✚ is between the ▲ and the ☺ .

m) An **✳** is to the left of the ☀ .

n) A ☹ is between the 🎈 and the ☺ .

TEST 78

1. **Draw one line of symmetry for each shape.**

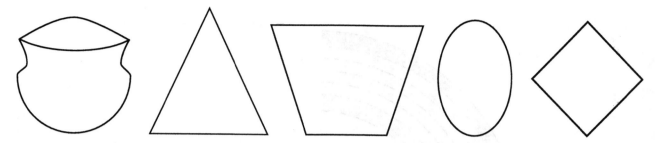

2. **Colour this pattern with two different colours.**

3. **Mira and her friends are playing Hide and Seek. Mira is "it". While she is counting, Roger runs 15 steps north and 5 steps west to hide in a closet; Lara runs 12 steps east and 5 steps south to hide behind a curtain; and Mona runs 17 steps west and 6 steps south to hide behind a couch. Who is furthest away from Mira? Draw and explain.**

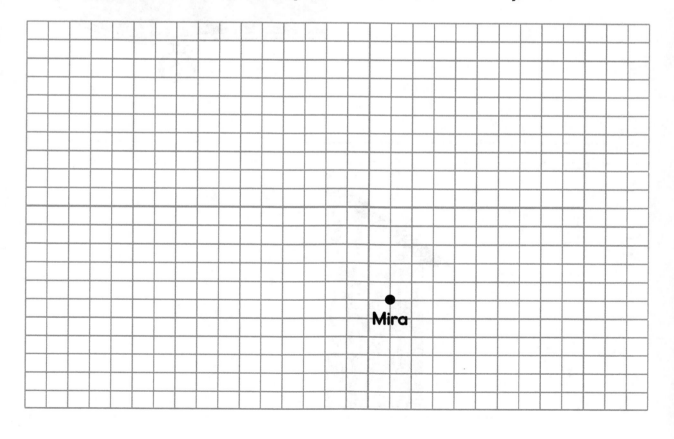

Mira

Mathematics

1. Complete and colour the missing half of each illustration.

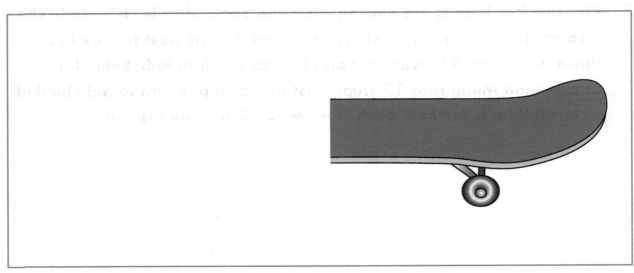

2. **Colour the pattern with colours of your choice. Make sure that the colouring is symmetrical, so that every shape has the same colour in both mirror halves.**

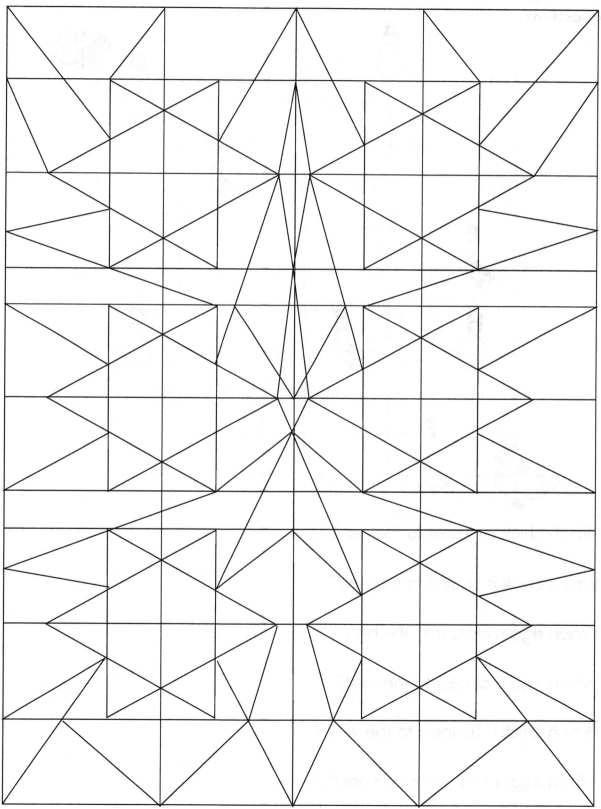

3. **The hen needs to find her chicks and eggs and take them to her nest. Look at the location of every object on the grid and then answer the questions.**

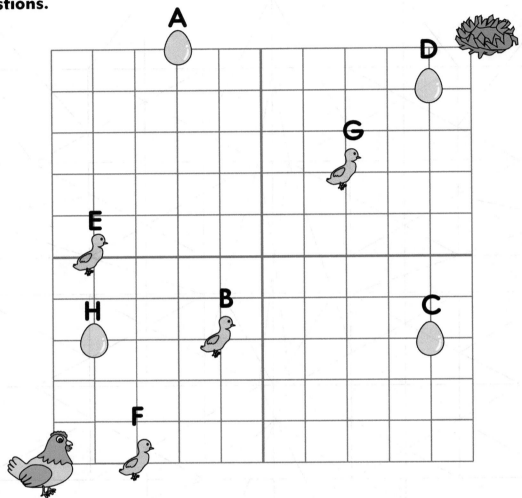

a) Which chick is closest to the hen? _____

b) Which chick is closest to the nest? _____

c) Which egg is closest to the hen? _____

d) Which egg is closest to the nest? _____

e) Which chick is furthest to the west? _____

f) Which egg is furthest to the north? _____

TEST 79

1. Estimate in centimetres the length of the following images. Use your ruler to verify your estimation.

a)

Estimate: _____

Length: _____

c)

Estimate: _____

Length: _____

b)

Estimate: _____

Length: _____

d)

Estimate: _____

Length: _____

2. Find the area and the perimeter of the shaded space in each figure.

a)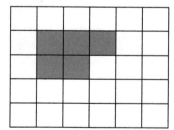

Area: _____ square units

Perimeter: _____ units

c)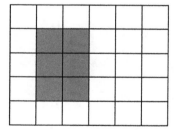

Area: _____ square units

Perimeter: _____ units

b)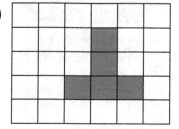

Area: _____ square units

Perimeter: _____ units

d)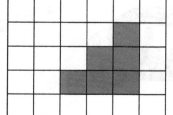

Area: _____ square units

Perimeter: _____ units

1. Put an X in the column that you would use to measure the length of the following objects.

	m	cm
a) a train		
b) a straw		
c) a worm		
d) a car		
e) your foot		

2. Draw lines of the following lengths.

a) 2 cm

b) 1 cm

c) 7 cm

d) 10 cm

3. Circle what you think is the correct measurement for each object in real life.

a) 5 m 20 cm 1 cm　　　b) 500 m 2 m 20 cm　　　c) 10 cm 26 m 1 km

Exercises

Mathematics

4. Calculate the area and the perimeter of the shaded squares.

a)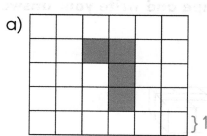
} 1 unit

Area: _____ square units

Perimeter: _____ units

e)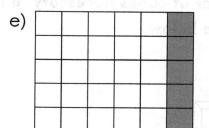

Area: _____ square units

Perimeter: _____ units

b)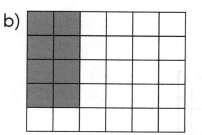

Area: _____ square units

Perimeter: _____ units

f)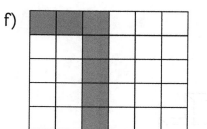

Area: _____ square units

Perimeter: _____ units

c)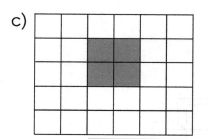

Area: _____ square units

Perimeter: _____ units

g)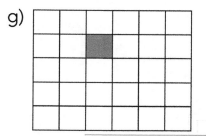

Area: _____ square units

Perimeter: _____ units

d)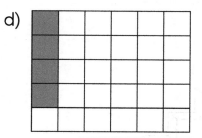

Area: _____ square units

Perimeter: _____ units

h)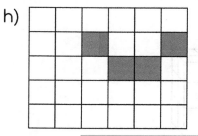

Area: _____ square units

Perimeter: _____ units

5. Bonus! Try this new challenge – finding volume! To find the volume, count the number of cubes necessary to build each shape and write your answer on the line below.

a) _____

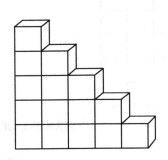

b) _____

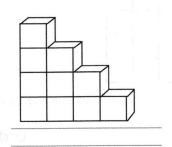

c) _____

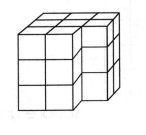

d) _____

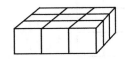

e) _____

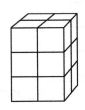

f) _____

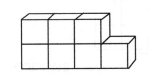

g) _____

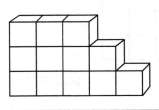

h) _____

TEST 80

1. Colour 10 cm of the line below.

_____

2. Find the area and the perimeter of the shaded regions.

a)

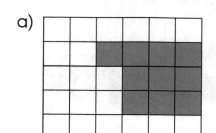

Area: _____ square units

Perimeter: _____ units

d)

Area: _____ square units

Perimeter: _____ units

b)

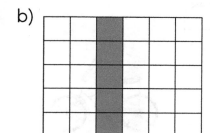

Area: _____ square units

Perimeter: _____ units

e)

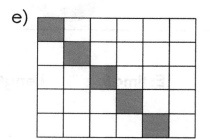

Area: _____ square units

Perimeter: _____ units

c)

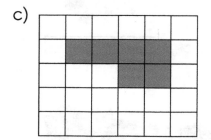

Area: _____ square units

Perimeter: _____ units

f)

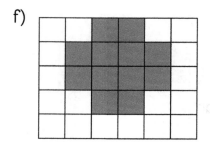

Area: _____ square units

Perimeter: _____ units

1. **Estimate the length of the following images in millimetres (mm). Then, verify your estimate with the help of a ruler. Complete the chart below.**

		Estimate	Length
a)	car		
b)	sailboat		
c)	snake		
d)	bicycle		
e)	caterpillar		
f)	plane		

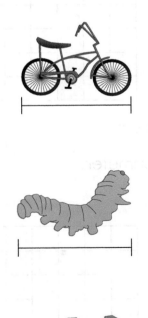

2. **Calculate the area and perimeter of the shaded regions.**

a)

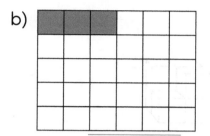

Area: _____ square units

Perimeter: _____ units

b)

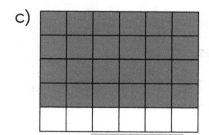

Area: _____ square units

Perimeter: _____ units

c)

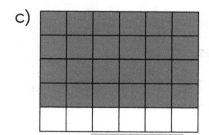

Area: _____ square units

Perimeter: _____ units

d)

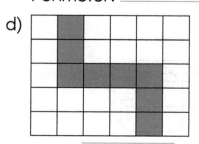

Area: _____ square units

Perimeter: _____ units

e)

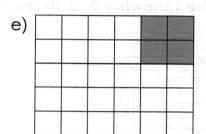

Area: _____ square units

Perimeter: _____ units

f)

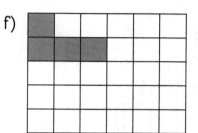

Area: _____ square units

Perimeter: _____ units

g)

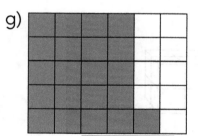

Area: _____ square units

Perimeter: _____ units

h)

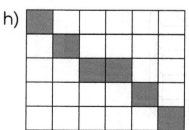

Area: _____ square units

Perimeter: _____ units

Exercises

Mathematics

3. Bonus! To find the volume, count the number of cubes necessary to build the following 3-D shapes.

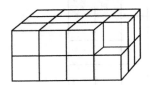

a) _____

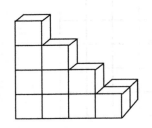

b) _____

c) _____

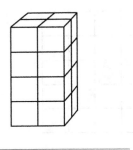

d) _____

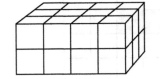

e) _____

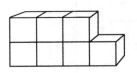

f) _____

g) _____

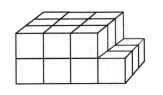

h) _____

TEST 81

1. Write the time of day when you would do the following:

a) eating breakfast _____

b) going to bed _____

c) eating lunch at school _____

2. Write the time shown on the clocks.

a) _____

b) _____

c) _____

3. Answer the questions.

a) How many months are there in a year? _____

b) How many days are there in a week? _____

c) How many days are there in a year? _____

d) How many minutes are there in an hour? _____

e) How many hours are there in a day? _____

f) How many seasons are there in a year? _____

g) How many seconds are there in a minute? _____

h) How many years are there in a century? _____

i) How many weeks are there in a month? _____

Mathematics

1. Draw the hands to show the time.

a) 12:15 pm

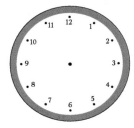

f) 1:05 pm

k) 9:40 am

b) 11:05 am

g) 10:45 pm

l) 12:25 am

c) 10:15 am

h) 2:50 pm

m) 6:50 pm

d) 9:15 pm

i) 8:55 pm

n) 7:45 pm

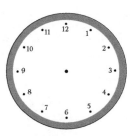

e) 1:20 am

j) 5:55 pm

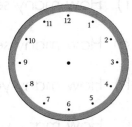

o) 11:55 pm

2. Write the time shown on each clock.

a) _____

c) _____

e) _____

b) _____

d) _____

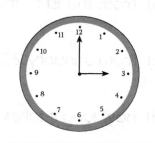

f) _____

3. How many minutes are there in...

a) 1 hour? _____

b) 1 and a half hours? _____

c) 2 hours? _____

4. Write the time of day you would do the following:

a) getting dressed for school _____

b) putting on your pyjamas _____

5. **Choose and write the correct unit of time to measure each of the following. You may use the words in the word bank more than once.**

| second | minute | hour | day | week | month | year |

a) from one Wednesday to the next Wednesday _____

b) from the 1st to the 31st of May _____

c) from January 2020 to December 2020 _____

d) how long it takes to say hello _____

e) the length of a song _____

f) the length of a phone conversation _____

g) from sunrise to sunset _____

h) how long it takes to paint a house _____

i) how long you play after school _____

j) how long it takes to brush teeth _____

k) how long it takes to build a snowman _____

l) from one birthday to the next _____

Exercises

Mathematics

6. Draw a line to match each clock with the correct time.

 •

 •

 •

 •

 •

 •

 •

 •

 •

 •

• It's three o'clock.

• It's eight o'clock.

• It's a quarter past nine.

• It's six o'clock.

• It's noon (twelve o'clock).

• It's ten o'clock.

• It's five o'clock.

• It's eleven thirty.

• It's four thirty.

• It's a quarter past two.

7. Fill in the blanks to complete each series.

a) Monday, _____ , Wednesday

b) Saturday, _____ , Monday

c) Tuesday, _____ , Thursday

d) Wednesday, _____ , Friday

e) Sunday, _____ , Tuesday

f) Thursday, _____ , Saturday

g) Friday, _____ , Sunday

8. Fill in the blanks to complete each series.

a) October, _____ , December

b) January, _____ , March

c) February, _____ , April

d) August, _____ , October

9. Place the months of the year in the correct season columns.

January, February, March, April, May, June, July, August, September, October, November, December

Winter	Spring	Summer	Fall

TEST 82

1. Solve the following problems.

a) Elaine started working at 8 am. She took a coffee break at 10 am. How many hours did she work from 8 am to 10 am?

_____

_____

b) Shyamal began working at midnight. He finished at 7 am. How many hours did he work last night?

_____

_____

c) It is 6:15 am. Lila's soccer match is at 8:00 pm. How much time is left until the beginning of her soccer game?

_____

_____

2. Write the time shown on each clock in two ways.

a) _____

_____

c) _____

_____

e) _____

_____

b) _____

_____

d) _____

_____

f) _____

_____

1. Solve the following problems.

a) Ron jogs for one hour every day. How many hours does he jog a week?

Show your work: _____ Answer: _____

b) Maggie goes to the doctor one hour a day from Monday to Friday. How many hours a week does she see the doctor?

Show your work: _____ Answer: _____

c) Lola practises singing one time a week with the choir. How many times does she practise singing in a year?

Show your work: _____ Answer: _____

d) Ricardo goes to his friend Pedro's house two times a week. How many times a month does Ricardo go to Pedro's?

Show your work: _____ Answer: _____

e) Anna spends fifteen minutes a day taking a shower. How many minutes a week does she spend taking a shower?

Show your work: _____ Answer: _____

f) Alyssa makes her bed every day. How many days a year does she make her bed?

Show your work: _____ Answer: _____

Mathematics | Exercises

2. Put an X on the clock that is showing the wrong time.

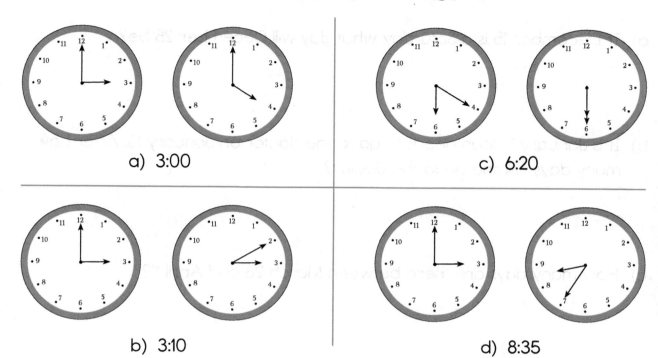

a) 3:00

c) 6:20

b) 3:10

d) 8:35

3. Draw the hands on the clock to show the given time.

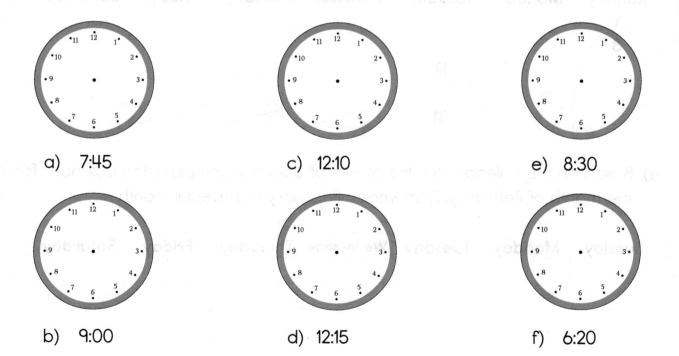

a) 7:45

c) 12:10

e) 8:30

b) 9:00

d) 12:15

f) 6:20

4. Answer the following questions.

a) If December 15 is a Saturday, what day will December 25 be?

           _____

           _____

b) It is January 1. Joan needs to go to the doctor on January 13. After how many days will she go to the doctor?

           _____

           _____

c) How many days are there between March 28 and April 11?

           _____

           _____

d) Complete the calendar for the month of January.

Sunday	Monday	Tuesday	Wednesday	Thursday	Friday	Saturday
1						
8						
		17				
		31				

e) Based on the calendar for the month of January, complete the calendar for the month of February. Remember: February is a special month.

Sunday	Monday	Tuesday	Wednesday	Thursday	Friday	Saturday

TEST 83

1. **Here are the types of books that have been borrowed from the school library. Use the graph to answer the questions.**

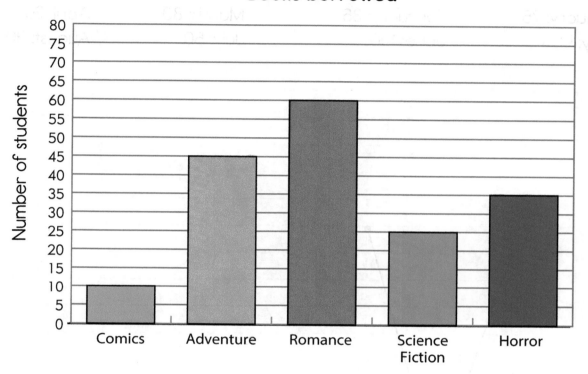

Books borrowed

Number of students / *Types of books*

a) How many students borrowed adventure books? _____

b) How many students borrowed romance books? _____

c) How many students borrowed horror books? _____

d) How many students borrowed science fiction books? _____

e) How many students borrowed comics? _____

f) Write the books in order, from least popular to most popular.

_____

_____

_____

_____

1. **Here is the number of stamps Yori bought between January and August. Complete the graph and answer the questions on the next page.**

January: 75   February: 35   March: 80   April: 25
May: 40   June: 100   July: 50   August: 90

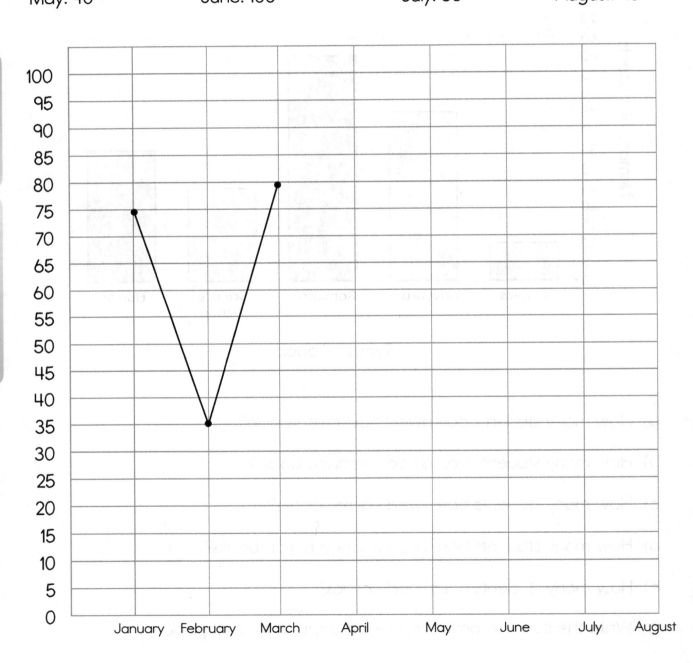

a) In which month did he buy the most stamps?

_____

_____

b) In which month did he buy the least stamps?

_____

_____

c) How many stamps does Yori have in total?

_____

_____

d) What is the difference between the number of stamps bought in February and in June?

_____

_____

e) How many more stamps did he buy in August than he did in April?

_____

_____

f) Write the months in order from lowest to highest number of stamps bought.

_____

_____

_____

_____

2. Justine works in a bakery. The graph below shows the number of desserts she baked on Monday. Answer the questions below.

Desserts Baked on Monday

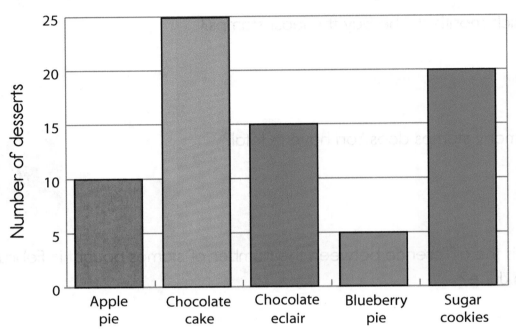

a) How many apple pies did she make? _____

b) How many sugar cookies did she make? _____

c) How many chocolate cakes did she make? _____

d) How many blueberry pies did she make? _____

e) How many chocolate eclairs did she make? _____

f) Why do you think she made more chocolate cakes?

_____

_____

_____

_____

_____

1. **Meg works in a flower shop. The graph shows how many flowers she sold last week. Use the graph to answer the questions below.**

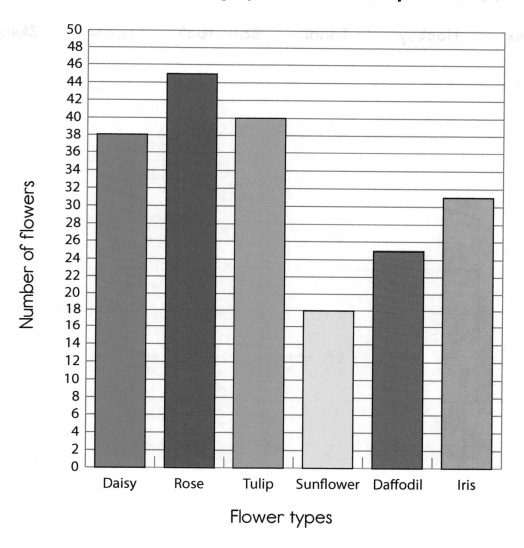

a) How many roses did she sell? _____

b) How many tulips did she sell? _____

c) Which flower did she sell the least of? _____

d) What was the most popular flower she sold? _____

e) How many more daisies did she sell than daffodils? _____

f) How many flowers in total did she sell last week? _____

1. **Complete a survey with your friends to find out their favourite sports.**
   You may place an X in more than 1 column for each friend.

Names	Hockey	Tennis	Basketball	Soccer	Skiing
Example: Anthony	X			X	
Total					

a) How many like hockey? _____

b) How many like tennis? _____

c) How many like basketball? _____

d) How many like soccer? _____

e) How many like skiing? _____

f) How many friends did you survey in total? _____

2. Now draw a bar graph with the results of your survey.

Favourite Sports

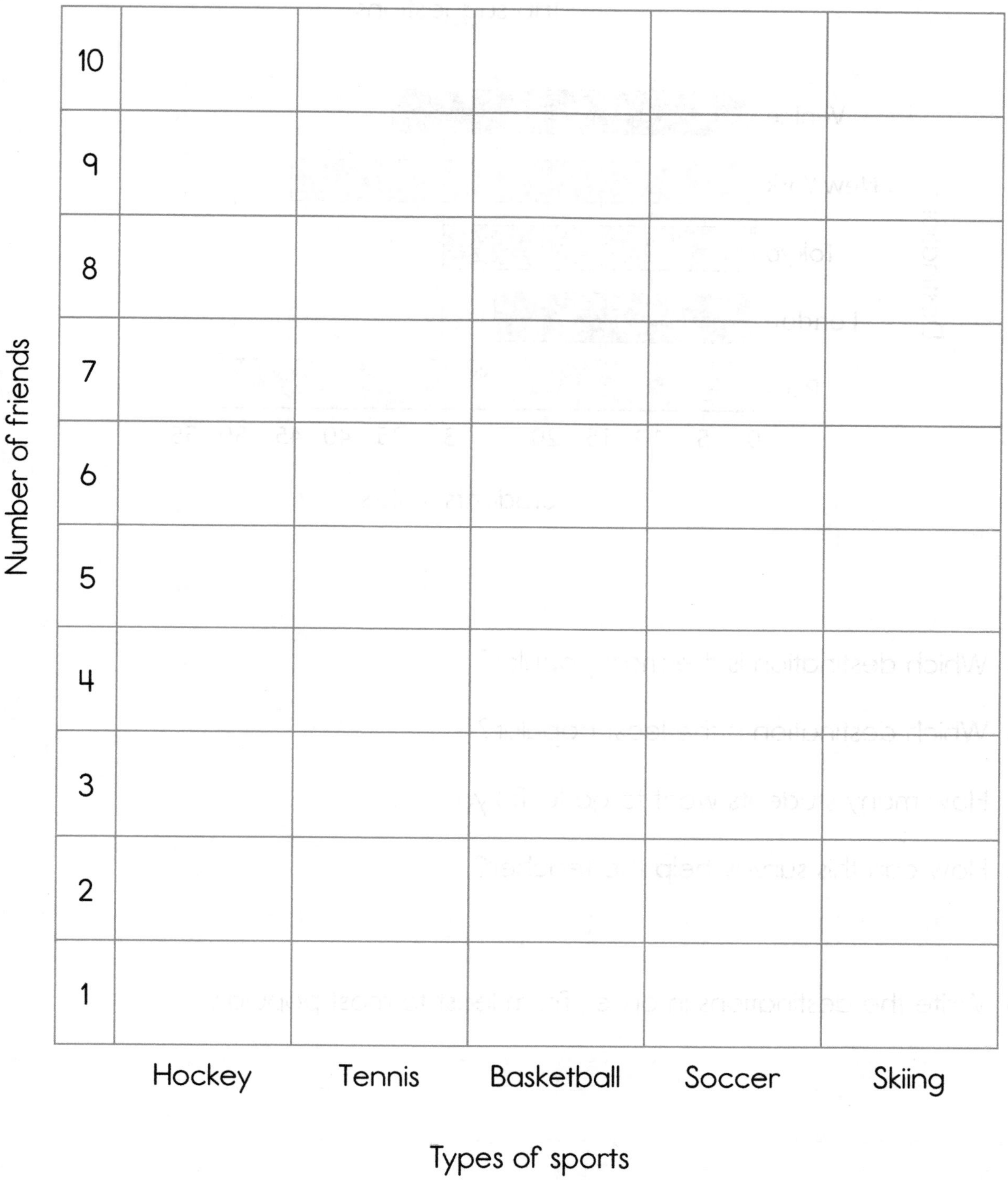

Number of friends	Hockey	Tennis	Basketball	Soccer	Skiing
10					
9					
8					
7					
6					
5					
4					
3					
2					
1					

Types of sports

3. The students of Grade 3 want to go on a trip, and a number of destinations are discussed. Look at the graph and answer the questions.

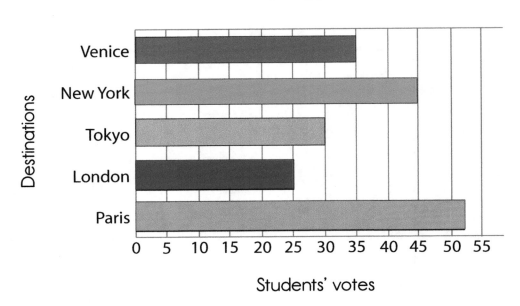

a) Which destination is the most popular? _____

b) Which destination is the least popular? _____

c) How many students want to go to Tokyo? _____

d) How can this survey help the teacher? _____

_____

e) Write the destinations in order, from least to most popular.

_____

_____

TEST 85

1. Check the correct box for each sentence below.

	Certain	Possible	Impossible
I can watch a movie.			
I can fly like a bird.			
I can drive a school bus some day.			
I can scratch my nose.			
I can help my mother bake cookies.			
I can sleep.			
I can participate in the Olympic Games some day.			
I can finish my homework.			
I can talk.			

Mathematics

Exercises

Mathematics

1. **Bob asks Dylan to pick two cards from the four in his hand. Show all the possible combinations.**

a)

d)

b)

e)

c)

f)

2. Asha threw two dice nine times in a row. Here is what she got.

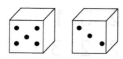 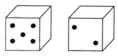 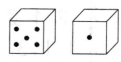

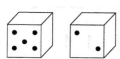 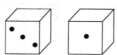 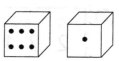

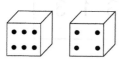 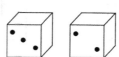 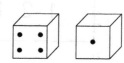

What do you notice? _____

_____

_____

3. Put an X on the illustrations that are impossible.

a)

c)

b)

d)

4. Look closely at the following boxes.

(1)

```
2 1 2 2 2 2 1 2
1 1 3 1 2 2 1 2 1
  1 2 1 1 2 3 2
```

(4)

```
3 3 1 3 2 2 3 1
2 2 3 2 3 2 2 3
1 3 3 2 3 3 1 3
```

(2)

```
2 2 1 1 1 3 1 3 1
  1 1 1 3 2 1 2 3
  1 3 3 1 2 2 1
```

(5)

```
1 1 3 1 3 2 1 1
2 3 1 1 1 1 1 1
3 1 1 2 1 2 1 1
```

(3)

```
1 2 1 3 3 2 3 1
2 1 2 2 3 2 1 3
1 3 2 3 2 1 3 1
```

(6)

```
3 3 3 3 2 3 1
3 3 3 3 1 3 1 3
3 1 2 3 3 3 1 1 3
```

a) How many numbers does each box have? _____

b) If you want a 3, in which box do you have the highest chance of getting it? In which box do you have the lowest chance of getting a 3?

_____

c) In which box do you have the highest chance of getting a 1?

_____

d) In which box do you have an equal chance of getting a 1 or a 2?

_____

TEST 86

1. Using yellow, blue and black, colour the circles so that each series is different.

a)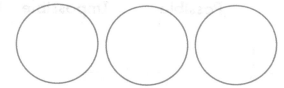

d)

b)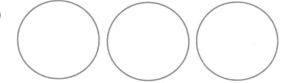

e)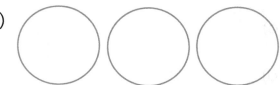

c)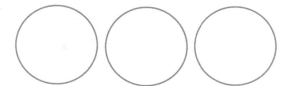

f)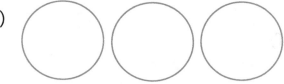

2. Place an X in the box that makes the most sense.

		Certain	Possible	Impossible
a)	I can visit the planet Mercury some day.			
b)	I can drink two small glasses of water.			
c)	I can eat a whole cow at breakfast.			
d)	I can recite the alphabet.			
e)	I can win a card game.			

Mathematics

1. **Fill in the boxes with situations of your choice that match the X in each column.**

	Certain	Possible	Impossible
a)		X	
b)	X		
c)			X
d)	X		
e)		X	
f)			X

2. **Look at each circle below and its yellow target area. If you were to throw a ball ten times at each yellow target, which one do you think you would hit the most?**

a)   b)   c)

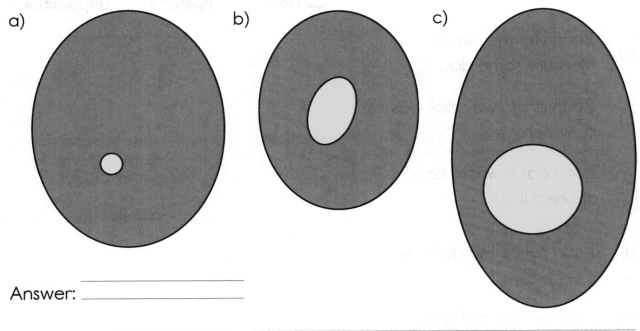

Answer: _____

Explain why: _____

3. **Create combinations with the numbers 2, 6, 5, 4, 7, 1. You may repeat the numbers.**

a) 2-digit combinations:

_____ _____ _____ _____ _____ _____
_____ _____ _____ _____ _____ _____
_____ _____ _____ _____ _____ _____
_____ _____ _____ _____ _____ _____
_____ _____ _____ _____ _____ _____
_____ _____ _____ _____ _____ _____
_____ _____ _____ _____ _____ _____

b) 3-digit combinations:

_____ _____ _____ _____ _____ _____
_____ _____ _____ _____ _____ _____
_____ _____ _____ _____ _____ _____
_____ _____ _____ _____ _____ _____
_____ _____ _____ _____ _____ _____
_____ _____ _____ _____ _____ _____
_____ _____ _____ _____ _____ _____

4. **Create combinations with the numbers 6, 3, 2, 4.**

a) 2-digit combinations:

_____ _____ _____ _____ _____
_____ _____ _____ _____ _____
_____ _____ _____ _____ _____

b) 3-digit combinations:

_____ _____ _____ _____ _____
_____ _____ _____ _____ _____

5. **Look at the picture, then answer the questions.**

a) What is the total number of fruits in the jar? _____

b) What is the probability of selecting an apple from this jar? _____

c) What is the probability of selecting an orange? _____

d) What is the probability of selecting a kiwi? _____

e) What is the probability of selecting either a pear **or** a banana? _____

f) If you picked a fruit at random, which fruit do you have the highest probability of getting? And which fruit has the lowest probability of being selected?

_____

_____

SOCIAL STUDIES

Pioneers in Canada, 1780–1850

Graphing and Mapping

Canada and the World

CANADIAN CURRICULUM PRESS

Forward Learning

The earliest European settlers who made their homes in Canada, mostly near the Great Lakes and major rivers, are known as pioneers. Pioneers made their homes from the materials that were around them. Some lived in tents or simple wooden-board shacks, while others built mud huts or log cabins.

1. **Choose one of the types of pioneer homes mentioned above. Draw it and the area around the home.**

   Hints: Think about how the pioneers protected themselves and their animals, how they stored their grain, and where they got water from.

1. **Write a story about a day in the life of a pioneer child in Canada in the early 1800s.**

   Hints: Think about the responsibilities of such children within the family and their chores around the home; about what they did in their free time; and how, if at all, they were educated.

   _____

   _____

   _____

   _____

   _____

   _____

   _____

   _____

   _____

   _____

   _____

   _____

   _____

   _____

   _____

   _____

   _____

   _____

   _____

   _____

   _____

   _____

Exercises

Social Studies

2. **How did the pioneers interact with Aboriginal groups in Canada in the early 1800s? Do some research online or at your local library for help.**

3. **Farming was an important part of pioneer life in Canada. Draw a pioneer farm below, and then describe how the farm was run.**

   Hints: What animals lived there and what did they provide? How was the planting done? What tools did pioneer farmers have to use?

TEST 88

1. **Imagine you are a pioneer living in Canada in 1795. Design a poster that you think would encourage other people to move to Canada in the early 1800s.**

   Hints: Think about what you could describe as the advantages for pioneers living in Canada at that time – natural resources in your surrounding area, land for farming and building a house of your own, freedom to live your life as you wish, etc. You may draw pictures to illustrate some of these points.

Social Studies

1. **Use your imagination to write a letter from a pioneer to a person in this time.**

   Hints: Think about how pioneers lived, what they ate and what clothes they wore, as well as what they did in their daily life, what challenges they faced, etc.

   _____
   _____
   _____
   _____
   _____
   _____
   _____
   _____
   _____
   _____
   _____
   _____
   _____
   _____
   _____
   _____
   _____
   _____

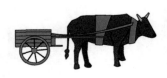

2. **Many pioneers in Canada came from European countries like England, France, and Germany. Imagine you are a pioneer whose relatives live in one of these countries. Write a letter to a relative about your journey to Canada and your life in a pioneer village.**

Hints: Think about how pioneers got to Canada, where they settled, and the differences between life in Canada and life in Europe in the early 1800s.

Exercises

Social Studies

3. **In the box below, draw a map of a pioneer village. Write about your village below.**

Hint: Think about what resources a village needs and what jobs people had.

TEST 89

1. **Create your own map with a title, a legend of the symbols used and their coordinate points [for example: (A,1), (B,2)].**

Title: _____

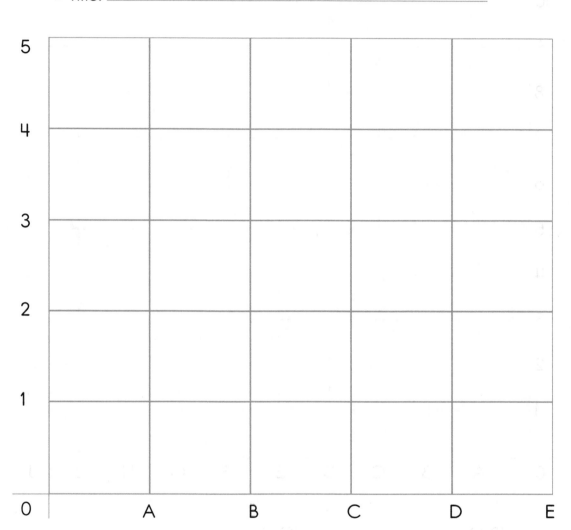

Legend	Coordinate points	Legend	Coordinate points

1. **Place coloured dots on the graph at the following coordinate points. The first one is done for you.**

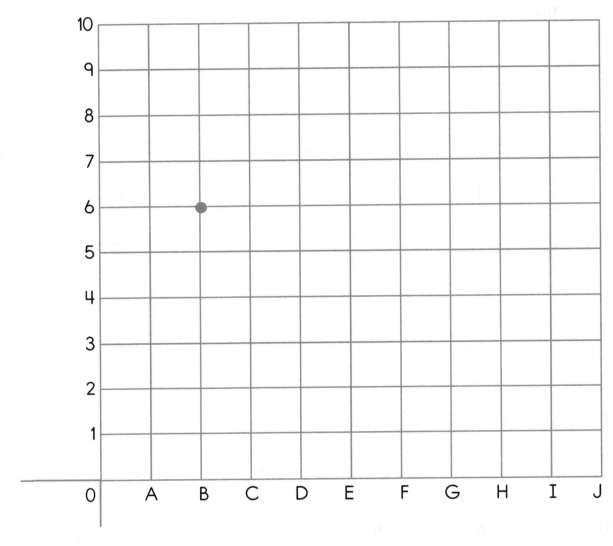

(B,6)

(A,2)

(E,9)

(G,7)

(I,10)

(C,8)

(D,5)

(F,4)

(H,3)

(J,1)

A **legend** gives information on a map. A legend has symbols for places.

For example: 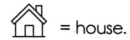 = house.

2. **Create symbols for the following places that could be on a map.**

a) apartment building

b) railway tracks

c) road

d) forest

e) school

f) church

g) river

h) hotel

i) bus stop

j) restaurant

GRAPHS AND MAPPING

3. Colour the boxes that match the coordinates.

a)

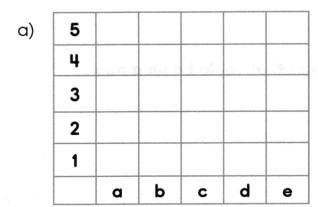

(b,2) (b,3) (b,4) (b,5)
(c,2) (d,2) (d,3) (d,4) (d,5)

c)

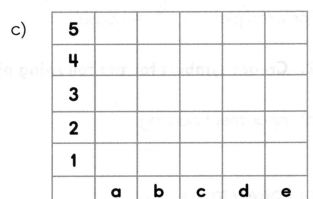

(b,4) (d,3) (e,5) (a,1)
(a,4) (b,2) (c,2) (c,4)

b)

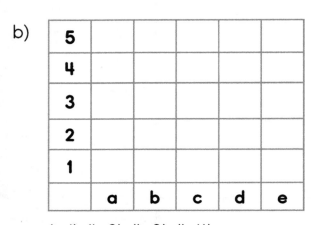

(a,1) (b,2) (b,3) (b,4)
(c,2) (d,2) (d,4) (e,1)

d)

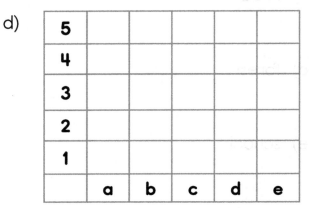

(a,5) (b,3) (c,5) (d,2)
(e,1) (d,4) (e,3) (b,5)

4. Place points on the graph to match these coordinates and then join them.

a)

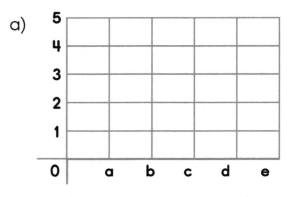

(a,1) to (b,3) to (c,4) to (d,2) to (a,1)

b)

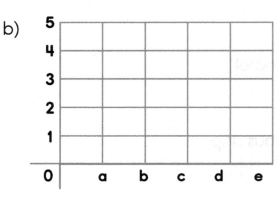

(a,5) to (b,4) to (c,1) to (d,3)
to (e,4) to (a,5)

5. **Here is the pirate's map of where all the treasure and other objects are. Write the coordinates of each object. The first one is done for you.**

fish: _____ (D,13) _____ island: _____ palm tree: _____

treasure: _____ hook: _____ flag: _____

mermaid: _____

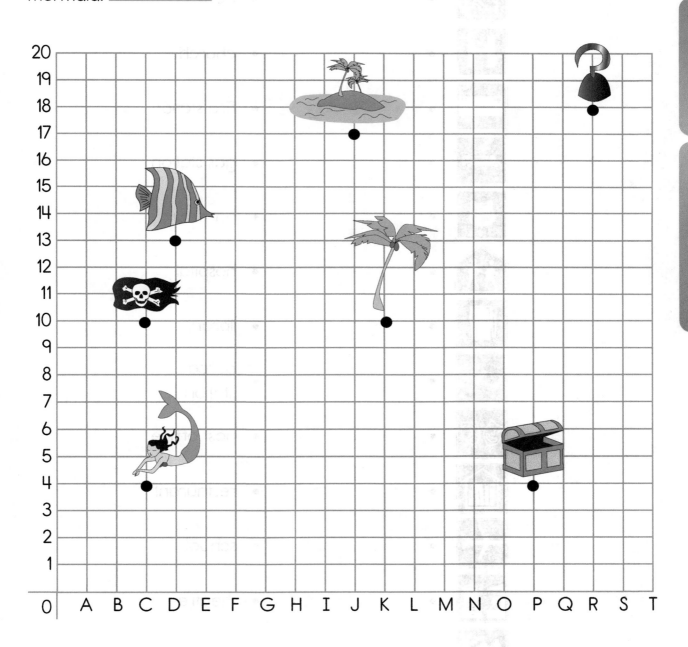

6. Draw a line from each map symbol to what it represents.

- airport
- skating arena
- bank
- church
- fire station
- gas station
- harbour
- hospital
- library
- police station
- post office
- restaurant
- school
- theatre
- train station

TEST 90

1. Place points on the graph to match the following coordinates.

(1,G), (4,E), (18,E), (17,G), (10,H), (9,L), (10,L), (5,L), (13,L), (10,Q)

Now connect the following points:

(1,G) to (4,E) to (18,E) to (17,G) to (1,G) to (9,L) to (10,H)
to (10,L) to (13,L) to (10,Q) to (5,L)

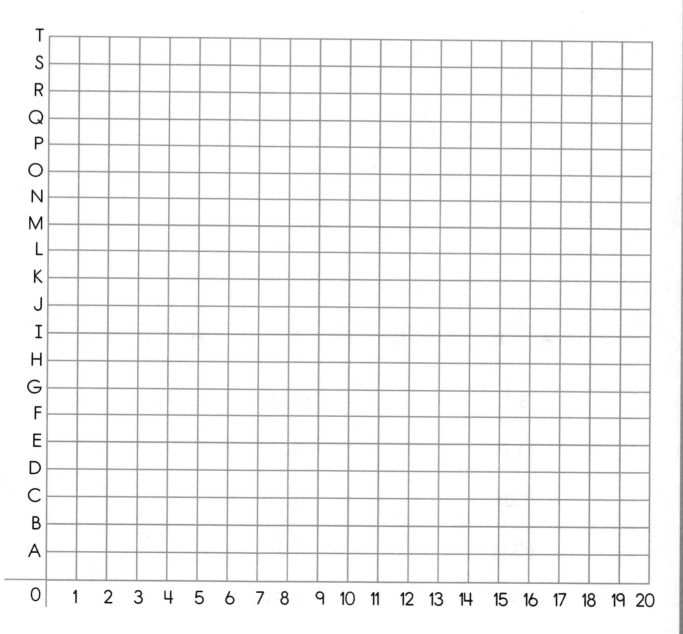

1. Colour the squares on the graph that match the following coordinate points. Cross each one off the list below as you complete it.

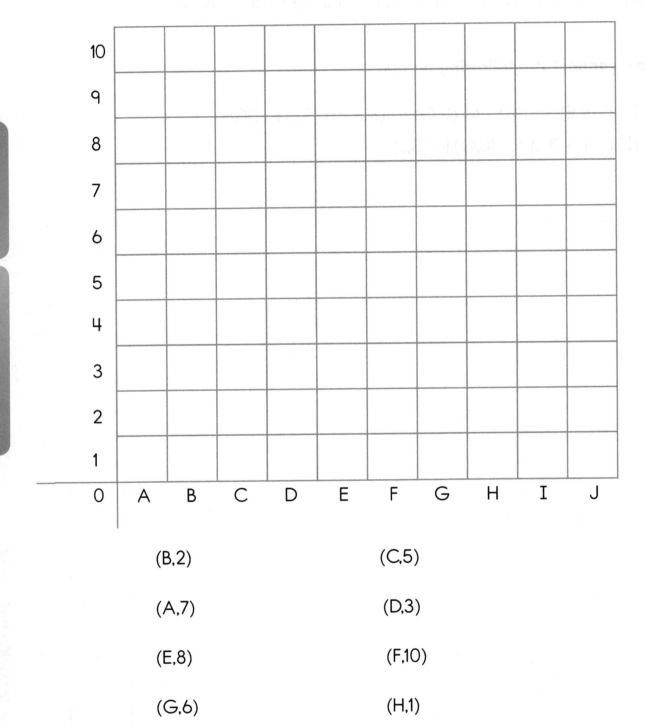

(B,2)	(C,5)
(A,7)	(D,3)
(E,8)	(F,10)
(G,6)	(H,1)
(I,4)	(J,9)

2. **Place the following symbols on the graph at the given coordinate points. Cross each one off as you complete it. The first one is done for you.**

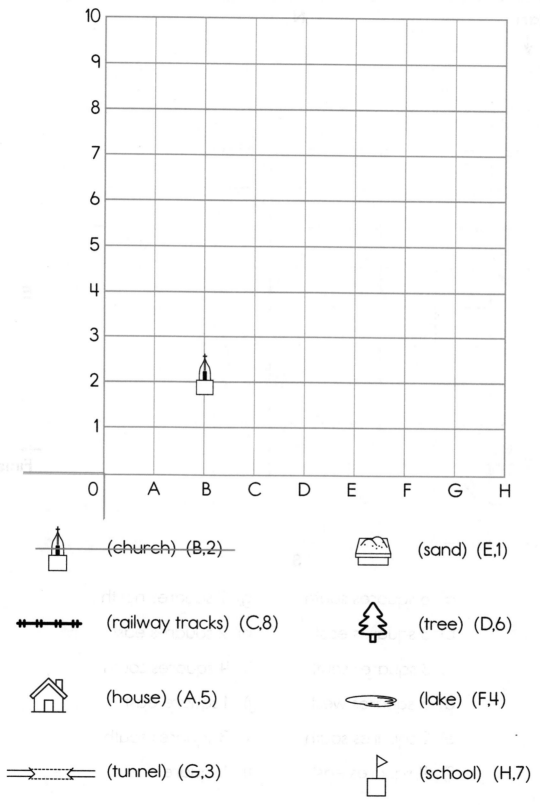

(church) (B,2)

(sand) (E,1)

(railway tracks) (C,8)

(tree) (D,6)

(house) (A,5)

(lake) (F,4)

(tunnel) (G,3)

(school) (H,7)

3. **Follow the instructions from a) to l) to move through the graph and reach the Finish.**

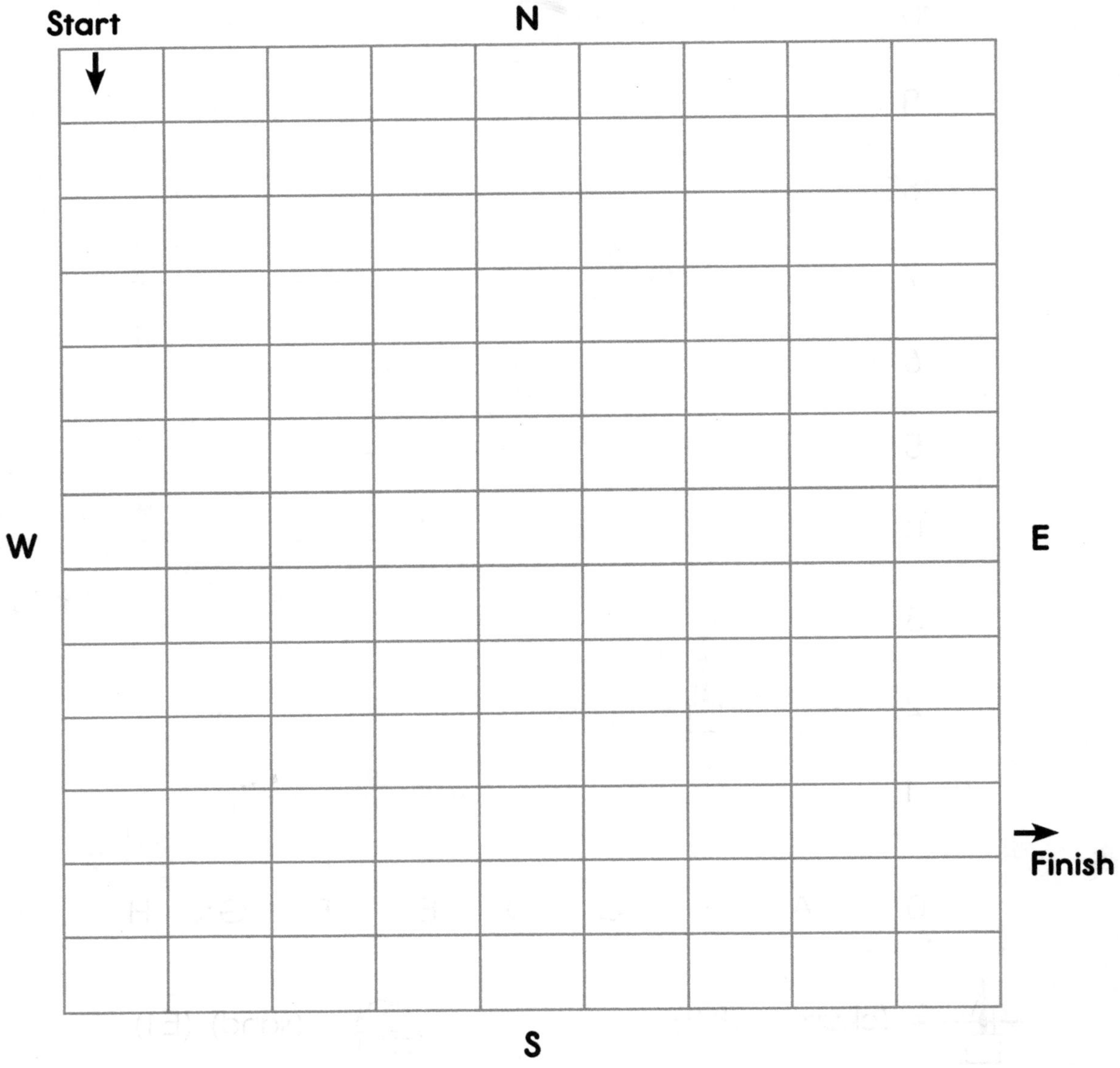

Start

N

W

E

Finish

S

a) 6 squares south

b) 3 squares east

c) 3 squares south

d) 3 squares west

e) 2 squares south

f) 4 squares east

g) 7 squares north

h) 2 squares east

i) 4 squares south

j) 1 square east

k) 3 squares south

l) 1 square east

1. **Label the seven continents in the world map. Then, colour each continent a different colour.**

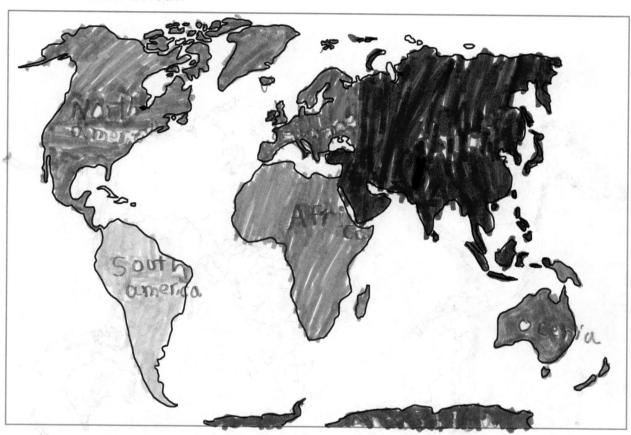

2. **Which continent do you live in? Locate and mark your home place (roughly) on the map. Now look at a map of your continent in an atlas and check if you were correct.**

3. **Which is the frozen continent?** _Aantartica_

4. **Which continent is the biggest in land and population?** _Asia_

5. **What are the official languages of Canada?** _English and French_

6. **In which continent is the Amazon Rainforest located?** _South america_

7. **Name the world's second-smallest continent, which has a rich history of kings and castles, knights and wars.** _Eerope_

1. Colour all the oceans in the world map. Then, name any three oceans.

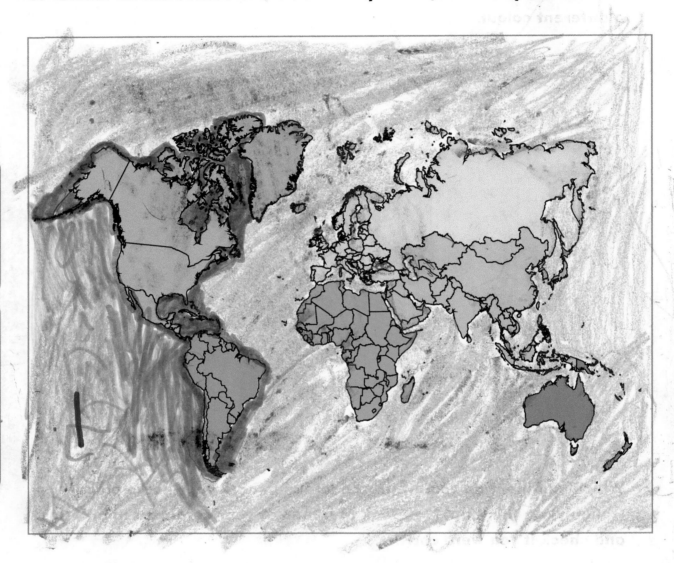

<u>Oceans:</u>

a) Pacific ocean

b) Antlantic ocean

c) Indian ocean

2. Label the following provinces and territories in the map of Canada. Then mark and label Ottawa, Canada's capital, on the map.

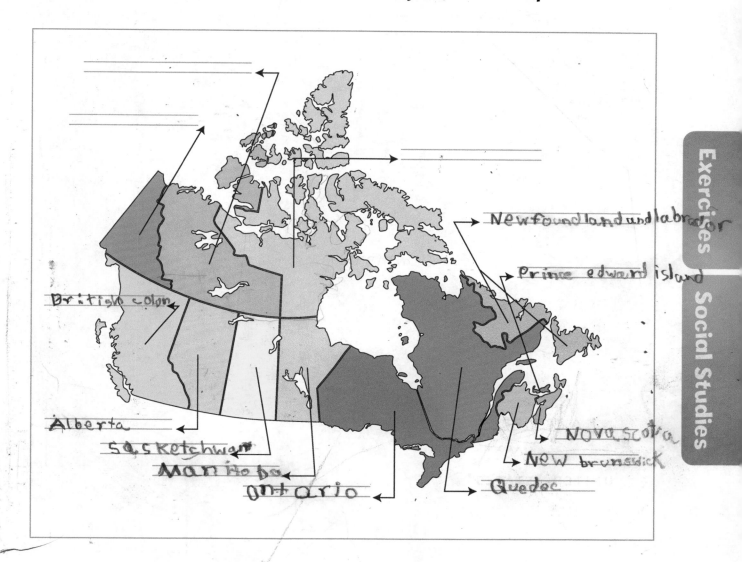

Handwritten labels on map: Newfoundland and labrador, Prince edward island, British colon, Alberta, Sasketchwan, Manitoba, Ontario, Nova scotia, New brunsdick, Quebec

a) Newfoundland and Labrador

b) New Brunswick

c) Prince Edward Island

d) Nova Scotia

e) Quebec

f) Ontario

g) Manitoba

h) Saskatchewan

i) Alberta

j) British Columbia

k) Nunavut

l) Northwest Territories

m) Yukon

3. **Look at the map of Ontario and the list of lakes and rivers below. Then, find them in the map and label them correctly.**

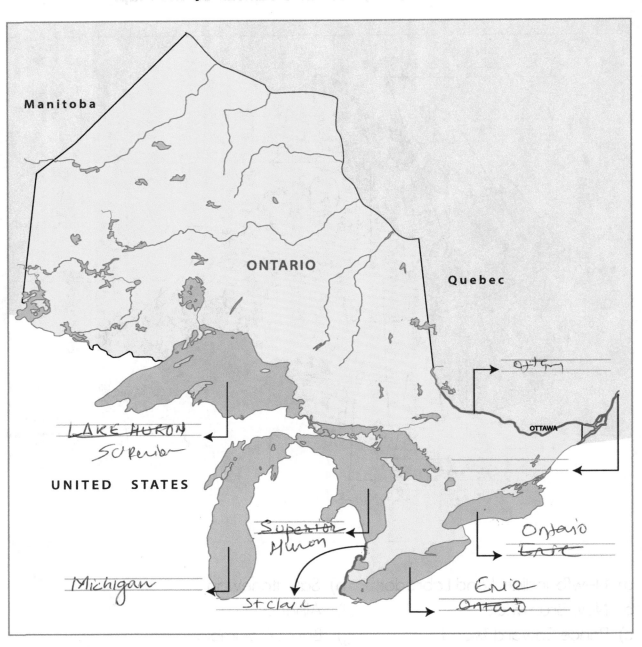

Great Lakes

Lake Huron

Lake Ontario

Lake Michigan

Lake Erie

Lake Superior

Rivers

St. Lawrence River

Ottawa River

St. Clair River

4. Use a globe or an atlas and answer the following:

a) What is the country south of the United States of America?

_____

_____

b) What is the biggest country in South America?

_____

c) What is the sea between Europe and Africa called?

_____

d) Name any two countries in Europe.

_____

_____

e) Name the sea to the west of India.

_____

f) What is the horizontal line that runs around the middle of the earth?

_____

_____

g) Name the continent at the South Pole.

_____

_____

h) What is the big island country east of Africa?

_____

_____

i) Name any three countries in Africa.

_____

_____

j) Name the ocean to the west of North America.

_____

_____

5. Find the names of Canada's provinces, territories and the capital cities in the word search.

```
S G F T N S I H O V I C T O R I A A S C T W S Q
N O R T H W E S T T E R R I T O R I E S I H O U
S E N U Q T C H A R L O T T E T O W N W N I E E
P R I N C E E D W A R D I S L A N D C N O T O B
W E Q U E B E C E E D M O N T O N L W T V E I E
I G E N B I U I A L N T O R O N T O U B A H Q C
N R I A N E E R O N N S T J O H N S L E S O A C
K S A S K A T C H E W A N F N E O G L R C R L I
O Q O I A E R E G I N A W S K U Y L W T O S U T
B R I T I S H C O L U M B I A D E E A R T E I Y
N A E R U T N Y A A N W V I M E L L U L I A T T
E N E W F O U N D L A N D A N D L A B R A D O R
I E Y T T V N O A P C C D N I N O B E A M K A R
E A U C R C A S N E A H I H U B W Y N W A E B N
W I K R B T V E A I K I H L A S K V A U A R R T
K A O W N A U U M A N I T O B A N I A A Q R H O
H D N A S E T H A L I F A X B R I I N F N W T A
A G O N T A R I O A L B E R T A F O T A A D M E
F R E D E R I C T O N I T U E R E T R I Q W N B
N E W B R U N S W I C K W I N N I P E G W E T T
```

Newfoundland and Labrador	Ontario	Nunavut
St. John's	Toronto	Iqaluit
New Brunswick	Manitoba	Northwest Territories
Fredericton	Winnipeg	Yellowknife
Prince Edward Island	Saskatchewan	Yukon
Charlottetown	Regina	Whitehorse
Nova Scotia	Alberta	
Halifax	Edmonton	
Quebec	British Columbia	
Quebec City	Victoria	

1. **On which continent did the first human beings live?** _____

2. **Which continent is called the "Land Down Under"?** _____

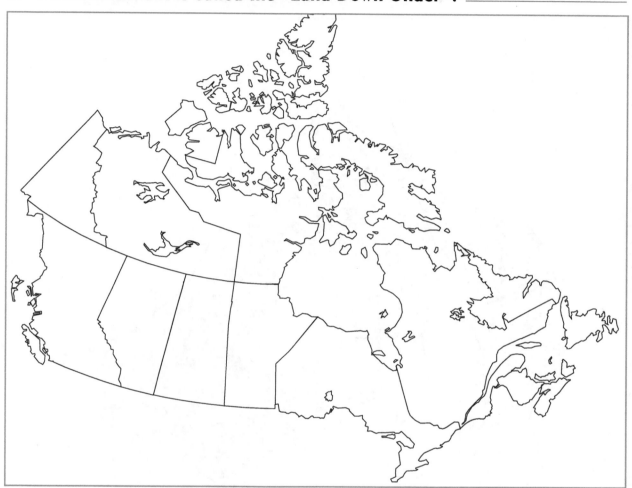

3. **What is the capital of Canada? Mark it on the map.** _____

4. **How many provinces and territories does Canada have? Name them and label them on the map.**

_____

_____

_____

_____

_____

5. **Colour the province/territory you live in red on the map and the rest of Canada green.**

1. Label the following provinces, territories and their capital cities on the map of Canada. The arrows are for the provinces and territories. The dots on the map are for the capitals.

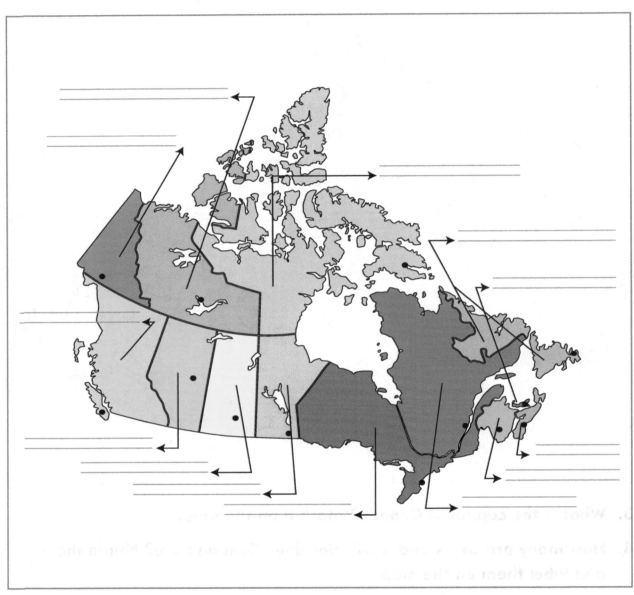

a) Newfoundland and Labrador: St.John's

b) New Brunswick: Fredericton

c) Prince Edward Island: Charlottetown

d) Nova Scotia: Halifax

e) Quebec: Quebec City

f) Ontario: Toronto

g) Manitoba: Winnipeg

h) Saskatchewan: Regina

i) Alberta: Edmonton

j) British Columbia: Victoria

k) Nunavut: Iqaluit

l) Northwest Territories: Yellowknife

m) Yukon: Whitehorse

Exercises

Social Studies

2. **Create your own map. Include a legend, cities, rivers and lakes. Cross off each item as you complete it. Remember to include coordinate points.**

Legend					

Cities

Names	Coordinates

Rivers and Lakes

Names	Coordinates

Exercises

Social Studies

3. Trace and colour the flag of Canada.

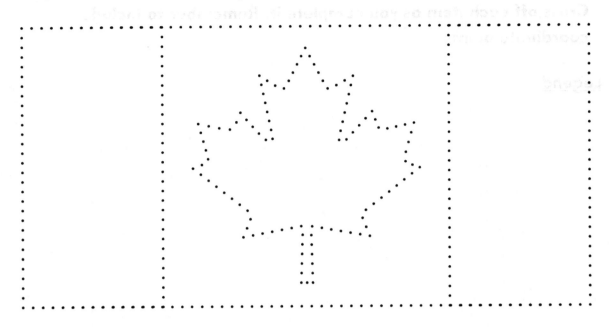

4. Complete the colouring of the flags of the territories of Canada. Then, name the territories on the lines below the flags.

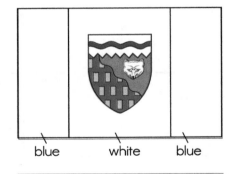

blue   white   blue

_____

_____

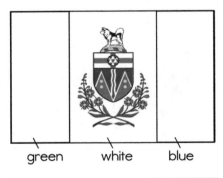

green   white   blue

_____

_____

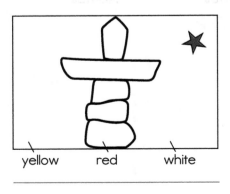

yellow   red   white

_____

_____

5. a) Complete the colouring of these flags of the provinces of Canada. Then, name the provinces on the lines below the flags.

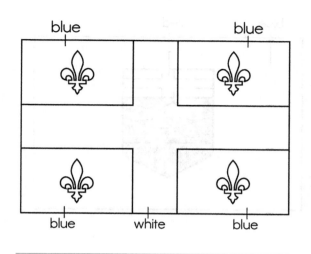

_____

_____

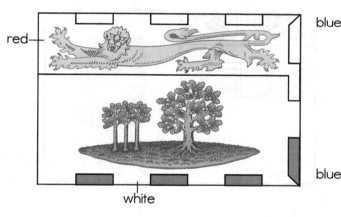

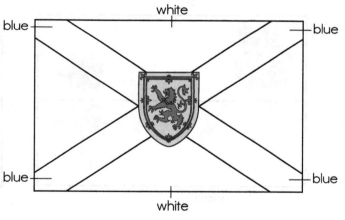

_____

_____

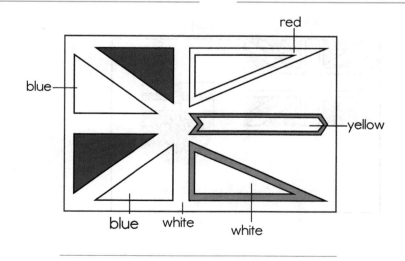

_____

_____

b) **Complete the colouring of these flags of the provinces of Canada.**
Then, name the provinces on the lines below the flags.

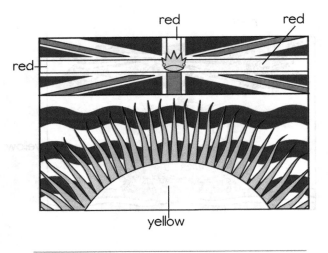

red   red

red

yellow

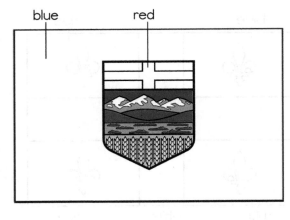

blue   red

_____

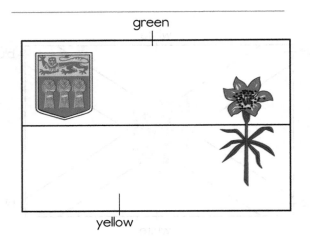

green

yellow

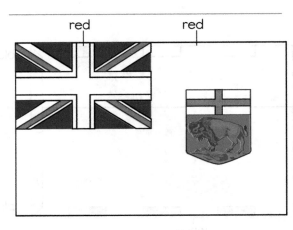

red   red

_____

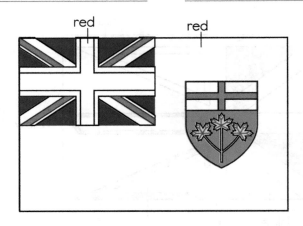

red   red

_____

SCIENCE

Plants, Trees and Soils

Matter: Structures and Forces

Food Groups

Animal Kingdom

TEST 93

1. Which plant form do the following words refer to: branch, crown, trunk?

_____

2. Why is it important to have a compost bin in your home?

_____

3. Name three things you *cannot* put in the green bin.

a) _____

b) _____

c) _____

4. Name three things you *can* put in the green bin.

a) _____

b) _____

c) _____

5. Using the word bank, label the parts of a plant.

roots	stem	flower	leaves

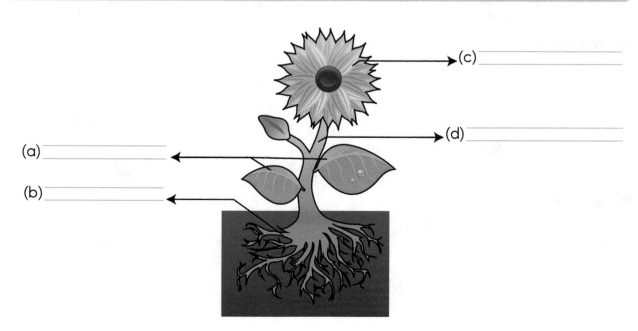

(c) _____

(d) _____

(a) _____

(b) _____

1. **The basic needs for any plant are: air, water, light, warmth and space. Write a few sentences to explain how each is important to the growth of a plant.**

a) air: _____

_____

_____

b) water: _____

_____

_____

c) light: _____

_____

_____

d) warmth: _____

_____

_____

e) space: _____

_____

_____

_____

2. **Draw a plant that has been given all the needs mentioned on the previous page.**

3. **Draw a plant that has not received one of the above needs.**

4. Recycling and Compost

Recycling is essential for the survival of our planet. Do you recycle at home? At school? That's good! However, we need to do more than just recycling. We must also reduce what we use and waste. Here are some things you can do:

Lunchbox: Instead of putting your sandwich in a plastic bag that you throw away, put it in a reusable, washable container. Take juice to school in a reusable, washable container. Do the same thing with yogurt. Do not use plastic cutlery. Instead, take metal forks and spoons from home and make sure you bring them back.

Compost: Composting the food waste in the kitchen reduces the amount of garbage sent into the landfills. Read through the items below and place an X in the correct column to show what items can be placed in a green bin.

	Yes	No
a) peel from vegetables and fruits		
b) egg shells		
c) coffee grinds and filter		
d) meat leftovers		
e) tea bags		
f) oil		
g) lawn clippings		
h) milk products		
i) hay		
j) hair and animal's fur		

	Yes	No
k) wilted flowers		
l) kleenex and paper towels		
m) animal waste		
n) leaves		
o) branches cut into small pieces		
p) metal		
q) nut shells		
r) sick plants		
s) fish leftovers		
t) wilted herbs		

5. Draw four different types of trees. If you know their names, write them.

a)

b)

c)

d)

Science Lab 1: Germination

Seeds **germinate** (change into a seedling) with the help of light and warmth (from the sun), water and air.

6. Try to germinate some seeds. You will need help from an adult to complete the following lab work. You will need: seeds and a peat-pots tray. Follow the directions on the peat pots to correctly prepare your lab. Record everything you do for the next 14 days and complete the following chart with the results.

Seed name: _____

	Date	Height (mm & cm)	Sunlight	Water (yes/no)
1.				☐
2.				☐
3.				☐
4.				☐
5.				☐
6.				☐
7.				☐
8.				☐
9.				☐
10.				☐
11.				☐
12.				☐
13.				☐
14.				☐

Exercises

Science

TEST 94

1. Design a poster to encourage people to protect plants and trees. Include a reminder in your poster about the importance of plants and trees to help our environment. You may draw or paste images to support your points. Use the lines to brainstorm ideas and then create your poster in the box.

Exercises

Science

1. **Some plants are grown as food. Research how the following fruits and vegetables are grown. Draw what you find.**

a) potato

d) apple

b) pineapple

e) strawberry

c) rice

f) carrot

2. Using the word bank, label the parts of a tree.

| branch | crown | leaves | roots | trunk |

(a) _____

(b) _____

(c) _____

(d) _____

(e) _____

3. Using the word bank, label the parts of a flower.

| stamen | petal | pistil | stem |

(a) _____

(b) _____

(c) _____

(d) _____

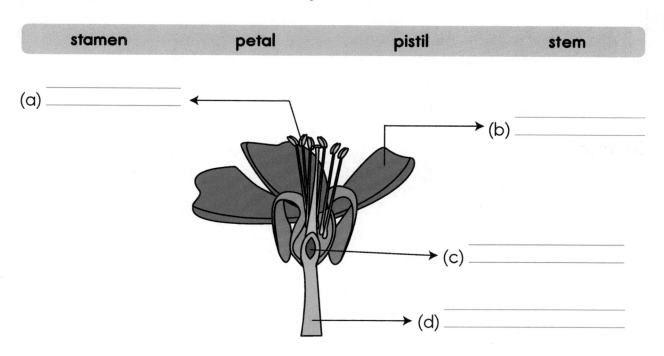

4. How do trees help our environment?

_____

_____

5. How are trees important in summer?

_____

_____

6. How are trees important in winter?

_____

_____

7. Choose an area you know well, maybe near your home. Draw how that same area looks in winter and summer. Include trees and plants.

Winter

Summer

Science Lab 2: Plant Needs

8. **You will need to use two similar plants to complete this science lab. One plant will receive all of the usual care (sun, water, and air). The second plant will have one of those needs removed (sun, water or air). Record the changes you notice over the next two weeks in the chart below.**

	Plant 1	Plant 2
Day 1		
Day 4		
Day 7		
Day 10		
Day 14		

Explain what you noticed.

_____

_____

_____

_____

_____

_____

_____

_____

9. Science Lab 3: Soils

Do beans grow better in potting soil, sand or water? Try the experiment and note your results.

What you'll need:
2 little pots for the plants
A small glass pot
Rocks, potting soil, sand
Cotton
3 bean seeds

Place some rocks at the bottom of the two pots. Put potting soil in one pot and sand in the other. In each pot, plant a bean seed 1 cm below the surface.

Put cotton at the bottom of the glass pot. Place the last seed inside and fill the pot halfway with water.

Place the pots in a sunny area and water the first two regularly. Measure how much all the plants grow and write it down below.

In the sand:

After one week: _____

After two weeks: _____

After one month: _____

In the potting soil:

After one week: _____

After two weeks: _____

After one month: _____

In the water:

After one week: _____

After two weeks: _____

After one month: _____

Which plant grew the most? _____

1. Define the word "structure". Use a dictionary to find the answer.

2. Define the word "stability". Use a dictionary to find the answer.

3. Choose the correct word to describe each object below.

a)

(hot, light)

b)

(heavy, soft)

c)

(fleshy, hard)

4. Which of these is bigger in real life? Circle it.

a)  b)  c)

5. Draw two things in the world that show the force of *push*.

a)

b)

6. Draw two things in the world that show the force of *pull*.

a)

b)

Science

1. Matter can have many different properties. Use the word bank to help you describe each item below.

cold	wet	light	dry	soft	furry

a)

_____

_____

d)

_____

_____

b)

_____

_____

e)

_____

_____

c)

_____

_____

f)

_____

_____

2. Which of these is bigger in real life? Circle it.

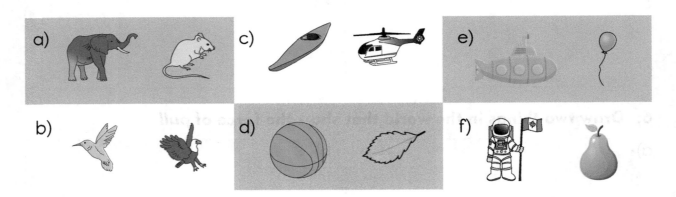

3. **Research two different kinds of bridges and draw them. Then, answer the questions below.**

Bridge 1

a) Where is the area of strength for this bridge? _____

b) Mark that area of strength in your drawing.

c) Where is this bridge? _____

d) What type of bridge is it? _____

Bridge 2

a) Where is the area of strength for this bridge? _____

b) Mark that area of strength in your drawing.

c) Where is this bridge? _____

d) What type of bridge is it? _____

4. Science Lab 4: Bridge

Collect items to build with, like cardboard rolls, newspapers, toothpicks, popsicle sticks, chopsticks or wooden skewers, cardboard, tape, etc. Using the materials you collected, create a bridge. Draw your bridge, then use the lines below to describe your bridge and how you built it.

Exercises

Science

5. Science Lab 5: Rain Gauge

What you'll need:

A 2-litre bottle (like a big, empty pop bottle)
Scissors
Measuring cup

Start this experiment at the beginning of a month.

a) Cut off the top one-third of the open, empty bottle.

b) Insert the top part into the bottom part, with the neck downwards. This will prevent dirt getting into the bottle.

c) Ask your parents' permission and dig a hole in a quiet corner of your backyard. Place the bottle in the hole.

d) After each day of rainfall, empty the container into a measuring cup. Measure the level of the water in mm using a ruler. Note the quantity in the chart below. Write the date in each little square.

e) After one month, add all the quantities of water you recorded in the chart. That will be the quantity of rain that fell during that month. You can verify your measurements against the rainfall data for that month published on weather sites online.

Monday	Tuesday	Wednesday	Thursday	Friday	Saturday	Sunday
☐	☐	☐	☐	☐	☐	☐
☐	☐	☐	☐	☐	☐	☐
☐	☐	☐	☐	☐	☐	☐
☐	☐	☐	☐	☐	☐	☐
☐	☐	☐	☐	☐	☐	☐

6. Science Lab 6: Thumbprints

What you'll need:

Ink pad

Ask each of your friends to press his or her thumb on the ink pad and then place the thumbprint in one of the empty boxes below. Write your friends' names above their fingerprints. Look closely at all the thumbprints.

What do you notice? _____

_____

_____

_____

_____

Name:	Name:	Name:
Name:	Name:	Name:
Name:	Name:	Name:
Name:	Name:	Name:
Name:	Name:	Name:

Exercises

Science

7. Science Lab 7: Static Electricity

What you'll need:

A plastic comb
A woollen shirt
A ping-pong ball
A balloon

a) Rub a comb on a woollen shirt several times. Turn on the sink faucet and run a thin stream of water. Bring the comb close to the water without touching it. Make sure to not get the comb wet.

Describe what happens: _____
_____
_____

Why do you think it happens?
_____
_____

b) Rub the comb on the woollen shirt many times. Bring the comb close to a ping pong ball without touching it.

Describe what happens: _____
_____
_____

Why do you think it happens?
_____
_____

c) Inflate the balloon. Rub it against your hair. Try to touch it to the wall.

Describe what happens: _____
_____
_____

Why do you think it happens?
_____
_____

d) Rub the balloon on different surfaces and try to touch it to a wall.
   Write down the results and your thoughts about them in the chart below.

Surface	Result	Reason for the result

TEST 96

1. Look around your home or environment and draw two structures that show _stability_. Remember: things that are stable do not tip over easily.

a)

b)

2. Define _push_. Use a dictionary to find the answer. Then, name two things in your life where you use the force of pushing.

3. Define _pull_. Use a dictionary to find the answer. Then, name two things in your life where you use the force of pulling.

4. Read the words, look at the picture and then fill in on each thermometer what temperature you think it is on that day. Use a red marker.

a) A hot day in summer

b) A rainy day in spring

c) A cool day in November

d) A very cold day in January

1. **Design a device that shows the force *of pushing or pulling*. Draw the device.**

2. **Explain how you built your device and how it works.**

_____
_____
_____
_____
_____
_____
_____
_____
_____
_____
_____

Exercises

Science

Temperature

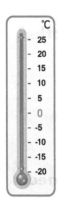

We can measure the outside temperature with a thermometer. Temperatures can sometimes be above 0° and sometimes below 0°. We measure in Celsius degrees (°C).

Here are some examples: -5°C: you would need your mittens and a scarf. 15°C: you would need a light jacket and your running shoes. Water freezes at 0°C and boils at 100°C. When you bake a cake in the oven, you would set the oven to 375°C. That's hot! Don't touch the inside of the oven!

3. Write the temperature shown on each thermometer.

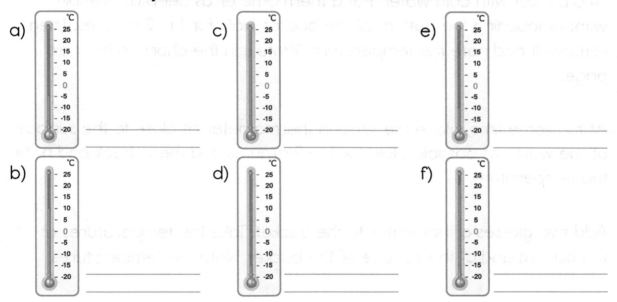

4. Mark each thermometer to show the temperature. Use a red marker.

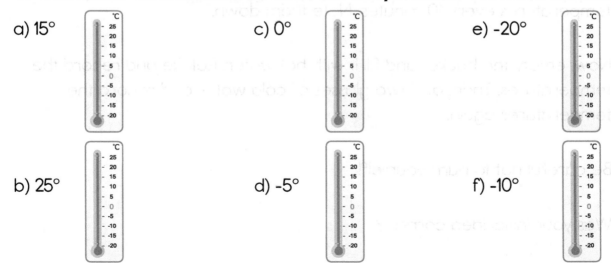

439

5. Science Lab 8: Water Temperature

a) Do you think the temperature of water varies at different depths?

Write what you think here: _____

_____

_____

Now let's see if you're correct. Ask an adult for help. What you'll need:

A bucket

Thermometers – 2

Fill a bucket with cold water. Put a thermometer as deep as possible without touching the bottom of the bucket. Hold for 1 to 2 minutes. Then, remove it and note the temperature. Write it in the chart on the next page.

At the same time, place the second thermometer as close to the surface of the water as possible. Hold for 1 to 2 minutes and then check and note the temperature.

Add two glasses of hot water to the bucket. Take the temperatures at the bottom and at the surface of the bucket. Note the temperatures.

Take the bucket outside your home. Leave it there and check the temperatures every 10 minutes. Note them down.

Now, empty the bucket and fill it with hot water. Retake and record the temperatures. Then, add two glasses of cold water and record the temperatures again.

Be careful not to burn yourself!

Was your initial idea correct? _____

5. b) Note the temperatures and your observations below.

Type of water in bucket (hot, cold, hot + cold, cold + hot, etc.)	Temperature at the bottom of water level	Temperature near the surface	Notes

6. Science Lab 9: Air Temperature

If you have a thermometer, place it outside on six different days at six different times and record the temperatures. If you do not have a thermometer, ask an adult to help you check temperatures online. Write them down below and mark the temperatures on the thermometers with a red marker.

a)

Date, Time: _____

Temperature: _____

b)

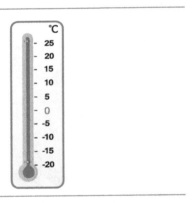

Date, Time: _____

Temperature: _____

c)

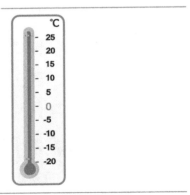

Date, Time: _____

Temperature: _____

d)

Date, Time: _____

Temperature: _____

e)

Date, Time: _____

Temperature: _____

f)

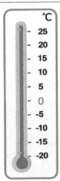

Date, Time: _____

Temperature: _____

Exercises

Science

7. Science Lab 10: Volcano

Here are two fun ways to make a volcano. Use an adult's help.

a) **What you'll need:**

Vinegar – 60 ml ($\frac{1}{4}$ cup)
Red food colouring – a few drops
Liquid dishwasher soap – a few drops
Baking soda – 15 ml (3 teaspoons)
Modelling clay

Work outside, or cover the table you will be working on with newspaper.
Shape the clay like a volcano (with a crater at the top). You can add red clay as well, to make it seem like there is lava.
Put the baking soda in the crater hole.
Add the drops of red food colouring.
Then, add the drops of dishwashing detergent.
Now, pour in the vinegar and watch the "eruption"!

b) **What you'll need:**

Newspaper
Small plastic bottle, empty
Baking soda – 15 ml (3 teaspoons)
Sand
Red food colouring – a few drops
Vinegar – 125 ml ($\frac{1}{2}$ cup)
Bottle of juice – $\frac{1}{2}$ full

Work outside, or cover a table with newspaper before you begin.
Put the baking soda in the bottle.
Place the bottle in the middle of the newspaper. Shape a mountain of sand around the bottle. Mix the vinegar and the red food colouring with the juice in the bottle. Pour the mixture into the plastic bottle in the sand. Stand back and enjoy the "eruption"!

8. **Science Lab 11: Bridge Strength**

   a) **Use the bridge you created in Science Lab 4. Test your bridge for strength. What can your bridge hold (for example: books, a shoe, a toy car)? Write your answers in the chart.**

Items	Bridge strength (yes/no)

b) Draw "before" and "after" pictures of your bridge.

BEFORE:

AFTER:

c) How can you improve the strength and stability of your bridge?

9. Science Lab 12: Crazy Soap

What you'll need:

Ivory Soap – 1 bar
Soap of any another brand – 1 bar
A deep bowl
Paper towels
Microwave

Fill a bowl with water.

Put the two soap bars in the bowl. You will notice that the Ivory soap will float while the other one sinks.

Break the Ivory soap in two. Put the two pieces on a paper towel in the microwave.

Cook the soap on high power for 2 minutes. Observe the soap in the microwave to see what happens. Make sure it does not cook too much!

Wait for the soap to cool before touching it. Impressive, is it not?

Draw the results below and describe what happened. Why do you think it happened?

_____
_____
_____
_____
_____

1. **Draw four different fruits and label them. Then, colour them as you wish.**

2. **Draw four different vegetables and label them. Then, colour them as you wish.**

3. **Name three foods from each food group below.**

Grains	Fruits and Vegetables	Meat and Alternatives	Dairy

FOOD GROUPS

1. **Write under each picture what it shows — a *fruit* or a *vegetable*.**

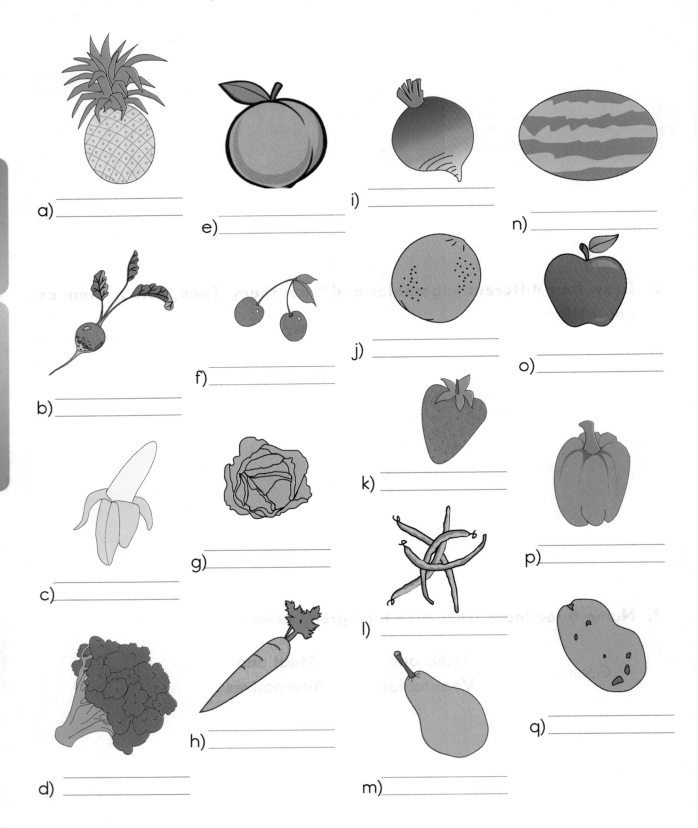

a) _____

b) _____

c) _____

d) _____

e) _____

f) _____

g) _____

h) _____

i) _____

j) _____

k) _____

l) _____

m) _____

n) _____

o) _____

p) _____

q) _____

2. Complete the crossword puzzle by looking at the pictures below. Use the word bank if you need help. Name the food group these foods belong to:

_____

_____

banana	celery	bell pepper	turnip
blueberry	grapes	pineapple	watermelon
broccoli	lemon	raspberry	pear
cherry			

Exercises

Science

Across

6.   10.   13.

9.   12.

Down

1.   4.   8.

2.   5.   11.

3.   7.

449

3. Name the food items shown below. Then, write which food group each one belongs to.

a)

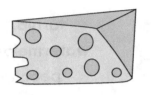

_____

_____

b)

_____

_____

c)

_____

_____

d)

_____

_____

e)

_____

_____

f)

_____

_____

g)

_____

_____

h)

_____

_____

i)

_____

_____

j)

_____

_____

k)

_____

_____

l)

_____

_____

m)

_____

_____

n)

_____

_____

o)

_____

_____

1. Name each food item shown below. Then, write if it is a fruit, vegetable, meat or alternative, grain, or dairy product.

a)

_____

b)

_____

c)

_____

d)

_____

e)

_____

f)

_____

g)

_____

h)

_____

i)

_____

j)

_____

k)

_____

l)

_____

m)

_____

n)

_____

o)

_____

p)

_____

q)

_____

r)

_____

Science

1. Find and circle these food words in the word search.

apple	cabbage	grape	pear
banana	carrot	green beans	potato
bell pepper	celery	orange	strawberry
broccoli	cherry	onion	watermelon

L	M	E	R	C	M	L	R	A	E	R	E	T	G
C	A	A	O	A	E	A	N	T	O	P	O	E	R
O	E	A	A	R	W	P	B	A	N	A	N	A	E
C	A	Y	W	R	T	P	O	T	A	T	O	O	E
L	L	E	N	O	G	R	A	P	E	R	R	R	N
R	A	B	N	T	R	Y	O	P	G	P	N	A	B
R	W	A	T	E	R	M	E	L	O	N	L	N	E
E	E	E	A	E	A	P	P	L	E	R	A	G	A
S	A	S	T	R	A	W	B	E	R	R	Y	E	N
B	E	L	L	P	E	P	P	E	R	C	P	Y	S
T	O	C	H	E	R	R	Y	N	A	A	E	P	A
R	C	A	B	B	A	G	E	E	L	T	A	A	O
E	A	O	N	I	O	N	C	E	L	E	R	Y	B
R	A	B	R	O	C	C	O	L	I	E	E	N	A

2. Write the name of each food item below and classify it as a fruit or a vegetable.

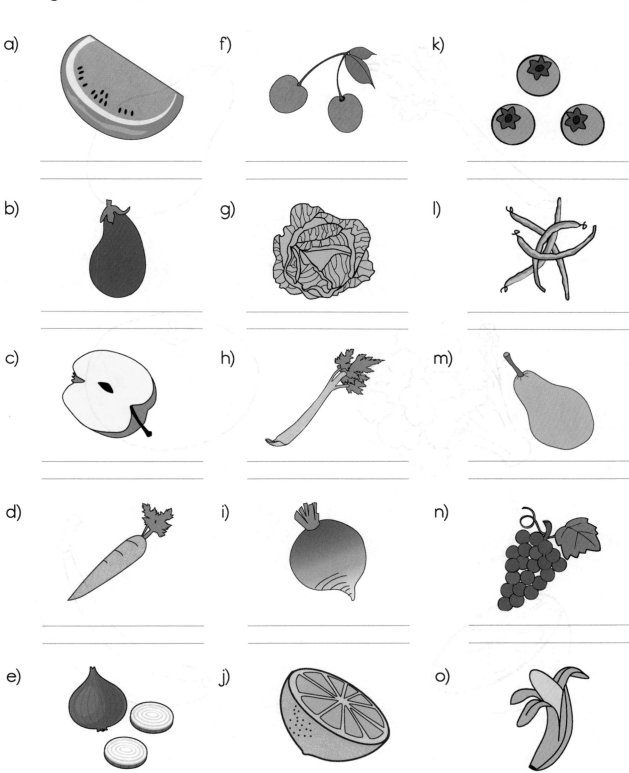

a)

f)

k)

b)

g)

l)

c)

h)

m)

d)

i)

n)

e)

j)

o)

3. Colour and label each of the following fruits and vegetables.

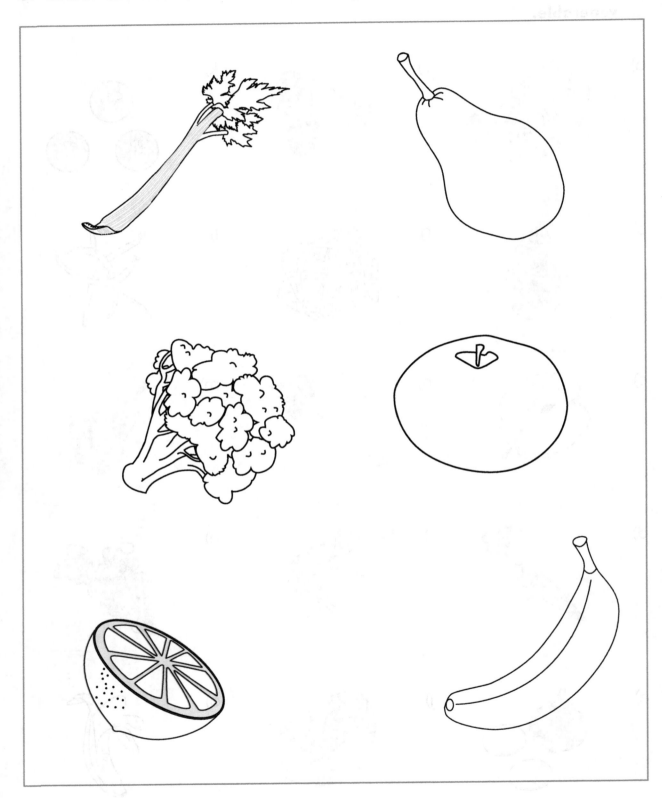

TEST 99

1. Draw two animals that eat only plants.

2. Draw two animals that eat both plants and animals.

3. List three animals that give birth to live babies.

_____   _____   _____

4. List three animals that lay eggs.

_____   _____   _____

1. Read the text and answer the questions on the following pages.

Animals

There are six types of animals. They are mammals, birds, reptiles, fish, amphibians, and insects. They have different characteristics.

Mammals: The characteristics of mammals are:
- they have fur or hair
- they give birth to live babies
- they feed their young milk

Birds: The characteristics of birds are:
- their babies hatch from eggs
- most fly
- they have feathers and wings

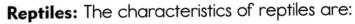

Reptiles: The characteristics of reptiles are:
- they have scales
- their babies hatch from eggs

Fish: The characteristics of fish are:
- they live underwater
- they have gills and fins

Amphibians: The characteristics of amphibians are:
- they live in water when they are babies
- they live on land when they are adults

Insects: The characteristics of insects are:
- they have three main body parts — head, thorax, and abdomen
- they have six legs and a pair of antennae

Exercises

Science

Look at the text on the previous page and answer the following questions.

a) What is one characteristic that both birds and reptiles have?

_____

_____

b) Fish live underwater. Which other animal group lives underwater when they are babies?

_____

_____

c) What is your favourite animal group? Write about two characteristics of your favourite animal group. Why are they your favourite?

_____

_____

_____

_____

_____

_____

d) Draw a picture of your favourite animal.

2. Draw a ◯ around each insect,

a ▢ around each mammal,

a ◇ around each bird

and an **X** on each reptile.

TEST 100

1. **Write under each picture whether the animal is a mammal, a bird, a fish, an amphibian, a reptile, or an insect.**

a) _____

f) _____

k) _____

o) _____

g) _____

b) _____

h) _____

l) _____

p) _____

c) _____

i) _____

m) _____

q) _____

d) _____

n) _____

r) _____

e) _____

j) _____

s) _____

1. Draw, label and colour a mammal, a bird, an insect, a reptile, a fish and an amphibian.

2. Name each animal shown below. Then, write whether it is a mammal, bird, amphibian, reptile, insect or fish.

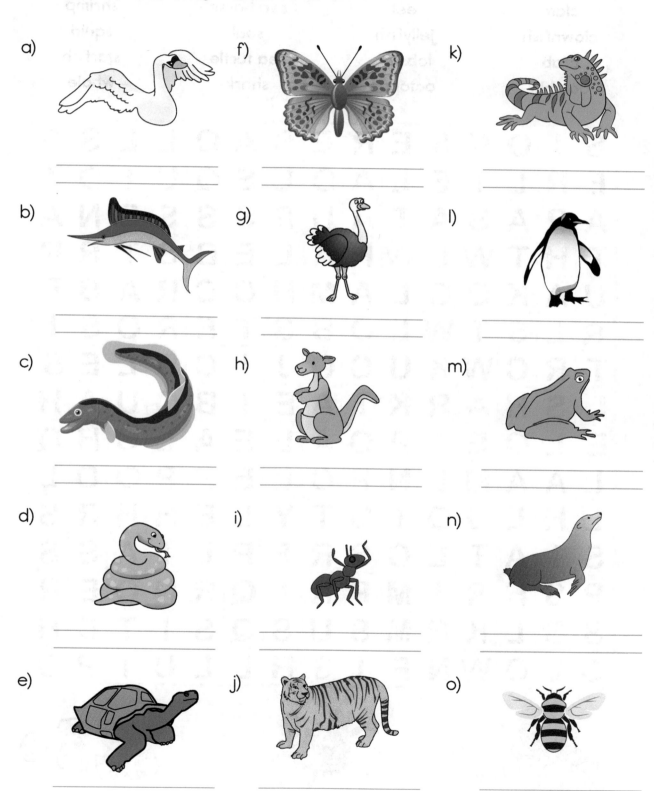

a)

f)

k)

b)

g)

l)

c)

h)

m)

d)

i)

n)

e)

j)

o)

3. Find and circle the animal words below in the word search.

clam	eel	sea horse	shrimp
clownfish	jellyfish	seal	squid
crab	lobster	sea turtle	starfish
dolphin	octopus	shark	whale

S	I	O	N	S	E	R	E	S	A	O	L	L	S	S
E	R	L	I	E	L	A	D	L	S	Q	U	I	D	T
A	P	A	S	A	T	A	U	P	S	S	E	N	A
T	H	T	W	L	W	H	A	L	E	B	S	T	R	R
U	A	K	O	C	L	A	M	H	C	C	R	A	B	F
R	L	S	T	W	L	O	B	S	T	E	R	O	S	I
T	R	C	W	K	U	C	O	J	I	C	D	L	E	S
L	S	H	A	R	K	T	A	E	I	B	O	U	A	H
E	L	O	E	I	P	O	A	L	E	A	L	C	H	Q
L	A	A	M	L	N	P	O	L	E	P	P	O	O	L
L	H	L	O	O	I	U	T	Y	L	E	H	H	R	S
S	I	A	T	L	C	S	R	F	P	L	I	A	S	S
P	S	H	R	I	M	P	K	I	Q	R	N	Q	E	R
S	B	L	K	R	M	S	U	S	Q	S	I	T	C	H
C	L	O	W	N	F	I	S	H	L	L	U	I	P	D

ANSWERS

Test 1

Page 11

1. a) art b) ball c) crayon d) dinner
   e) erase f) frog g) gate h) house i) jug
   j) lamp k) mat l) neck m) octagon
   n) paper o) queen p) right q) shell
   r) television s) umbrella t) vein u) water
   v) zipper

Exercises

Page 12

1. a) begin can paddle soup
   b) best concert hopeful world
   c) computer delight race thunder
   d) half hobby piece reward
   e) mask math monster moon
   f) polite purple quickly quiet
   g) dark deep dictionary dock
   h) addition address astronaut automatic

Exercises

Page 13

2. a) Alexander b) Aliya c) Bill d) Catherine
   e) Danny f) Gina g) Iqbal h) Jeremy
   i) Joan j) Joey k) Justine l) Karina
   m) Kevin n) Lalita o) Lydia p) Marika
   q) Martha r) Mary s) Oliver t) Paul
   u) Quinn v) Ram w) Samantha x) Tony

Exercises

Page 14

3. a) band, bear, black, board, break
   b) car, chord, cop, cry, cup
   c) sap, shallow, simple, special, stick
   d) girl, gold, great, gum, gym
   e) tackle, team, time, track, tyre
   f) racket, real, right, road, rude
   g) hat, heart, hip, home, hurt
   h) pail, pear, please, post, pram

Test 2

Page 15

1. a) author b) book c) chapter
   d) dictionary e) edition f) ending
   g) index h) library i) page j) series
2. a), c), f), g)

Exercises

Page 16

1. a) baby b) elephant c) eraser d) fall
   e) fellow f) flower g) girl h) hat i) ice
   j) ink k) jacket l) joke m) laugh n) lower
   o) magic p) magnificent q) orange r) out
   s) pass t) possible u) shoe v) toe
   w) tomato x) train y) yell z) yellow

Exercises

Page 17

2.

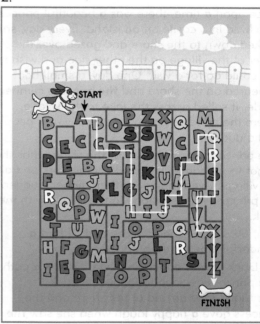

Exercises

Page 18

3. a) debit, decorate, demand, dentist, detail
   b) balloon, bandage, barbecue, basket, bath
   c) pedal, peel, pen, pest, pet
   d) train, treasure, trip, trot, try
   e) sea, seep, sell, send, set
   f) ready, record, red, reply, rescue
   g) chain, cheer, child, chocolate, chute
   h) light, limb, linger, lip, list

Test 3

Page 19

1. a) An/The b) a/the c) a/the d) an
   e) the/a f) a/the g) a/the h) an
2. a) the b) an c) the d) The, the
   e) an f) the

Exercises
Page 20

1. a) an eagle   b) a bottle c) an apron
   d) the farms   e) an elephant   f) a notebook
   g) an accident   h) an island   i) an element
   j) an inspector   k) the roots   l) a flower
   m) an action   n) a truck   o) a test
   p) an effort   q) an absence   r) the homes
   s) a mountain   t) the pencils   u) the chair

Exercises
Page 21

2. Once upon **a** time, there was **a** beautiful princess who lived in a castle on **an** island. Every day, she walked down to the shore and gazed over the water at the village on the other side and wished she could go for a visit. One day, a small boat appeared on the shore and **the** princess climbed inside. It sailed across the lake to the village, where the princess got to meet many new people and a duck.

The princess was so happy at **the** village that she forgot to go home. The sky became dark and all the villagers went home for their dinner. Suddenly, the princess was left alone in the village with the duck.

"Oh, Mr. Duck!" the princess said. "I had **a** wonderful time today, but I miss my home."

Mr. Duck gave a quack and set off down **a** path. The princess decided to follow the duck. Eventually, they arrived at the shore and the princess gave **a** happy laugh when she saw **the** boat. She and the duck got in the boat and sailed back to the castle, where they lived happily ever after, with many more trips to **the** village.

Exercises
Page 22

3. Some of the answers may vary.
   a) the, the   b) an/the   c) an/the, a   d) the
   e) an   f) the, the

4. b), c), e)

Test 4
Page 23

1. Answers will vary.

Exercises
Page 24

1. a) an/the   b) a/the   c) the   d) the   e) an/the
   f) an/the   g) a/the   h) an/the   i) a/the
   j) a/the   k) an/the   l) an/the   m) an/the
   n) an/the   o) a/the   p) the   q) the   r) the

Exercises
Page 25

2.

Start					
an		can	his	her	it
not	the	to	him	she	he
me	a	be	the	the	a
they	an	an		my	a

Finish

3.

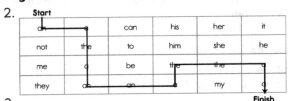

Exercises
Page 26

4. How Many Seconds? – Christina Rossetti

How many seconds in **a** minute?
Sixty, and no more in it.

How many minutes in **an** hour?
Sixty for sun and shower.

How many hours in **a** day?
Twenty-four for work and play.

How many days in **a** week?
Seven both to hear and speak.

How many weeks in **a** month?
Four, as **the** swift moon runn'th.

How many months in **a** year?
Twelve **the** almanack makes clear.

How many years in **an** age?
One hundred says **the** sage.

How many ages in time?
No one knows **the** rhyme.

Test 5
Page 27

1. a) cat, bird   b) woman, telephone
   c) house   d) boy, bicycle

2. ~~My~~ friend (Tara) moved to (Thunder Bay) (Ontario). Since she left, ~~I~~ have often sent ~~her~~ emails. ~~I~~ miss ~~her~~ and ~~her~~ dog, (Milo). This summer, ~~I~~ will visit ~~her~~ and ~~we~~ will go walking along the shore of the (Current River). ~~I~~ have many things to tell ~~her~~ when ~~we~~ meet.

Exercises
Page 28

1. a) king — He
   b) people — They
   c) girl — She
   d) Mark — I
   e) Anita and I — We
   f) Jim — you

2. a) She b) They c) They d) It e) They
   f) It g) He

Exercises
Page 29

3. He, It, He, They

4. a) (Bella) loves her white goat.
   b) (Flowers, grass and hay) grow in the fields.
   c) (My grandmother) often tells me the same story.
   d) (Jack and Mary) would really like to have a bike.
   e) In this story, (fairies) are nice.

5. a) True b) True

Exercises
Page 30

6. a) Malika is my (sister.)
   b) Mark lived in Montreal before moving to England.
   c) The Titanic hit an (iceberg.)
   d) I love (chocolate) (ice cream.)
   e) My (dog)'s (name) is Rex.
   f) I will go play at Fountain Park after (school.)

Common Nouns	Proper Nouns
sister	Malika
iceberg	Mark
chocolate	Montreal
ice cream	England
dog	Titanic
name	Rex
school	Fountain Park

Test 6
Page 31

1. Answers will vary.

2. Answers will vary.

3. Answers will vary.

4. a) Where is it?
   b) He went home.
   c) She loves her hat.
   d) They went to the park.
   e) We play the piano.

Exercises
Page 32

1.

Places	People	Animals
Hamilton	Jackie	Max
Toronto	Paula	Cinnamon
University of Toronto	Emily	

2. Mary and her dog Candy are walking on Granville Street in Vancouver.

Exercises
Page 33

3.

One day, a boy and his father planned on going fishing. They went to find their gear. They looked in the garage for the fishing rods. They found them. Then they looked for their boots. The boy asked his mother to help find his boots. She found them. The boy went looking for his hat. He found it. The father looked for his fishing net. He found it. They were ready to go. Wait a minute – where are the car keys? The father found them. Off they went.

Pronoun	Noun it replaces
They	a boy and his father
them	fishing rods
She	mother
them	boots
He	boy
it	hat
He	father
it	fishing net
them	car keys

Exercises
Page 34

4. a) She likes her bicycle.
   b) He rode his horse into the stable.
   c) It is tall.
   d) They barked loudly.

5. a) They b) I c) She d) We e) you
   f) He g) It

Test 7
Page 35

1.

Singular	Plural
flower	flowers
foot	feet
book	books
mat	mats
lamp	lamps
puppy	puppies
man	men
child	children
lady	ladies
hand	hands
cookie	cookies
candy	candies

Exercises
Page 36

1. Answers will vary.

Exercises
Page 37

2. a) knives b) toys c) letters d) kittens
   e) cars f) dogs g) tomatoes h) phones
   i) shoes j) houses k) jugs l) horses
   m) women n) bikes o) maps p) stairs
   q) keys r) glasses s) pizzas t) chairs
   u) tables v) wives w) potatoes x) leaves
   y) balls z) children

Exercises
Page 38

3. a) potatoes b) feet c) mice d) crises
   e) children f) foxes g) boxes h) men
   i) babies j) stories k) wives l) families
   m) teeth n) women o) buses p) knives
   q) wolves

Test 8
Page 39

1. a) a plane b) two cherries c) ten mice
   d) three leaves e) all the children
   f) many buses g) a few oranges h) one man
   i) a key j) two shoes

2. a) geese b) boats c) mice d) shoes
   e) tables f) men g) boys h) cats
   i) heads j) telephones k) foxes l) cameras
   m) books n) ladies o) friends p) armies

3. a) number b) page c) car d) story
   e) child f) team g) man h) tooth i) pen

Exercises
Page 40

1. a) knives b) birds c) erasers d) children
   e) stories f) monkeys g) dates h) mice
   i) movies j) blueberries k) foxes l) boys
   m) babies n) heads o) feet p) lions
   q) teeth r) ties s) stars t) spoons u) men
   v) potatoes w) dishes x) words y) shoes
   z) shirts

Exercises
Page 41

2. a) knives b) prizes c) halves d) tomatoes
   e) feet f) women g) shelves h) bracelets
   i) children j) cups k) scissors l) wires
   m) nieces n) houses o) boys p) lighters
   q) dresses r) hammers

Exercises
Page 42

3. Start

king	boy	pens	paws	light	window
squirrels	man	queens	finger	stars	daughter
ear	host	couch	moons	eye	widowers
spoon	lion	house	ship	months	walk
smiles	father	thought	lakes	lions	aunt
boys	uncle	tiger	hospital	suits	ducks
phone	walls	prince	departure	plane	flowers
mice	feet	emperor	grandfather	bird	woman
songs	printers	glasses	actor	feather	foxes
paper	computers	lioness	nephew	crocodiles	accidents
tree	girl	apple	waiter	bull	plates
curtains	cow	chewing gum	books	husband	television
oranges	necklace	drawers	horses	hero	tigress
file	table	chairs	flute	son-in-law	caterpillars
piano	leaf	notes	pear	wizard	black

Finish

Test 9
Page 43

1. a) went b) go c) studied d) plays
   e) gave f) snowed g) baked h) love

2.

	Past	Present
Steven played in the orchestra at school.	X	
Jim went to Italy this summer.	X	
Nadine is watching television.		X
We play outside all day.		X
I read a book yesterday.	X	
Do you want to go for a swim?		X

Exercises
Page 44

1. a) ate b) studied c) like d) looked e) be
   f) flew g) swam h) built i) wrote
2. a) The boy buys a candy.
   b) The lady bakes cookies.
   c) The teacher tells a story.
   d) I play a song.
   e) The student packs his books.

Exercises
Page 45

3. a) skipped: past b) was: past
   c) picks: present d) see: present
   e) created: past f) finished: past
   g) visited: past h) want: present
   i) am: present j) am: present
   k) served: past
4. Answers will vary.
5. Answers will vary.

Exercises
Page 46

6. a) Mark plays hockey. b) The child talks.
   c) The lady smiles. d) The boy runs.
   e) The man swims. f) Sarah drinks.
   g) The mother reads. h) Rick sings.
   i) The father washes the dishes.
   j) Joshua eats. k) Nathan talks.
   l) Anna paints.

Exercises
Page 47

7. a) pays b) cries c) watches d) listens
   e) writes f) walks g) slide h) skate
   i) puts j) takes

Exercises
Page 48

8. a) eats b) is c) wants d) bought
   e) listens f) close g) was
9.

	Past	Present
a) I am a good dancer.		X
b) Laura was with us yesterday.	X	
c) Susan is reading a book at this moment.		X
d) They gave a present to their father last week.	X	
e) Claudio went to Italy last year.	X	
f) Benjamin wrote a letter last night.	X	
g) I am leaving the house.		X

Test 10
Page 49

1.   Jennifer was a doctor. She liked helping people get better. She worked in a big hospital. One day, she saw a young girl trip and fall as she crossed the street. Jennifer quickly took her to the hospital. She cleaned the scrapes on the girl's arms and legs. She put a special ointment on them and bandaged them. Then, she talked cheerfully with the girl till her mother came to pick her up. The girl told her mother on the way home that she wanted to become a doctor when she grew up.

Exercises
Page 50

1. fixing, eating, yanked, underlined, sleeping, running, see, looking
2. Max watches television while doing his homework. His mom tells him it is not a good idea. He agrees and turns off the television. He turns on the radio to listen to music. His dad comes and tells him it is really not a good idea. Max agrees and turns off the radio. He understands and does his homework in silence.

Exercises
Page 51

3. a) The birds flew away.
   b) A terrible tsunami hit Indonesia yesterday.
   c) My neighbour planted beautiful flowers.
   d) Jack saw a deer on the side of the road.
   e) They watched television all night long.
   f) We finished our homework very quickly.
4. Answers will vary.

Exercises
Page 52

5.

```
F I L L C H O O S E J U M P T
O T T C O M O V E D L O O K E
A R S H A K E P E A T E N S U
U S L R A T U R N E D R A N F
R L W R O T E S A Y L O V E D
E L B O S A I O P E N E D B M
A L A G D L A U G H P F L W
D L U U T W I L I K E T O R I
A B I T E H A P C R Y I L O N
E U D H S O R T P E M H L I G
W E E I H L T E E E R E O R U
S A A E O L S V W R D D W E C
W N L I U B O U G H T P L A Y
U N B R T D A N C E M P T X S
T M S T O P H O S M I L E E L
```

Exercises
Page 53

6. a) skate b) surf c) play d) cry
   e) smile f) tie g) shuffle h) brush i) eat
   j) wake up k) dress l) blow

Exercises
Page 54

7.

	Past	Present
a) Please, don't do that.		X
b) Thomas was a great dancer when he was young.	X	
c) William joined us later in the evening.	X	
d) My friends were at my birthday party yesterday.	X	
e) Emily went shopping last weekend.	X	
f) Jim watches a good movie.		X
g) Gabrielle and Rachel did their chores last night.	X	

8. b), c), e)

9. a) cried b) sleeps c) stopped d) laughed
   e) sang f) eats g) danced h) read

Test 11
Page 55

1. a) The queens are tired.
   b) My nieces are fixing the car.
   c) The waitresses were very nice to the women.
   d) The heroines saved the girls.
   e) The cows glared at the geese.
   f) The wives spoke to the mothers.
   g) The landladies are not home.
   h) The grandmothers spoke to their daughters.
   i) The princesses waved to the crowd.

Exercises
Pages 56 & 57

1.

Noun	Plural noun	Feminine noun
uncle	uncles	aunt
king	kings	queen
lion	lions	lioness
grandfather	grandfathers	grandmother
policeman	policemen	policewoman
husband	husbands	wife
grandson	grandsons	granddaughter
bull	bulls	cow
man	men	woman
stepfather	stepfathers	stepmother
peacock	peacocks	peahen
rooster	roosters	hen
buck	bucks	doe
wizard	wizards	witch
son	sons	daughter
fox	foxes	vixen
nephew	nephews	niece
prince	princes	princess
emperor	emperors	empress
gander	ganders	goose
gentleman	gentlemen	lady
brother	brothers	sister
father	fathers	mother
boy	boys	girl
hero	heroes	heroine

Exercises
Page 58

2. a) lamb b) farmer c) wolves d) zebras
   e) buses f) orange g) house h) friend
   i) gems j) actress k) waitress

Test 12
Page 59

1.

```
P G M S T O N E S S C W O S A S G V P C
A A F R N I E C E S S N T K P A W C
I O W O M A N L I E O E K O A R E E
V D G F E O W K S U N C L E C R C A P L
A H O A E N X T E L E U G X D L B B T
S T O B O X D T I G L G N K G E C T U S
A B S E E P C R O C K S I A W T K R L O
H L E L N E P H E W K U S R E U T F L I
P P B O Y S A R F A T H E R G A N D E R
N A E C N P T W K E H M O T H E R R C N
O H B A H E N U S G L E N S A H S R
S O R N O N E C P Z H T R I I C A V T H
L B A G E C E O L L A G U A R D A N A S
E C N P O I S E P L E R O C K H A P L
E C R S E S T O N E R O N S E P N L P
E O G U A R D S V T F U S B O X E S E D
G L I A O N X E C S T U I A U N T E R S
S P T R M L O A S W D P W M A N D U R S
P E N C I L S S O N C O W K N I V E S A
P B I K N I F E F R O T B E N C A P S E
```

Exercises
Page 60

1.

Singular	Plural
cat	cats
book	books
mouse	mice
shoe	shoes
goose	geese
strawberry	strawberries
activity	activities
daisy	daisies
fork	forks
gift	gifts
elf	elves
roof	roofs
wheel	wheels
owl	owls
computer	computers
carrot	carrots

Exercises
Page 61
2. Answers will vary.

Exercises
Page 62

3.
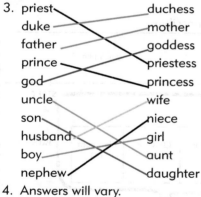

priest — priestess
duke — duchess
father — mother
prince — princess
god — goddess
uncle — aunt
son — daughter
husband — wife
boy — girl
nephew — niece

4. Answers will vary.

Test 13
Page 63

1. low, tall, delicious, clever, mouth-watering, beautiful, shiny, soft, conceited, happy, quiet, kind, clever, delicious

2. Answers may vary.
   a) tasty b) pretty c) social d) smart
   e) expensive f) little

3. Answers may vary.
   a) brave b) ugly c) happy d) huge
   e) large f) hard

Exercises
Page 64
1. Answers will vary.
2. Answers will vary.

Exercises
Page 65
3. Answers will vary.
4. Answers will vary.

Exercises
Page 66
5. a) hates b) unfriendly c) hot, outside
   d) sad e) short f) boring g) white
   h) forgot

Test 14
Page 67
1. a) dark b) clean c) outside d) pleasant
   e) first f) happy g) black h) woman
2. a) glad b) tale c) fast d) nice
   e) clever f) jump g) mistake h) little
3. a) beautiful red b) long, black, curly
   c) beautiful d) tall e) smart f) wonderful

Exercises
Page 68
1. cute, little, golden, reddish, sunny, neighbouring, beach (for ball), excited, stubby, warm, blue, lovely
2. a) cute b) majestic African c) little, delicious
   d) striped
3.
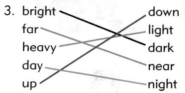

bright — dark
far — near
heavy — light
day — night
up — down

Exercises
Page 69
4. Answers will vary. Be creative!

Exercises
Page 70
5. Answers will vary.

6. loyal — faithful
   mad — angry
   draw — sketch
   delicious — tasty
   awful — horrible
   loving — caring
   cold — icy

7.
early → morning
shiny, silver → spaceship
three huge → ailens
first → alien
curly red → hair
three → eyes
long, bony → fingers
second → alien

pointy → ears
round → nose
blue → bumps
third → alien
six short → arms
six short → legs
longest → tail
crazy → snacks

Test 15
Page 71

1. a) in b) between c) to the left of
   d) under e) on f) to the right of

Exercises
Page 72

1. a)
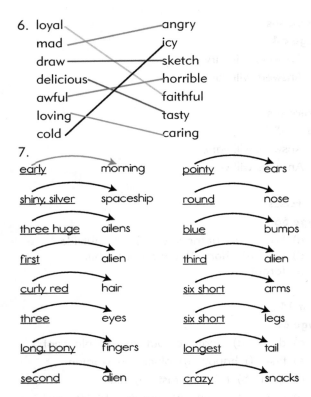

Exercises
Page 73

2. a) on b) under c) above
   d) in e) below f) in front of

Exercises
Page 74

3.

SCHOOL

Math Room	Gymnasium	Science Room
	Library Cafeteria Computer Room	
English Room	Geography Room	Principal's Office	Staff Room

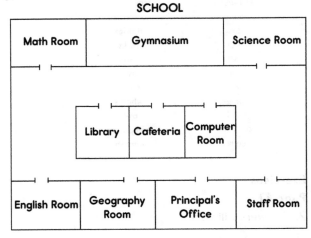

Test 16
Page 75

1. Two paths are possible:

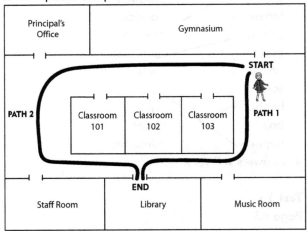

2. For Path 1, Samra needs to walk straight, then turn right in front of the Music Room, then turn left into the Library. For Path 2, Samra needs to turn right and pass the three classrooms, then turn left in front of the Principal's Office, turn left again in front of the Staff Room and turn right into the Library.

Exercises
Page 76

1. a) 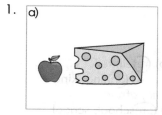 d)

   b)  e)

   c)  f)

Exercises
Page 77

2. a) before b) left c) up d) down
   e) between f) right g) after h) on i) in
   j) under

Exercises
Page 78

3.

4.

Test 17
Page 79

1. pizza, woman, tradition, fork
2. Answers will vary.
3. a) I'm b) You won't do c) She didn't
4. a) St. b) ft. c) Aug. d) hr. e) Fri. f) Mr.

Exercises
Page 80

1. a) under(ground)   (grounds)keeper
   b) (super)market   (super)man
   c) foot(ball)   basket(ball)
   d) (school) bus   (school) bag
   e) (life)guard   (life)like
   f) dining (table)   (table) tennis
   g) fish (tank)   water (tank)
   h) (tooth)paste   (tooth)brush
   i) black(board)   key(board)
   j) full (moon)   (moon)light
   k) back(street)   (street)light
   l) birth(day)   (day)light
   m) (lamp) post   table (lamp)

2. a) back+bone b) after+noon
   c) ham+burger d) some+where e) with+out
   f) day+light g) hill+side h) shoe+lace

Exercises
Page 81

3. a) we're b) don't c) doesn't d) you're
   e) it's
4. Answers may vary.
   a) Mon. b) Tues. c) Wed. d) Thurs.
   e) Fri. f) Sat. g) Sun.

Exercises
Page 82

5. a) we've b) won't c) they're d) I'll
   e) weren't
6. Answers may vary.
   a) Jan. or JA b) Feb. or FE
   c) Mar. or MR d) Apr. or AL e) May or MA
   f) June or JN g) July or JL h) Aug. or AU
   i) Sep. or SE j) Oct. or OC k) Nov. or NO
   l) Dec. or DE

Test 18
Page 83

1. Answers may vary. a) handshake
   b) sunshine c) seashore d) flyaway
   e) weekend f) daylight g) forehead
   h) blackboard i) sandbox j) eyeball
   k) policeman l) boathouse m) icebox
   n) homeschool o) rubber band p) crosswalk

2. a) They don't b) I didn't c) She isn't
   d) I'm not e) They're f) They won't

3. a) Jr. b) Sun. c) in. d) Dec.

Exercises
Page 84

1. a) waterfalls b) keyboard c) underground
   d) nearby e) skydive f) weekend
   g) toothpaste h) airplane i) babysitter
   j) alongside k) backpack l) forehead
   m) walkway n) upstairs o) haircut
   p) bookstore q) pancake r) rainbow

Exercises
Page 85

2. a) I'm not your best friend.
   b) They won't see a movie tonight.
   c) We haven't eaten dinner yet.
   d) She hasn't seen her grandmother in two years.
   e) She didn't fix her broken bicycle.
   f) I haven't studied for my test yet.
   g) You don't want to share your candy.
   h) She isn't ready to go out.
   i) It's not/It isn't my turn to speak in front of the class.
   j) They don't want to play outside.

Exercises
Page 86

3. a) NL b) NB c) NS d) PEI e) QC
   f) ON g) MB h) SK i) AB j) BC k) NU
   l) YT m) NT

4. March ———— ON
   Doctor ———— Thu.
   Pound ———— Hwy.
   Highway ———— Mar. or MR
   Thursday ———— lb.
   Ontario ———— Dr.

5. a) haven't b) wouldn't c) isn't
   d) hasn't e) didn't

Test 19
Page 87

1. a) unhappy, happy b) retell, tell
   c) impossible, possible d) unkind, kind
   e) redo, do f) unafraid, afraid
   g) triangle, angle h) preschool, school

2. a) going, go b) talked, talk c) saying, say
   d) teaches, teach e) reading, read
   f) doing, do g) walking, walk h) circles, circle

3. a) allow, act b) inside, interest
   c) running, reach d) obtuse, obey
   e) about, able

Exercises
Page 88

1. a) return, turn b) dishonest, honest
   c) replay, play d) preschool, school
   e) misbehave, behave f) preheat, heat
   g) untie, tie h) underwater, water
   i) unable, able j) disagree, agree

2. a) joyful, joy b) youngest, young
   c) worthless, worth d) fearless, fear
   e) careful, care f) smaller, small
   g) slower, slow h) likeable, like i) singer, sing
   j) oldest, old

Exercises
Page 89

3. a) unwrap b) preheat c) return d) unable

4. a) boundless b) longest c) careful d) doable
   e) boxer f) worthless

Exercises
Page 90

5. imperfect, imperfection, imperfectly, perfection, perfecting, perfecter, perfectable, perfectly, impossible, impossibility, possibility, possibly, reuse, reusing, reusable, using, user, usable, useful, misuse, misusing, misuser, disuse, underuse, review, reviewing, reviewer, reviewable, viewing, viewer, viewable, preview, previewing, previewer, retake, retaking, retaker, taking, taker, takable, mistake, mistaking, mistakable, mistakeful, intake, undertake, undertaking, undertaker, reagree, reagreeing, agreeing, agreer, agreement, agreeable, misagree, disagree, disagreeing, disagreement, disagreeable, recover, recovering, recoverer, recoverable, covering, coverer, coverable, uncover, uncovering, covering, coverer, coverable, discover, discovery, discovering,

discoverer, discoverable, undercover, renew, renewing, renewer, renewment, renewable, newer, newest, newly, reform, reforming, reformer, reformable, forming, former, preform, preforming, misform, misforming, misformation, inform, informity, informing, informer, informable, recorrect, recorrecting, correction, correcting, correcter, correctable, correctly, miscorrect, miscorrection, miscorrecting, incorrect, incorrectly, replace, replacing, replacer, replaceable, placing, placer, placement, placeable, unplace, preplace, preplacing, misplace, misplacing, misplacement, displace, displacing, displacer, displacement, reread, rereading, re-reader, rereadable, unread, unreadable, misread, misreading, misreader, retest, retesting, pretest, pretesting, recook, recooking, cooking, cooker, cookable, pre-cook, pre-cooking, miscook, miscooking, undercook, recomfort, recomforting, comforting, comforter, comfortable, uncomfortable, miscomfort, discomfort, discomforting, discomforter, discomfortable, unable, ability, disable, disability, disabling, disabler, inability, dissimilar, dissimilarity, dissimilarly, similarity, similarly, dishonest, dishonesty, dishonestly, honesty, honestly, understand, understanding, understander, understandable, standing, stander, caring, carer, careful

Test 20
Page 91

1. a) un b) pre c) ful d) ex e) est f) ly
2. a) tall b) spoke c) like d) farm e) laugh f) stood g) joy h) different or differ
   Sentences will vary.

Exercises
Page 92

1. a) mismatched b) preview c) unlock
   d) redo
2. Answers will vary.

Exercises
Page 93

3. a) re b) Be c) al d) un e) ful f) er
   g) er h) dis
4. a) refill, fill b) painter, paint c) refinish, finish
   d) misbehave, behave e) action, act
   f) softness, soft g) moveable, move
   h) preschool, school i) disagree, agree
   j) neatly, neat k) selection, select
   l) rename, name m) incorrect, correct
   n) restless, rest o) wooden, wood
   p) impolite, polite q) unfair, fair

r) southern, south s) sunny, sun
t) underground, ground u) musical, music
v) subtraction, subtract w) friendship, friend
x) nonsense, sense

Exercises
Page 94

5.

Test 21
Page 95

1. a) bank b) drowning c) tree d) leaf
   e) climbed f) under g) dove h) hunter
   i) pain j) flew

Exercises
Page 96

1. a) summer b) family c) flew d) airplane
   e) seats f) great g) window h) city i) nice
   j) ate k) pizza l) day m) Another n) boat
   o) went p) really q) bought r) main
   s) new t) trip

Exercises
Page 97

2. a) The children go <u>to</u> school every day.
   b) A plane flies <u>across</u> the sky.
   c) The owl hunts at <u>night</u>.
   d) The <u>project</u> will soon be finished.
   e) The <u>princess</u> goes to the ball.
   f) I listen to the radio to <u>hear</u> my favourite songs.
   g) I am <u>going</u> to the park.
   h) The curtain is blowing in the <u>wind</u>.
   I) Matt was <u>driving</u> too fast.
   j) I will be home <u>soon</u>.

Exercises
Page 98

3. a) papaya b) bottle c) backpack
   d) calendar e) chair f) roof g) house

475

h) window i) slipper j) video k) match
l) flag m) paper n) potato o) plant
p) tissue q) floor r) laugh s) notebook
t) ground

Test 22
Page 99

1. Sentences will vary.
   a) look   b) school bus   c) marvellous
   d) blender
2. a) My cousin has a <u>beautiful</u> cat and <u>two</u> dogs.
   b) I admire this dancer <u>because</u> he dances <u>very</u> well.
   c) I wanted <u>new</u> skates for my <u>birthday</u>.
   d) My sister baked <u>cookies</u>. She made them <u>all</u> day.

Exercises
Page 100

1. Sentences will vary.
   a) night   b) whale   c) baggage   d) delicious
2. Sentences will vary.
   a) server   b) outfit   c) boat   d) notebook
   e) furniture   f) adjective   g) computer
   h) dishes   i) magnificent   j) student
   k) speak   l) class

Exercises
Page 101

3. a) cutting   b) river   c) crying   d) asked
   e) heard   f) gold   g) lost   h) brought
   i) happy   j) two   k) story   l) dropped
   m) down   n) reached   o) refused

Exercises
Page 102

4. a) robot   b) carton   c) store
   d) counter   e) money   f) arms
   g) legs   h) move   i) mother   j) house

Test 23
Page 103

1. Answers will vary.

Exercises
Pages 104 & 105

1. Answers will vary.

Exercises
Pages 106

2. a) Yes, I like watching movies. No, I do not like watching movies.
   b) Yes, I have visited Europe. No, I have not visited Europe.
   c) Yes, I have to ask permission to leave the classroom. No, I do not have to ask permission to leave the classroom.
   d) Yes, I got the cat down from the tree. No, I did not get the cat down from the tree.
   e) Yes, we have enough apples for snacks. No, we do not have enough apples for snacks.
   f) Yes, they did wrap their Christmas presents. No, they did not wrap their Christmas presents.

Test 24
Page 107

1. a) Are we reading a very interesting book?
   b) Did my uncle catch a big fish?
   c) Am I down with the flu?
   d) Did I close the windows?
   e) Did she pass the ball?
2. a) My sister did not replace the tire of her car.
   b) We are not tired.
   c) I do not like gardening.
   d) He did not give me the book.
   e) Mary does not go home tomorrow.

Exercises
Page 108

1. a) yes   b) yes   c) yes   d) no   e) yes   f) no
2.

	Positive	Negative
Do you want dessert?	X	
This medicine is great against colds.	X	
Fred is not happy.		X
Did you find what you were looking for?	X	
My grandfather does not work anymore.		X
My aunt picks rare flowers.	X	
Do not let the dog inside.		X
Martin is not scared of zoo animals.		X
Is your mother doing better?	X	
Are you going on vacation this summer?	X	

Exercises
Page 109

3. a) You play hockey.
   b) Stephanie received her exam.
   c) Your parents gave you permission to go to the cinema.
   d) Felix can come to play with me.
   e) Fatima and Omar chose their research subject.
   f) The students were nice during my absence.
   g) You reserved your airplane tickets.
   h) You like craftwork.

Exercises
Page 110

4. a), c), d)
5. Answers will vary.

Test 25
Page 111

1. a) My dad eats apples all day long.
   b) Matthew and I played in the garden.
   c) I do not like strawberry ice cream.
   d) I helped my mother bake cookies.
   e) I will not go to the match if it rains.
2. a) At the end of a statement.
   b) At the end of a question.
   c) At the end of an exclamation.
3. Answers will vary.

Exercises
Page 112

1. a) My mother's first name is Suzanne.
   b) My friend Ali lives in Oakville.
   c) My favourite animals are cats and dogs.
   d) We are going to see a movie tomorrow.
   e) I checked my friend's work in class.
2. a) ! b) ? c) ! d) . e) . f) ! g) ?

Exercises
Page 113

3. a) ? – question mark   b) . – period
   c) ! – exclamation mark   d) . – period
   e) . – period   f) ! – exclamation mark
   g) ? – question mark   h) . – period
   i) ? – question mark   j) ! – exclamation mark
   k) ? – question mark   l) ! – exclamation mark

m) ! – exclamation mark   n) . – period
o) ? – question mark

Exercises
Page 114

4. a) The kids, the parents, and their friends are all invited to the end-of-the-year show.
   b) Did you find the math textbook?
   c) What a marvellous invention!
   d) He chose a board game for his friend Pedro.
   e) The baker sells chocolate cakes, tarts, and croissants.
   f) All the children want to play with the ball.
   g) What a great dream I had!
   h) What is your name?
   i) Tomorrow, I will go to the cinema.
   j) Where are your shoes?
   k) I am happy today.
   l) The pen is blue.
   m) The family went on a picnic.
   n) What a great trip!
   o) How do you like your pizza?
   p) Wow, that was exciting!
   q) I like muffins.
   r) We are moving.
   s) Is it raining?
   t) What a game!

Test 26
Page 115

1. Answers may vary.
   a) The blue couch is very comfortable.
   b) The girl dived into the warm water in the pool.
   c) Jason made macaroni for dinner.
   d) I am going to a movie tomorrow with my friends.
   e) Rita flew a kite in the park.
   f) I had a lot of fun at the birthday party!
2. a) ? b) ! c) . d) ?
3. a) My brother is very good at hockey.
   b) Felix is eating a delicious orange.
   c) Marie had a beautiful trip.
   d) The school choir put on a great show.

Exercises
Page 116

1. Answers may vary.

a) She had to wade in the river to go rescue her dog.

b) My brother was feeling sad, so I decided to tell him jokes to cheer him up.

c) There was broken glass near the building and my mother told me to be careful to not step on it.

d) Roger goes to the library with his son every Tuesday for story time.

2. a) Last night, I saw the stars.

b) What a beautiful Halloween costume!

c) My sister bought socks, shoes, dresses, and skirts.

d) Have you been to Italy?

e) We need apples, oranges, bananas, and cherries.

f) I like my dog.

g) Go, Owen!

h) What are we eating?

Exercises
Page 117

3. a) light: noun, adjective, verb

b) glass: noun, verb, adjective

c) hear: verb

d) game: adjective, noun, verb

e) house: adjective, noun, verb

f) book: noun, verb

g) deer: noun

h) bun: noun

i) snow: noun, verb

j) golden: adjective

k) turning: noun, verb

l) pretty: adjective

Exercises
Page 118

4. a) My neighbour's son is a very good swimmer.

b) Her father felt very proud of her achievement.

c) The police car stopped at the red light.

d) The young boy read his new book.

e) The children eat the green apples.

f) The monkeys climbed up the tall tree.

g) My mother bakes delicious banana cookies.

h) Dark clouds hid the sky.

5. Sentences may vary slightly.

a) Sam and Jill rode their bikes to the park.

b) Where are my shoes?

c) Can you order pizza for dinner tonight?

d) The blue car is parked in front of our house.

e) What a beautiful morning!

Test 27
Page 119

1. Answers will vary.

2.

tap
work
hit
base
bear
season
blue

a big furry animal
hit gently
winter, spring, summer or fall
the colour of the sky
what a baseball player likes to steal
carry
sad
a job
a very popular song
water comes out of it
a piece of art
strike forcefully
the bottom part of something
add spices

3. Answers will vary. For example: bright, knight, night, sight, site, right

Exercises
Page 120

1. Once upon a sunny day,
I skipped along a grassy way.
I sang a song and bounced my ball,
While waiting for that special call.

Then came the yell, I turned to where
The sound had wafted through the air.
Dad gave a wave, and I had a hunch
The message was, "It's time for lunch!"

When I got home, I whispered, "Please,
I hope that Dad has made grilled cheese."
'Cause toast and cheese just can't be beat –
With ketchup, it's the perfect treat!

And there it was! My favourite meal!
I took a bite with happy zeal,
Ate every drippy, gooey crumb,
And wiped my plate with my thumb.

Some day, when I'm as tall as Dad,
I'll make him a meal like that one we had —
A perfect sandwich made with ease,
The most delicious kind, grilled cheese!

Exercises
Page 121

2. a) eight b) deer c) cent d) hear
   e) chews f) pear g) herd h) there i) ant
   j) piece k) tale l) bear m) two

Exercises
Page 122

3. a) bat: flying mammal/stick used for hitting a ball
   b) cold: a common illness/a low temperature (the opposite of hot)
   c) bowl: to throw a ball/a round, deep dish
   d) hide: an animal's skin/keep out of sight
   e) bark: surface of a tree trunk/the noise a dog makes
   f) low: lacking in height/a sad feeling
   g) ground: surface of the earth/to prevent from flying
   h) box: a container/to fight using fists
   i) train: a type of transportation/to teach or learn a skill

Test 28
Page 123

1. a) here b) flower c) sell d) waste e) no
   f) heel g) week h) sun i) one j) die
   k) ball l) break

2. drive — walk
   talk — bun
   ten — pen
   handle — alive
   fun — candle

3. a) bar: a long piece of wood or metal
      bar: a place where alcohol and refreshments are served
   b) address: details of where someone lives
      address: to speak to an audience
   c) beam: a long, sturdy piece of wood or metal
      beam: a ray or shaft of light
   d) bank: the land beside a river or lake
      bank: a financial establishment

Exercises
Page 124

1. a) wrap b) some c) weight d) great
   e) roll f) night g) meet h) steal

2. back — thin flat piece of wood
   reserve or buy in advance
   arm — get onto a vehicle
   drop down
   board — written or printed work
   autumn
   book — rear surface
   limb
   fall — supply equipment or weapons
   provide support

3. a) brake b) buy c) bear d) base
   e) ant f) board

Exercises
Page 125

4. Answers will vary. For example:
   a) share b) deed c) tale d) bite
   e) same f) crown g) main h) brother
   i) sun j) long k) dribble l) saw

5. Answers may vary.
   a) clam, dam, jam, ram, slam, tram, yam
   b) brook, cook, hook, look, nook, shook, took
   c) band, brand, fanned, grand, land, sand, stand
   d) flour, hour, our, power, shower, sour, tower
   e) blouse, grouse, doghouse, douse, louse, mouse, rouse
   f) bite, bright, fight, kite, night, right, white

Exercises
Page 126

6. a) happy b) shut c) unless d) meat
   e) treat f) heap g) gold

7. Answers may vary.
   a) hope, mope, rope b) hide, slide, tide
   c) ham, pram, slam d) gap, rap, tap
   e) dome, foam, roam f) bright, fight, sight
   g) low, mow, show

8. new — bore
   bye — scent
   boar — knew
   I — buy
   cent — eye

Test 29
Page 127
1. a) fact   b) opinion   c) fact   d) opinion
   e) fact   f) fact   g) opinion   h) fact
   i) opinion   j) opinion

Exercises
Page 128
1. a) opinion   b) opinion   c) fact   d) opinion
   e) opinion   f) fact   g) fact   h) opinion   i) fact
   j) opinion

Exercises
Page 129
2. Answers will vary.

Exercises
Page 130
3. Answers may vary.
   a) fact   b) fact   c) fact   d) opinion
   e) opinion   f) fact   g) opinion   h) fact
   i) opinion   j) opinion   k) opinion   l) fact
   m) fact   n) fact   o) opinion

Test 30
Page 131
1. Answers will vary.

Exercises
Page 132
1. a) true   b) true   c) true   d) false   e) true

Exercises
Page 133
2. i. d)   ii. d)   iii. b)   iv. a)   v. a)

Exercises
Page 134
3. Answers will vary.

Test 31
Page 135
1. a) 5   b) 2   c) 9   d) 12   e) 7   f) 3
   g) 11   h) 10   i) 6   j) 8   k) 1   l) 4

Exercises
Page 136
1. a) 3   b) 12   c) 1   d) 8   e) 6
   f) 10   g) 5   h) 9   i) 11   j) 2
   k) 4   l) 7

Exercises
Page 137

2.	whale	shore	mushroom
	trees	seaweed	hot
	lizard	starfish	oasis
	sand	maple tree	current
	thirst	shark	elm
	dune	moose	camel
	waves	tides	monkey
	cactus	bear	snake

3. ambulance, barn, lamb, tiger, restaurant, dentist, wave, cow, squirrel, lion

Exercises
Page 138
4. a) Why   b) Who   c) What   d) How
   e) Where   f) When

Test 32
Page 139
1. a) blue   b) dark   c) day   d) summer
   e) water
2. house, baby, man, school, pool, photo.
3. cinema, skyscraper, karate, robber
4. galaxy, window, eyelashes, sandwich

Exercises
Page 140
1. a) Why   b) How   c) Where   d) When
   e) How much   f) Who   g) Which   h) What

Exercises
Page 141
2. basketball, tennis, court, baseball, golf, running shoes, racket, net, rules, score, badminton, coach, team

3.

water bottle
jacket
orange
skates
chess
elephant
kite

Exercises
Page 142

4. sunny, clouds, thunder, snow, hot, lightning,mudslide, hail, overcast, tornado, windy, rain, tsunami
5. Answers will vary.

Test 33
Page 143

1. Answers will vary, depending on the dictionary used.
2. An author.
3. A surgeon.

Exercises
Page 144

1. a) 2 b) 8 c) 4 d) 3 e) 1 f) 7
   g) 5 h) 6

Exercises
Page 145

2. a) water polo b) diving c) karate d) hockey
   e) basketball f) volleyball g) soccer h) golf
   i) curling j) tennis k) lacrosse l) ping-pong

Exercises
Page 146

3. Answers will vary.

Test 34
Page 147

1. Answers will vary, depending on the dictionary used.
2. A director.

Exercises
Page 148

1. Answers will vary, depending on the dictionary used.

Exercises
Page 149

2. 1) author 2) title 3) series 4) publisher
3. Answers will vary.

Exercises
Page 150

4. a) ketchup b) noodle c) walnut d) cheese
   e) soup f) parsley g) beef h) lettuce
   i) ice cream j) chocolate k) apple l) pizza

Test 35
Page 151

1.

Exercises
Page 152

1. Answers and colouring will vary.

Exercises
Page 153

2.

Exercises
Page 154

3.
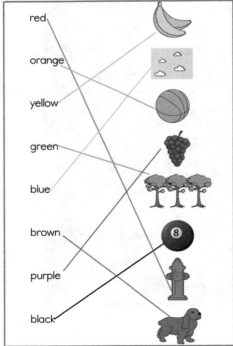

Test 36
Page 155

1.

a) Canada

e) Seychelles

b) Quebec

f) Lebanon

c) France

g) Switzerland

d) Italy

h) Japan

Exercises
Page 156

1. Colouring will vary.

Exercises
Page 157

2.
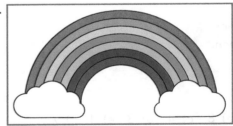

Colours of the rainbow: red, orange, yellow, green, blue, indigo, violet

Exercises
Page 158

3. a) blue b) green c) blue d) red e) green
   f) red g) blue h) red i) green j) blue
   k) green l) blue m) green n) red

Test 37
Page 159

1.

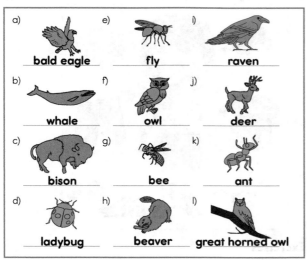

a) bald eagle	e) fly	i) raven
b) whale	f) owl	j) deer
c) bison	g) bee	k) ant
d) ladybug	h) beaver	l) great horned owl

Exercises
Page 160

1.

Herbivore (eats plants)	Carnivore (eats other animals)	Insectivore (eats insects)
cow	fox	frog
deer	tiger	bat
horse	wolf	hedgehog
zebra	lion	mole
moose	cheetah	salamander
giraffe	cougar	

Exercises
Page 161

2. a) eye   b) beak   c) talon   d) wing
   e) tail feathers   f) leg

Exercises
Page 162

3. a) ladybug   b) dragonfly   c) worm
   d) butterfly   e) caterpillar   f) moth   g) beetle
   h) ant   i) fly   j) bee   k) grasshopper
   l) mosquito

Test 38
Page 163

1.

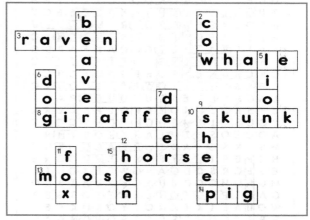

Exercises
Page 164

1. a) wing   b) beak   c) eye   d) antler   e) hoof
   f) fin   g) claw   h) paw   i) ear   j) nose
   k) snout   l) trunk   m) mane   n) wool   o) tail

Exercises
Page 165

2.

Animals	Male	Female	Young	Sound
bee	drone	queen	fry	buzz
bear	boar	sow	cub	growl
cat	tomcat	queen	kitten	meow/purr
chicken	rooster	hen	chick	cackle
dog	dog	bitch	puppy	bark
duck	drake	duck	duckling	quack
elephant	bull	cow	calf	trumpet
fox	dog	vixen	cub	bark
goose	gander	goose	gosling	honk
horse	stallion	mare	foal	neigh/whinny
lion	lion	lioness	cub	roar
ox	bull	cow	calf	bellow/moo
pig	hog	sow	piglet	grunt/squeal
sheep	ram	ewe	lamb	baa/bleat

Exercises
Page 166

3.

Test 39
Page 167

1. a) Bermuda shorts   b) sock   c) earmuffs
   d) T-shirt   e) hat   f) tie   g) shorts
   h) scarf   i) raincoat   j) skirt   k) glasses
   l) winter coat   m) pants   n) cap   o) jacket
   p) pyjamas

Exercises
Page 168

1.

```
G L O V E  N I G H T G O W N  C
J A C K E T S L  M I T T E N S  S
O  R A I N C O A T S  K I R T  T
S H I R T  W I N T E R C O A T
S A N D A L S H  S H O E S  I N
S L I P P E R  T U Q U E  C A P
B O O T  D R E S S  S H O R T S
B E R M U D A S  B L O U S E S
A P R O N S  E A R M U F F S  G
B A T H I N G S U I T  H A T S
```

Secret word: **CLOTHING**

Exercises
Page 169

2. Drawings will vary. For example:

Exercises
Page 170

3.

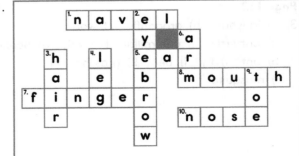

sight
smell
taste
touch
hearing

Test 40
Page 171

1.

```
1.n a v e l
      y      6.a
3.h  4.l  5.e a r
 a   e   b   8.m o u t h
7.f i n g e r       o
 r       r   10.n o s e
         o
         w
```

Exercises

Page 172

1. a) nose   b) ear   c) mouth/lips   d) tie
   e) scarf   f) tuque

Exercises

Page 173

2. Answers may vary based on where one lives.
   a) winter   b) summer   c) spring
   d) summer or fall   e) spring   f) winter
   g) summer   h) winter
   i) spring, summer or fall   j) summer
   k) winter   l) summer

Exercises

Page 174

3. a) hair   b) eye   c) nose   d) ear   e) mouth
   f) chin

Test 41

Page 175

1. a) scissors   b) backpack   c) blackboard
   d) triangle   e) eraser   f) protractor
   g) ruler   h) sharpener   i) paper clip   j) glue
   k) pencil case   l) pen

Exercises

Page 176

1.

B	A	C	K	P	A	C	K	S	P	E	N	C	I	L
B	L	A	C	K	B	O	A	R	D	C	H	A	I	R
C	S	H	A	R	P	E	N	E	R	R	U	L	E	R
B	I	N	D	E	R	S	H	J	A	N	I	T	O	R
T	E	A	C	H	E	R	S	C	I	S	S	O	R	S
P	E	N	O	G	L	U	E	O	E	R	A	S	E	R
N	O	T	E	B	O	O	K	S	N	U	R	S	E	S
D	E	S	K	S	P	A	P	E	R	C	L	I	P	S
W	A	S	T	E	B	A	S	K	E	T	B	E	L	L
C	O	M	P	U	T	E	R	S	T	U	D	E	N	T
A	R	T	T	E	A	C	H	E	R	C	H	A	L	K
S	E	C	R	E	T	A	R	Y	C	L	O	C	K	S
L	U	N	C	H	B	O	X	E	N	G	L	I	S	H
C	A	L	C	U	L	A	T	O	R	W	A	L	L	S
L	G	Y	M	N	A	S	I	U	M	D	O	O	R	S

Secret word: **S C H O O L**

Exercises

Page 177

2. a) gym class   b) English   c) science   d) math
   e) geography   f) history   g) social studies
   h) French

Exercises

Page 178

3. a) science   b) math   c) English   d) gym
   e) math   f) art   g) geography   h) music
   i) art   j) English   k) gym   l) science

Test 42

Page 179

1.

Exercises

Page 180

1. a) 2   b) 5   c) 6   d) 9   e) 7   f) 3
   g) 8   h) 1   i) 4

Exercises

Page 181

2. Answers will vary.

Exercises

Page 182

3. Answers will vary.

Test 43

Page 183

1. a) 5   b) 4   c) 1   d) 6   e) 2   f) 3
2. Answers will vary. For example: playing cards, singing, reading.
3. Answers will vary.

Exercises
Page 184

1. a) playing a board game
   b) acting
   c) playing dominoes
   d) playing snakes and ladders
   e) riding a bike
   f) camping
   g) playing the piano
   h) listening to music
   i) cooking

Exercises
Page 185

2. a) basketball   b) baseball   c) tennis
   d) hockey   e) skiing   f) badminton
   g) figure skating   h) running   i) boxing
   j) diving   k) golf   l) soccer

Exercises
Page 186

3. Answers and drawings will vary.

Test 44
Page 187

1. a) jumping rope   b) playing a computer game
   c) dancing   d) playing chess   e) snowboarding
   f) singing

Exercises
Page 188

1.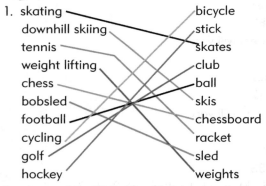
   skating   bicycle
   downhill skiing stick
   tennis   skates
   weight lifting   club
   chess   ball
   bobsled   skis
   football   chessboard
   cycling   racket
   golf   sled
   hockey   weights

2. a) watching TV   b) collecting hockey cards
   c) singing   d) reading a book
   e) collecting stamps   f) playing a card game

Exercises
Page 189

3.

Danica	Melanie	Peter
sweep the floor	wash the dishes	dry the dishes
fold the laundry	put away the laundry	put away the dishes
take out the garbage	take out the recycling	shovel the snow

Exercises
Page 190

4. Answers will vary.

Test 45
Page 191

1. Answers will vary.

Exercises
Page 192

1. a) ii)   b) iii)

Exercises
Page 194

2. a) The hare mocked the tortoise for being slow
      and the tortoise challenged him to a race.
      The tortoise won it by walking slow and
      steady, while the hare lost (though he was
      fast) by taking a nap.
   b) i) True   ii) False   iii) False   iv) True
      v) False   vi) False

Test 46
Page 195

1. a) The main idea is that pizza is a popular,
      versatile and healthy food.
   b) 2
   c) Answers will vary. For example,
      "Pizza: Popular and Healthy" – Because that
      is the main idea.

Exercises
Page 196

1. a) iii)   b) ii)   c) i)

Exercises
Page 197

2. a) The main idea is that Darren is a responsible big brother who walks his little brother safely to school every day.
   b) The main idea is that Mazari had a very enjoyable outing to the zoo with her father.

Exercises
Page 198

3. The main idea is that Roshawn has grown tall and is preparing as best he can to make the basketball team.
4. Answers will vary, but the main idea is that the seed is planted in the soil and, given water and sunlight, grows into a flowering plant.

Test 47
Page 199

1. 5, 7, 4, 3, 1, 6, 2

Exercises
Page 200

1. a) Samantha cleared the fire pit first.
   b) She set up lots of kindling to burn quickly and added two big logs to burn more slowly.
   c) Samantha cooked the hot dog last.

Exercises
Pages 201 & 202

2. Answers will vary.

Test 48
Page 203

1. a) Pick a pumpkin from the patch.
   b) Bring the pumpkin home.
   c) Get out a sharp knife.
   d) Cut off the top and scoop out the seeds.
   e) Carve a face into the pumpkin.
   f) Put a candle in the pumpkin.
   g) Light the candle and set the pumpkin outside when dark.

Exercises
Pages 204 & 205

1. Answers will vary.

Exercises
Page 206

2. First, mix together the flour, baking soda, nutmeg, cinnamon powder and sugar Secondly, add oats, mashed bananas and cocoa flakes.
   Thirdly, melt the butter and add it to the rest of the ingredients. Beat an egg lightly and add to the mix.
   Fourthly, mix well. Make little balls and place them on the baking sheet.
   Finally, cook in the oven at 180° Celsius for 12 to 15 minutes.

Test 49
Page 207

1. Countries: Germany, United States, France
   Ways to travel: plane, car, golf cart, train
   Clothing and Accessories: bathing suit, shoes, dress
   Food: pretzels, sausages, ice cream

Exercises
Page 209

1. a) Rob was so nervous because he was leaving to go to camp for the first time and he was always scared when trying new things.
   b) They made him a good breakfast and told him funny stories about their camp experiences.
   c) Answers will vary.
   d) Rob learned that he really did enjoy camping.

Exercises
Pages 211 & 212

2. a) Jack is 10 years old.
   b) Jack slept under a tree.
   c) Jack made a fire to stay warm.
   d) Jack threw a stick from the fire twice at the monster.
   e) Jack took shelter up a tree.
   f) Jack used the words "Whoomity whop, whoomity whop!" to describe the steps of the monster.

g) The monster couldn't climb the tree because it was too sticky.

h) The monster was eating the tree to get to Jack.

i) Jack woke up.

j) Drawings will vary.

Test 50
Page 213

1. b)

2. c)

3. "Hearing Bender purr always makes people smile."

4. Answers will vary.

Exercises
Page 215

1. a) Anika

b) Pine Lane School in Barrie

c) The students visited Julie's farm near Orangeville and fed the goats and chickens.

d) Seeing the small dog Bailey trotting beside the tall horse, Thunder, made Anika laugh.

e) Anika told her teacher she loves taking care of animals. The teacher replied that Anika could be a vet if she studied hard.

f) Answers will vary.

Exercises
Pages 217 & 218

2. a) Matthew was so nervous because the monkey bars wobbled and were quite high – he felt that he was not tall enough.

b) Matthew started counting to himself to help swing his way across the monkey bars using alternating hands.

c) Answers will vary.

d) Answers will vary – Daniel did help Matthew complete the monkey bars because he encouraged him by completing them first, and he suggested that Matthew should count "one hand, two hand" as he swung his way across.

e) Drawings will vary.

Test 51
Page 219

1. Answers will vary.

Exercises
Pages 220 & 221

1. Answers will vary.

Exercises
Pages 223 & 224

2. Answers will vary.

Test 52
Page 225

1. Answers will vary.

Exercises
Pages 226 to 228

1. Answers will vary.

Exercises
Pages 229 & 230

2. Answers will vary.

Test 53
Page 231

1. Answers will vary.

Exercises
Pages 232 & 233

1. Answers will vary.

Exercises
Pages 234 to 236

2. Answers will vary.

Test 54
Page 237

1. Answers will vary.

Exercises
Pages 238 & 239

1. Answers will vary.

Exercises
Pages 240 to 242

2. Answers will vary.

Test 55
Page 245
1. a) 175 b) 121 c) 300 d) 100 e) 280
2. a) 310 b) 270 c) 140 d) 480
3. a) 3 b) 3 c) 8
4. a) 300 + 1 b) 200 + 30 + 8
c) 400 + 20 + 4 d) 100 + 50 + 8

Exercises
Page 246

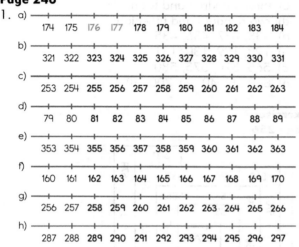

1. a) 174 175 176 177 178 179 180 181 182 183 184
b) 321 322 323 324 325 326 327 328 329 330 331
c) 253 254 255 256 257 258 259 260 261 262 263
d) 79 80 81 82 83 84 85 86 87 88 89
e) 353 354 355 356 357 358 359 360 361 362 363
f) 160 161 162 163 164 165 166 167 168 169 170
g) 256 257 258 259 260 261 262 263 264 265 266
h) 287 288 289 290 291 292 293 294 295 296 297

2. a) 454 = 400 + 50 + 4
b) 365 = 300 + 60 + 5
c) 187 = 100 + 80 + 7
d) 215 = 200 + 10 + 5
e) 471 = 400 + 70 + 1
f) 458 = 400 + 50 + 8
g) 438 = 400 + 30 + 8
h) 399 = 300 + 90 + 9
i) 452 = 400 + 50 + 2
j) 277 = 200 + 70 + 7
k) 402 = 400 + 2
l) 379 = 300 + 70 + 9

Exercises
Page 247
3. a) 90 b) 70 c) 400 d) 20 e) 200 f) 300
g) 80 h) 100 i) 9 j) 3 k) 30 l) 30

4.

		Hundreds	Tens	Ones
a)	489	4	8	9
b)	323	3	2	3
c)	474	4	7	4
d)	166	1	6	6
e)	225	2	2	5

5.
a) 120, 122, 124, 125 118 119 120 121 122 123 124 125 126
b) 52, 42, 46, 36 36 38 40 42 44 46 48 50 52
c) 424, 427, 430, 429 423 424 425 426 427 428 429 430 431
d) 236, 239, 238, 241 234 235 236 237 238 239 240 241 242
e) 195, 190, 210, 200 175 180 185 190 195 200 205 210 215

Exercises
Page 248
6.

7.

	Standard Form	Expanded Form
a)	212	200 + 10 + 2
b)	464	400 + 60 + 4
c)	395	300 + 90 + 5
d)	498	400 + 90 + 8
e)	196	100 + 90 + 6

8. a) fifty-two b) fifteen c) eleven d) seven
e) twenty-two f) seventy-eight g) sixty-six
h) one hundred i) ninety-two

Exercises
Page 249
9. i) eleven ii) thirty iii) five iv) fifty-five
v) nine vi) twenty-nine vii) fourteen viii) six
ix) forty x) nineteen xi) fifteen xii) twenty-one
xiii) thirty-three xiv) one hundred xv) twenty-five
xvi) thirty-seven xvii) twenty-six xviii) sixty-seven
xix) thirty-one xx) one xxi) seventeen
xxii) thirty-four xxiii) seven xxiv) seventy
xxv) two xxvi) sixty xxvii) twenty-seven
xxviii) twenty-two

Exercises
Page 250
10. i) 18 ii) 50 iii) 36 iv) 28 v) 12 vi) 38
vii) 90 viii) 35 ix) 24 x) 3 xi) 71 xii) 20
xiii) 10 xiv) 4 xv) 13 xvi) 39 xvii) 80
xviii) 8 xix) 26 xx) 16 xxi) 32 xxii) 19
xxiii) 14 xxiv) 60 xxv) 100 xxvi) 42
xxvii) 37 xxviii) 1

Answers

Mathematics

Test 56
Page 251
1. a) 130, 135, 140, 145, 150, 155
   b) 321, 346, 371, 396, 421, 446
   c) 320, 310, 300, 290, 280, 270
   d) 250, 300, 350, 400, 450, 500
   e) 242, 251, 260, 269, 278, 287
2. a) 180 b) 300 c) 401 d) 212 e) 194
3.

		Hundreds	Tens	Ones
a)	389	3	8	9
b)	236	2	3	6
c)	495	4	9	5
d)	152	1	5	2
e)	358	3	5	8

Exercises
Page 252
1. a) 310 b) 420 c) 231 d) 413 e) 112
   f) 307 g) 221 h) 473 i) 139 j) 309
2.

424	425	426	427	428	429	430	431	432
433	434	435	436	437	438	439	440	441
442	443	444	445	446	447	448	449	450
451	452	453	454	455	456	457	458	459
460	461	462	463	464	465	466	467	468
469	470	471	472	473	474	475	476	477
478	479	480	481	482	483	484	485	486
487	488	489	490	491	492	493	494	495
496	497	498	499	500	501	502	503	504

3. a) 240, 245, 250 b) 267, 277, 287
   c) 219, 221, 223 d) 242, 251, 260
   e) 492, 592, 692

Exercises
Page 253
4.

		Hundreds	Tens	Ones
a)	158	1	5	8
b)	387	3	8	7
c)	148	1	4	8
d)	432	4	3	2
e)	246	2	4	6

5. a) 100 b) 2 c) 8 d) 200 e) 80 f) 200
6. a) 1, 3, 9
   b) 13, 19, 31, 39, 91, 93
   c) 139, 193, 319, 391, 913, 931
7. a) four hundred and forty-seven
   b) three hundred and eighty-one
   c) two hundred and one

Exercises
Page 254
8. a) 9, 8, 3
   b) 8, 7, 4
   c) 9, 9, 1
   d) 1, 4, 2
   e) 9, 6, 3

Test 57
Page 255
1. a) 261, 262, 263, 264, 265
   b) 320, 275, 230, 185, 140
   c) 489, 609, 729, 849, 969
2. a) one hundred and twenty-three
   b) eight hundred and seventy-one
   c) three hundred and twenty-five
   d) two hundred and fifty-eight
3. a) 438, 437, 436, 435
   b) 128, 129, 130, 131
   c) 565, 570, 575, 580
4. a) 800 b) 40 c) 700 d) 5

Exercises
Page 256
1.

2.

		Hundreds	Tens	Ones
a)	589	5	8	9
b)	785	7	8	5
c)	148	1	4	8
d)	777	7	7	7
e)	333	3	3	3
f)	978	9	7	8

3. a) 4 b) 4 c) 9 d) 2

Exercises
Page 257
4. a) 790 b) 120 c) 340 d) 460 e) 1000
   f) 550
5. a) 300 b) 200 c) 200 d) 500 e) 800
   f) 700
6. a) 384 b) 712 c) 763 d) 655 e) 532
   f) 197
7. a) 228 b) 961 c) 355 d) 170 e) 323

Exercises
Page 258

8. a) 700 + 50
   b) 800 + 90 + 6
   c) 400 + 70 + 8
   d) 700 + 80 + 3
   e) 100 + 10 + 1
   f) 500 + 50 + 5

9.

		Hundreds	Tens	Ones
a)	587	5	8	7
b)	369	3	6	9
c)	581	5	8	1
d)	416	4	1	6
e)	236	2	3	6
f)	547	5	4	7
g)	123	1	2	3
h)	475	4	7	5
i)	347	3	4	7
j)	148	1	4	8
k)	563	5	6	3

Test 58
Page 259

1. a) 784 b) 991 c) 562 d) 784 e) 240
   f) 524 g) 248 h) 240 i) 259 j) 362
   k) 841 l) 240

2. a) Hundreds: 1, Tens: 5, Ones: 9
   b) Hundreds: 7, Tens: 4, Ones: 1
   c) Hundreds: 3, Tens: 6, Ones: 2

3. a) 2 b) 6 c) 5 d) 8

Exercises
Page 260

1.

221	222	223	224	225	226	227	228	229
230	231	232	233	234	235	236	237	238
239	240	241	242	243	244	245	246	247
248	249	250	251	252	253	254	255	256
257	258	259	260	261	262	263	264	265
266	267	268	269	270	271	272	273	274
275	276	277	278	279	280	281	282	283
284	285	286	287	288	289	290	291	292
293	294	295	296	297	298	299	300	301

2.

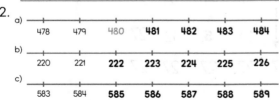

a) 478 479 480 481 482 483 484
b) 220 221 222 223 224 225 226
c) 583 584 585 586 587 588 589

Exercises
Page 261

3. a) 9, 8, 5 b) 1, 2, 1 c) 6, 5, 2 d) 8, 8, 7
   e) 7, 6, 3

Exercises
Page 262

4. a) Hundreds: 4, Tens: 7, Ones: 8
   b) Hundreds: 8, Tens: 2, Ones: 3
   c) Hundreds: 6, Tens: 6, Ones: 1

5. a) 9 b) 10

6. a) 1000 b) 500 c) 100 d) 400 e) 300
   f) 100

7.

326	327	328	329	330	331	332	333	334
335	336	337	338	339	340	341	342	343
344	345	346	347	348	349	350	351	352
353	354	355	356	357	358	359	360	361
362	363	364	365	366	367	368	369	370
371	372	373	374	375	376	377	378	379
380	381	382	383	384	385	386	387	388
389	390	391	392	393	394	395	396	397
398	399	400	401	402	403	404	405	406

Test 59
Page 263

1. a) 445>357 b) 254=254 c) 452>371
   d) 354>247 e) 187<279 f) 237>157

2. a) 458 b) 739 c) 415

3. a) 28, 125, 129, 215, 627
   b) 124, 128, 139, 236, 897
   c) 738, 752, 846, 947, 949

Exercises
Page 264

1. a) 198, 258, 358, 474, 478
   b) 111, 125, 136, 224, 378
   c) 174, 219, 247, 321, 421
   d) 114, 231, 321, 386, 497

2. a) 179<258 b) 258<487 c) 158<345
   d) 389<478 e) 258>189 f) 358<436

3. a) 995, 933, 539, 412 b) 834, 649, 645, 533
   c) 848, 721, 439, 369

Exercises
Page 265

4. a) 950 b) 631 c) 932 d) 789

5. 750

6. 927

7. a) 101, 236, 369, 478, 623
   b) 125, 269, 741, 789, 896
   c) 539, 632, 731, 769, 878
   d) 421, 593, 632, 718, 943
   e) 376, 538, 602, 749, 894

Exercises
Page 266

8. a) 966, 933, 716, 691, 411
   b) 800, 799, 737, 444, 291
   c) 942, 732, 563, 298, 137
   d) 800, 720, 432, 312, 245
   e) 940, 789, 635, 512, 133
   f) 949, 873, 781, 439, 264
   g) 973, 878, 519, 435, 115
   h) 944, 718, 466, 328, 178
   i) 890, 748, 533, 309, 158

Test 60
Page 267

1. a) 879>258   b) 258<587
   c) 158<745   d) 789>578
   e) 258<789   f) 458>236
   g) 139<472   h) 320<321
2. a) 587<789   b) 125<369
   c) 587=587   d) 375<376
   e) 135<421   f) 99<199
   g) 531>208   h) 399=399
   i) 398<399   j) 400<401

Exercises
Page 268

1. a) 952>950   b) 102<478
   c) 458=458   d) 139<148
   e) 726>258   f) 410>236
   g) 539>538   h) 416>329
   i) 632>519   j) 806>383

Exercises
Page 269

2. a) 125, 256, 523   b) 125, 458, 521
   c) 125, 214, 254   d) 129, 133, 256
   e) 135, 645, 710   f) 115, 728, 933
   g) 100, 699, 834   h) 128, 830, 909
   i) 208, 413, 577   j) 302, 383, 769

Exercises
Page 270

3. a) 411<412   b) 347>254   c) 123<147
   d) 654>547   e) 885>411   f) 521>171
   g) 306=306   h) 817>139   i) 239<700
   j) 573=573

Test 61
Page 271

1. a) 12   b) 15   c) 15   d) 18   e) 23   f) 22
   g) 27   h) 26   i) 26   j) 31   k) 39   l) 99
   m) 77   n) 322   o) 541   p) 911   q) 681   r) 901
   s) 710   t) 641   u) 470   v) 820   w) 66   x) 231

2. a) 500+125=625   b) 23+31+26=80
   c) 119+187=306

Exercises
Page 272

1.

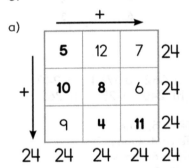

2. a) 6   b) 7   c) 6   d) 15   e) 6   f) 5   g) 5
   h) 7   i) 6

3.

a)

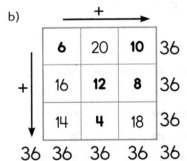

b)

c)

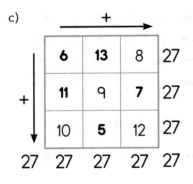

Exercises
Page 273
4. a) 80 b) 768 c) 436 d) 689 e) 815 f) 593
g) 562 h) 663 i) 368 j) 254 k) 240 l) 213
5. a) 117 b) 955 c) 141 d) 856

Exercises
Page 274
6. a) 127+284=411 b) 215+256+256=727
c) 136+127+58=321 d) 174+458+158=790

Test 62
Page 275
1. a) 13 b) 13 c) 13 d) 16 e) 16
f) 15 g) 13 h) 13 i) 469 j) 399
k) 811 l) 571 m) 251 n) 350 o) 512
p) 779
2. a) 184 b) 231 c) 386
d) 629 e) 433 f) 215
3. a) 684 b) 783 c) 553 d) 454 e) 856
f) 910 g) 701 h) 605
4. 258+712+12+3=985

Exercises
Page 276
1.

+	5	9	7	10	8
3	8	12	10	13	11
6	11	15	13	16	14
4	9	13	11	14	12
2	7	11	9	12	10
5	10	14	12	15	13
7	12	16	14	17	15
9	14	18	16	19	17

2. a) 15 b) 12 c) 9 d) 17 e) 11 f) 14
g) 16 h) 7 i) 13 j) 5 k) 9 l) 13
m) 14 n) 9 o) 13 p) 11 q) 7 r) 12
s) 6 t) 10 u) 15 v) 12 w) 9 x) 17
y) 11 z) 8

Exercises
Page 277
3. 75+75, 10+140, 125+25, 88+62, 61+89, 100+50, 98+52, 12+138
4. a) 618 b) 626 c) 661 d) 667

Exercises
Page 278
5. a) 452 b) 806 c) 569 d) 989 e) 785
f) 841 g) 982 h) 978 i) 984 j) 854
k) 772 l) 997 m) 240 n) 514 o) 630
p) 836 q) 914 r) 708 s) 543 t) 587

u) 780 v) 731 w) 951 x) 547
6. a) 459 b) 545 c) 442 d) 296 e) 540
f) 195

Test 63
Page 279
1. a) 16 b) 13 c) 13 d) 9 e) 4
f) 7 g) 3 h) 15 i) 1 j) 6
k) 6 l) 12
2. a) 812 b) 127 c) 333 d) 251 e) 500
f) 673 g) 270 h) 617 i) 519 j) 858
k) 232 l) 250 m) 565 n) 107 o) 677
p) 313
3. a) 23-15=8 b) 58-12=46

Exercises
Page 280
1. a) 7 b) 4 c) 3 d) 9 e) 7 f) 19
g) 3 h) 12 i) 2 j) 13 k) 5 l) 13
m) 8 n) 13 o) 13 p) 51
2.

3.

–	12	3	8	6	4	7	9	5	11
17	5	14	9	11	13	10	8	12	6
15	3	12	7	9	11	8	6	10	4
13	1	10	5	7	9	6	4	8	2
16	4	13	8	10	12	9	7	11	5
12	0	9	4	6	8	5	3	7	1
14	2	11	6	8	10	7	5	9	3

Exercises
Page 281
4. a) 28 b) 63 c) 30 d) 262 e) 506
f) 400 g) 505 h) 331 i) 264 j) 83
k) 441 l) 155
5. a) 348 b) 959 c) 531 d) 312 e) 656
f) 527 g) 133 h) 405 i) 514
6. a) 600-259-27=314 b) 125-48-68=9

Exercises
Page 282
7. a) 111 b) 207 c) 263 d) 424 e) 265
f) 235 g) 76 h) 314

8. a) 469 b) 155 c) 134 d) 406 e) 150
   f) 605
9. a) 557 b) 375 c) 442 d) 232 e) 1
   f) 307 g) 63 h) 68 i) 53 j) 248
   k) 153 l) 46 m) 454 n) 297 o) 78
   p) 474
10. a) 290 b) 63 c) 108 d) 121 e) 85
    f) 387 g) 385 h) 122

Test 64
Page 283

1.

–	12	3	8	6	4	7	9	5	11
18	6	15	10	12	14	11	9	13	7
20	8	17	12	14	16	13	11	15	9
24	12	21	16	18	20	17	15	19	13
19	7	16	11	13	15	12	10	14	8
25	13	22	17	19	21	18	16	20	14
23	11	20	15	17	19	16	14	18	12

2. a) 22 b) 231 c) 237 d) 35 e) 337
   f) 163 g) 51 h) 189 i) 170 j) 138
   k) 33 l) 20 m) 153 n) 143 o) 55
   p) 134 q) 43 r) 125 s) 132 t) 140

Exercises
Page 284

1. Answers will vary. Possible answers include:
   50-45=5, 76-45=31, 70-45=25, 69-45=24,
   49-45=4, 233-45=188, 68-45=23, 132-45=87,
   77-45=32, 48-45=3, 251-45=206,
   316-45=271, 58-45=13, 320-45=275,
   240-45=195, 59-45=14

2.
   24 - 8 = 16 s
   28 - 10 = 18 u
   20 - 9 = 11 b
   18 - 6 = 12 t
   16 - 7 = 9 r
   15 - 7 = 8 a
   18 - 12 = 6 c
   23 - 11 = 12 t

   23 - 6 = 17 i
   15 - 2 = 13 o
   20 - 6 = 14 n
   25 - 8 = 17 i
   30 - 14 = 16 s
   24 - 9 = 15 f
   20 - 2 = 18 u
   18 - 4 = 14 n

3. a) 52-37=15; 15+37=52
   b) 80-26=54; 54+26=80

Exercises
Page 285

4. a) 25-13=12 b) 144-72=72
   c) 274-14-36=224 d) 568-321=247
   e) 289-125=164 f) 425-178=247

Exercises
Page 286

5. a) 75 b) 615 c) 630 d) 177 e) 61

f) 303 g) 240 h) 248 i) 523 j) 757
k) 18 l) 39 m) 138 n) 252 o) 739
6. a) 252 b) 635 c) 289 d) 448 e) 755
   f) 527 g) 403 h) 597 i) 612

Test 65
Page 287

1. a) 2x4=8 b) 5x5=25 c) 3x2=6
   d) 9x3=27 e) 7x9=63
2. a) 12 b) 35 c) 24 d) 16 e) 21
   f) 8 g) 18 h) 6 i) 30
3.

x	0	1	2	3	4	5	6
0	0	0	0	0	0	0	0
4	0	4	8	12	16	20	24
2	0	2	4	6	8	10	12
5	0	5	10	15	20	25	30
3	0	3	6	9	12	15	18
6	0	6	12	18	24	30	36
7	0	7	14	21	28	35	42
9	0	9	18	27	36	45	54

Exercises
Page 288

1.

Table of 1	Table of 2	Table of 3
0	0	0
1	2	3
2	4	6
3	6	9
4	8	12
5	10	15
6	12	18
7	14	21
8	16	24
9	18	27
10	20	30

2.

x	1	5	8	4	3	9	6	10	2	7
4	4	20	32	16	12	36	24	40	8	28
5	5	25	40	20	15	45	30	50	10	35

Exercises
Page 289

3.

a) 7 x 2
b) 5 x 3
c) 4 x 4
d) 3 x 3
e) 6 x 3

4. a) $3 \times 4 = 12$ b) $2 \times 9 = 18$ c) $5 \times 5 = 25$
   d) $4 \times 6 = 24$ e) $3 \times 7 = 21$ f) $4 \times 9 = 36$

Exercises
Page 290
5. a) $3 \times 7 = 21$ b) $8 \times 2 = 16$ c) $9 \times 3 = 27$
   d) $3 \times 8 = 24$ e) $9 \times 8 = 72$

Test 66
Page 291
1. a) 30 b) 8 c) 32 d) 24 e) 36 f) 18
   g) 36 h) 16 i) 45 j) 14 k) 27 l) 28
2.

Table of 4	Table of 5	Table of 6
0	0	0
4	5	6
8	10	12
12	15	18
16	20	24
20	25	30
24	30	36
28	35	42
32	40	48
36	45	54
40	50	60

Exercises
Page 292
1.

Exercises
Page 293
2. a) 32 b) 35 c) 21 d) 18 e) 5
   f) 32 g) 6 h) 42

3. a)

x	3	5	8	6	4
7	21	35	56	42	28
3	9	15	24	18	12
4	12	20	32	24	16
6	18	30	48	36	24
5	15	25	40	30	20

b)

x	5	7	9	4	8
2	10	14	18	8	16
6	30	42	54	24	48
9	45	63	81	36	72
8	40	56	72	32	64

Exercises
Page 294
4. a) 40 b) 28 c) 24 d) 16 e) 12
   f) 10 g) 6 h) 9 i) 14 j) 10 k) 15
   l) 8
5. a) 7 b) 6 c) 8 d) 9 e) 3 f) 24
   g) 5 h) 5 i) 42 j) 7 k) 7 l) 21
   m) 6 n) 54 o) 8

6. a) 48 b) 9 c) 20 d) 54 e) 28
   f) 35 g) 72 h) 42 i) 16 j) 24
   k) 24 l) 27

Test 67
Page 295
1.

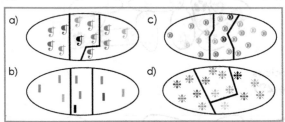

2.

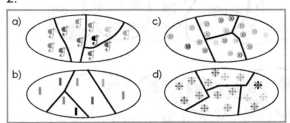

3. 9 marbles
   $36 \div 4 = 9$
4. a) 4 b) 3 c) 2 d) 3 e) 2 f) 4
   g) 10 h) 4 i) 4

Exercises
Page 296

1. a) 2

b) 5

c) 3

d) 3
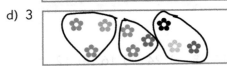

e) 3

f) 5

g) 4

h) 2

Exercises
Page 297

2.

3.
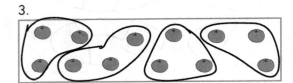

4.

5.

Exercises
Page 298

6. a) 7, 4   b) 5, 3   c) 9, 7   d) 4, 6   e) 5, 10
   f) 6, 8   g) 2, 4   h) 7, 9   i) 5, 6   j) 3, 7
   k) 9, 5   l) 6, 10   m) 2, 9   n) 7, 6   o) 9, 10
   p) 4, 12   q) 4, 11   r) 2, 12

Test 68
Page 299

1. a)
   b)
   c)
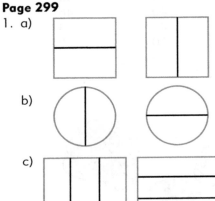

2. $48 \div 6 = 8$
3. $36 \div 4 = 9$

Exercises
Page 300

1. a) $24 \div 6 = 4$ b) $40 \div 8 = 5$ c) $12 \div 6 = 2$
   d) $36 \div 3 = 12$ e) $30 \div 2 = 15$

Exercises
Page 301

2. a) $12 \div 3 = 4$ b) $12 \div 4 = 3$ c) $30 \div 6 = 5$
   d) $24 \div 2 = 12$ e) $27 \div 3 = 9$ f) $25 \div 5 = 5$
   g) $9 \div 9 = 1$ h) $8 \div 2 = 4$ i) $20 \div 2 = 10$
   j) $24 \div 4 = 6$ k) $10 \div 2 = 5$ l) $16 \div 4 = 4$
   m) $14 \div 2 = 7$

Exercises
Page 302
3.

1) 1	2) 1	3) 1	4) 1
5) 2	6) 2	7) 2	8) 2
9) 3	10) 3	11) 3	12) 3
13) 4	14) 4	15) 4	16) 4
17) 5	18) 5	19) 5	20) 5
21) 6	22) 6	23) 6	24) 6
25) 7	26) 7	27) 7	28) 7
29) 8	30) 8	31) 8	32) 8
33) 9	34) 9	35) 9	36) 9
37) 10	38) 10	39) 10	40) 10
41) 11	42) 11	43) 11	44) 11
45) 12	46) 12	47) 12	48) 12

Test 69
Page 303
1. a) one half $\frac{1}{2}$ c) one third $\frac{1}{3}$

   b) one quarter $\frac{1}{4}$ d) one sixth $\frac{1}{6}$

2.
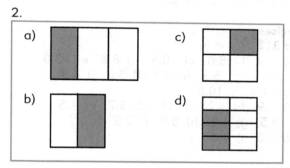

3.

Exercises
Page 304
1. a) $\frac{1}{2}$ b) $\frac{1}{2}$ c) $\frac{1}{3}$ d) $\frac{1}{4}$ e) $\frac{1}{3}$ f) $\frac{1}{4}$

2.
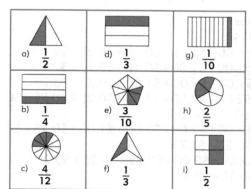

Exercises
Page 305
3.
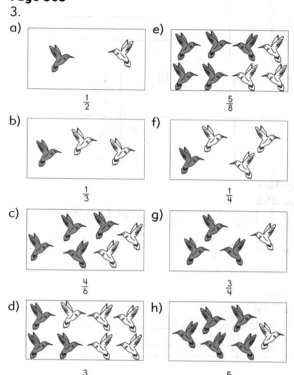

Exercises
Page 306
4. b)
5.
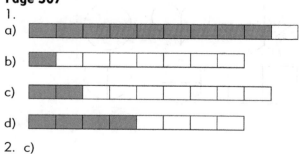

Test 70
Page 307
1.

a) ▬
b) ▬
c) ▬
d) ▬

2. c)

3.

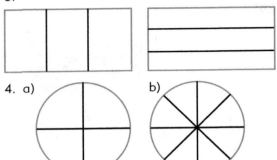

4. a)   b)

Exercises
Page 308

1. a) $\frac{3}{8}$ b) $\frac{1}{4}$ c) $\frac{2}{5}$ d) $\frac{4}{6}$ or $\frac{2}{3}$ e) $\frac{1}{3}$ f) $\frac{3}{4}$

   g) $\frac{2}{4}$ or $\frac{1}{2}$ h) $\frac{1}{2}$

Exercises
Page 309

2.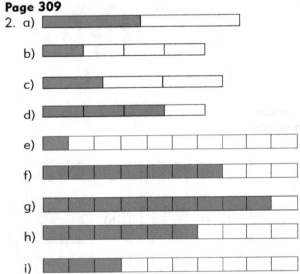

Exercises
Page 310

3. Answers may vary.

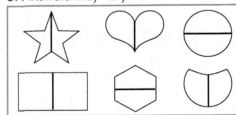

4.
a)
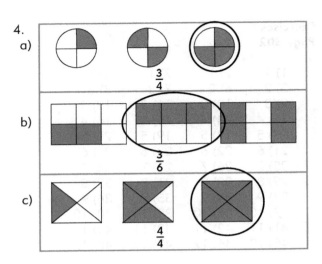
$\frac{3}{4}$

b)
$\frac{3}{6}$

c)
$\frac{4}{4}$

Test 71
Page 311

1. a) 6.9 b) 10.6 c) 17.9 d) 7.5 e) 9.0
   f) 11.4 g) 8.3 h) 3.4
2. a) 1.5 b) 7.1 c) 6.3 d) 3.4 e) 5.9
   f) 1.4 g) 2.6 h) 2.5

Exercises
Page 312

1. a) 4.9 b) 8.6 c) 10.9 d) 8.5 e) 10.0
   f) 10.5 g) 5.3 h) 8.7 i) 5.8 j) 4.8
   k) 11.2 l) 10.5
2. a) 4.9 b) 4.7 c) 2.8 d) 3.7 e) 1.5
   f) 5.5 g) 1.5 h) 5.0 i) 2.2 j) 3.2
   k) 5.3 l) 4.5

Exercises
Page 313

3.

| Anne: 1.65 m | Ram: 1.25 m | Justin: 1.80 m |
| Jenny: 1.55 m | Laura: 1.79 m | Michelle: 1.78 m |

4. a) $2.00 b) $3.40 c) $0.65 d) $3.85
   e) $5.00 f) $2.70 g) $5.00

Exercises
Page 314

5. a) $1.00+$1.00+$0.25+$0.25=$2.50
   b) $1.00+$1.00+$0.10+$0.10=$2.20
   c) $1.00+$1.00+$1.00+$0.25=$3.25
   d) $2.00+$2.00+$1.00+$0.25+$0.25+$0.10+
      $0.05=$5.65
   e) $2.00+$2.00+$2.00+$1.00+$0.25+$0.25+
      $0.25=$7.75
   f) $2.00+$2.00+$0.25+$0.25+$0.25+$0.10+
      $0.10=$4.95

g) $1.00+$1.00+$1.00+$0.25+$0.10+$0.10+
$0.05+$0.05=$3.55

h) $2.00+$1.00+$1.00+$1.00+$0.25+$0.25+
$0.10+$0.10+$0.05+$0.05+$0.05=$5.85

Exercises
Page 315
6. a) $14.50, Ben b) $11.35, Anna
   c) $13.55, Zoe d) $12.25, Tony

Exercises
Page 316
7. a) $30.00 b) $4.00 c) $1.40 d) $29.00
   e) $50.00 f) $80.00 g) $6.00 h) $2.35

Test 72
Page 317
1. a) $2.00+$1.00+$0.25=$3.25
   b) $5.00+$0.25+$0.25+$0.05+$0.05+$0.05+
      $0.10+$0.10+$0.10=$5.95
   c) $10.00+$0.25=$10.25
   d) $5.00+$5.00+$1.00+$0.25+$0.25+
      $0.25=$11.75
   e) $0.25+$0.25+$0.25+$0.10+$0.10+$0.10+
      $0.05=$1.10
   f) $5.00+$2.00+$1.00+$1.00+$0.25+$0.25+
      $0.25=$9.75
   g) $2.00+$2.00+$2.00+$0.05+$0.05=$6.10
   h) $5.00+$1.00+$1.00+$0.10+$0.10+
      $0.05=$7.25

Exercises
Page 318
1. a) 9.0 b) 13.7 c) 9.0 d) 3.6 e) 5.7
   f) 7.7 g) 7.5 h) 10.6 i) 2.9 j) 7.1
   k) 9.9 l) 9.9 m) 7.4 n) 9.7
2. a) 5.1 b) 3.3 c) 3.2 d) 5.6 e) 2.7
   f) 4.6 g) 1.9 h) 2.7 i) 2.2 j) 3.3
   k) 1.5 l) 4.5 m) 5.2 n) 0.9

Exercises
Page 319
3. a) $6.65 b) $5.20 c) $7.35 d) $4.45
   e) $9.75 f) $5.50 g) $2.95 h) $8.40

Exercises
Page 320
4. a) 10.0 b) 15.2 c) 9.3 d) 12.9 e) 8.6
   f) 5.8 g) 7.5 h) 9.0 i) 9.0 j) 7.6
   k) 9.7 l) 6.0 m) 10.1 n) 6.0 o) 11.4
5. a) 1.6 b) 6.2 c) 5.2 d) 1.7 e) 2.1
   f) 3.7 g) 1.5 h) 6.2 i) 5.5 j) 4.3
   k) 4.4 l) 4.7 m) 2.5 n) 0.3

Exercises
Page 321
6. a) $1.05 b) $3.15 c) $7.15 d) $6.00
   e) $5.30 f) $3.00 g) $6.30 h) $2.05

Exercises
Page 322
7. a) 1 nickel (5¢) and 1 dime (10¢)
   b) 1 toonie ($2) and 1 loonie ($1)
   c) 1 five-dollar bill ($5), 1 ten-dollar bill
      ($10) and 1 twenty-dollar bill ($20)
   d) 2 nickels (5¢), 2 dimes (10¢) and
      2 loonies ($1)
   e) 1 fifty-dollar bill ($50) and 2 hundred-dollar
      bills ($100)
   f) 1 loonie ($1), 1 five-dollar bill ($5) and
      1 quarter (25¢)
   g) 1 dime (10¢), 3 loonies ($1) and
      4 quarters (25¢)
   h) 3 ten-dollar bills ($10), 1 twenty-dollar bill
      ($20) and 1 fifty-dollar bill ($50)
   i) 1 loonie ($1)
   j) 1 toonie ($2)

Test 73
Page 323
1. b), c), d) – colouring will vary.
2. c)
3. a) 8 b) 3 c) 4 d) 5

Exercises
Page 324
1. Drawings will vary.

a) 2 figures with 3 sides   c) 2 figures with 4 angles

b) 2 figures with 4 sides   d) 2 figures with 5 sides

Exercises
Page 325

2. a)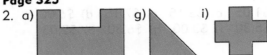

3. Squares – 3, Diamonds – 2, Triangles – 2, Rectangles – 6, Circles – 8

Exercises
Page 326

4. a) b) c) d)

f) g) h)

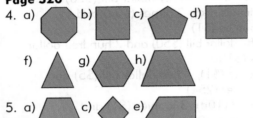

5. a) c) e)

6. b)

7. a) b) c) d)

Test 74
Page 327

1. a) 8 b) 4 c) 3 d) 5 e) 4 f) 4
2. Answers will vary.

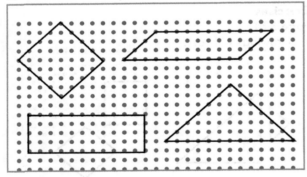

Exercises
Page 328

1. Drawings will vary.

2. Answers will vary.

a) b)

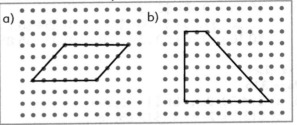

Exercises
Page 329

3. a), c), e) — colouring will vary.
4. Drawings will vary.

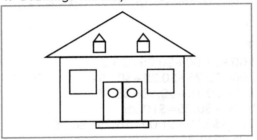

Exercises
Page 330

5. Drawings will vary.

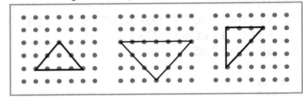

6. Drawings will vary.

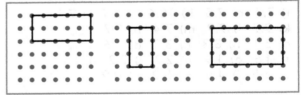

7. Drawings will vary.

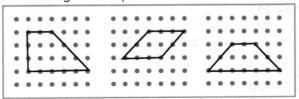

8. Drawings will vary.

Exercises
Page 331
9. Colouring will vary.

Triangles: green   Rectangles: yellow   Circles: pink   Squares: purple

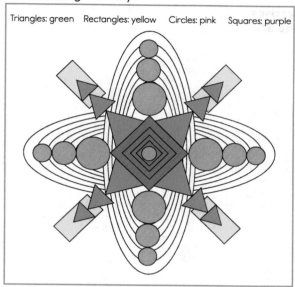

Exercises
Page 332
10. Drawings will vary.

Test 75
Page 333
1. a) triangular pyramid
   b) square pyramid
   c) cube
   d) rectangular prism
   e) triangular prism
   f) rectangular pyramid
2. a) Faces: 3, Edges: 2   b) Faces: 6, Edges: 12
3. cylinder or sphere
4. cube, square pyramid or square prism

Exercises
Page 334
1. a) 8, 12   b) 0, 2   c) 8, 12   d) 6, 9   e) 5, 8
   f) 8, 12   g) 4, 6

Exercises
Page 335
2.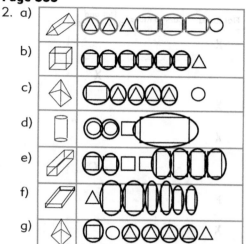

Exercises
Page 336
3.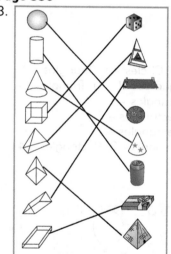

Test 76
Page 337
1. a) Faces: 1, Vertices: 0
   b) Faces: 5, Vertices: 5
   c) Faces: 5, Vertices: 5
   d) Faces: 3, Vertices: 0
   e) Faces: 5, Vertices: 6
   f) Faces: 6, Vertices: 8
2. a) cylinder   b) rectangular pyramid
3. d)

Exercises
Page 338
1. a) 6, 12, 8   b) 2, 1, 1   c) 5, 8, 5
   d) 4, 6, 4   e) 3, 2, 0   f) 5, 9, 6
   g) 5, 8, 5   h) 1, 0, 0   i) 6, 12, 8

Exercises
Page 339

2.

		Flat faces	Curved faces	Flat and curved faces
a)		X		
b)				X
c)		X		
d)		X		
e)				X
f)		X		
g)		X		
h)			X	
i)		X		

Exercises
Page 340

3. a) Squares – 6   b) Circles – 1, Triangles – 1
   c) Triangles – 4, Squares – 1   d) Triangles – 4
   e) Circles – 2, Rectangles – 1
   f) Triangles – 2, Rectangles – 3
   g) Triangles – 4, Rectangles – 1
   h) Circles – 1   i) Squares – 2, Rectangles – 4

Test 77
Page 341

1.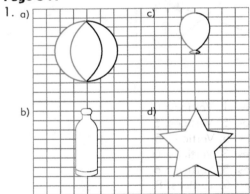

2. I will be 3 miles west from where I started.

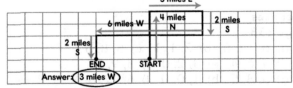

3.

Exercises
Page 342

1.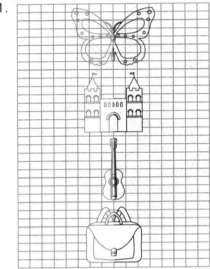

Exercises
Page 343

2.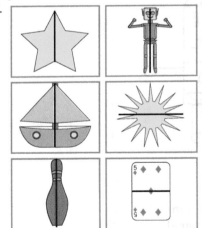

Exercises
Page 344

3.

		*	
▲	♥		X
+	■	◆	★
☺	☹		

Test 78
Page 345
1.

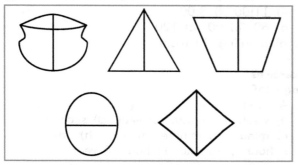

2.

3. Mona is furthest away from Mira.

Exercises
Page 346
1.

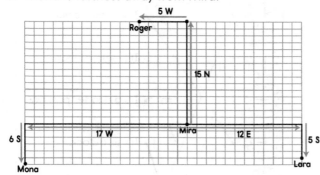

Exercises
Page 347
2. Answers will vary. For example:

Exercises
Page 348
3. a) F b) G c) H d) D e) E f) A

Test 79
Page 349
1. a) Estimate will vary; 3 cm
   b) Estimate will vary; 6 cm
   c) Estimate will vary; 5 cm
   d) Estimate will vary; 3 cm
2. a) 5; 10 b) 5; 12 c) 6; 10 d) 6; 12

Exercises
Page 350
1.

	m	cm
a) a train	X	
b) a straw		X
c) a worm		X
d) a car	X	
e) your foot		X

2. Use your ruler to draw and verify your answers.
3. a) 5 m b) 20 cm c) 26 m

Exercises
Page 351
4. a) 4; 10 b) 8; 12 c) 4; 8 d) 4; 10
   e) 5; 12 f) 7; 16 g) 1; 4 h) 4; 14

Exercises
Page 352
5. a) 3 b) 15 c) 10 d) 24 e) 9 f) 12
   g) 7 h) 12

Test 80
Page 353
1. Use your ruler to verify your answer.
2. a) 10; 14   b) 5; 12   c) 6; 12   d) 4; 10
   e) 5; 20   f) 12; 16

Exercises
Page 354
1. Estimates will vary.
   a) 50 mm   b) 60 mm   c) 119 mm
   d) 29 mm   e) 30 mm   f) 60 mm

Exercises
Page 355
2. a) 4; 14   b) 3; 8   c) 24; 20   d) 8; 18
   e) 4; 8   f) 4; 10   g) 21; 20   h) 6; 22

Exercises
Page 356
3. a) 23   b) 11   c) 8   d) 16   e) 24   f) 7
   g) 7   h) 21

Test 81
Page 357
1. a) morning   b) night   c) afternoon
2. a) 1:00   b) 2:00   c) 10:00
3. a) 12   b) 7   c) 365 or 366   d) 60
   e) 24   f) 4   g) 60   h) 100   i) 4 or 5

Exercises
Page 358
1.

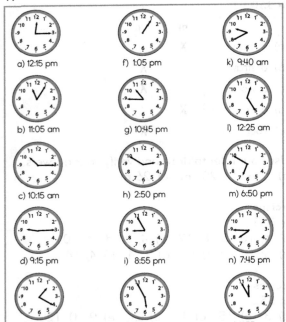

a) 12:15 pm   f) 1:05 pm   k) 9:40 am
b) 11:05 am   g) 10:45 pm   l) 12:25 am
c) 10:15 am   h) 2:50 pm   m) 6:50 pm
d) 9:15 pm   i) 8:55 pm   n) 7:45 pm
e) 1:20 am   j) 5:55 pm   o) 11:55 pm

Exercises
Page 359
2. a) 4:00   b) 6:00   c) 10:00   d) 9:00
   e) 11:00   f) 3:00
3. a) 60   b) 90   c) 120
4. a) morning   b) night

Exercises
Page 360
5. Answers may vary.
   a) week   b) month   c) year   d) second
   e) minute   f) minute   g) hour   h) day
   i) hour   j) minute   k) hour   l) year

Exercises
Page 361
6.

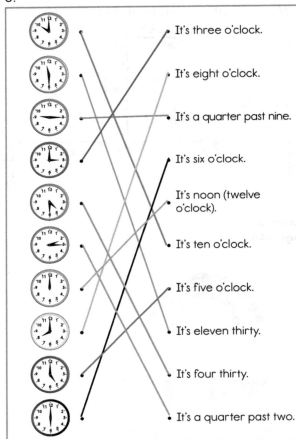

It's three o'clock.
It's eight o'clock.
It's a quarter past nine.
It's six o'clock.
It's noon (twelve o'clock).
It's ten o'clock.
It's five o'clock.
It's eleven thirty.
It's four thirty.
It's a quarter past two.

Exercises
Page 362
7. a) Tuesday   b) Sunday   c) Wednesday
   d) Thursday   e) Monday   f) Friday
   g) Saturday
8. a) November   b) February   c) March
   d) September

9.

Winter	Spring	Summer	Fall
December	March	June	September
January	April	July	October
February	May	August	November

Test 82
Page 363

1. a) 2 hours   b) 7 hours
   c) 13 hours and 45 minutes
2. a) 3:00, 3 o'clock   b) 5:00, 5 o'clock
   c) 10:00, 10 o'clock   d) 9:00, 9 o'clock
   e) 8:00, 8 o'clock   f) 11:00, 11 o'clock

Exercises
Page 364

1. a) 1x7=7   b) 1x5=5   c) 1x52=52
   d) 2x4=8   e) 15x7=105
   f) 1x365=365 or 1x366=366 (for leap years)

Exercises
Page 365

2.

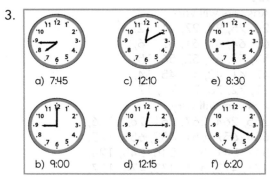

a) 3:00   c) 6:20
b) 3:10   d) 8:35

3.

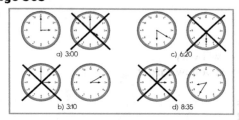

a) 7:45   c) 12:10   e) 8:30
b) 9:00   d) 12:15   f) 6:20

Exercises
Page 366

4. a) Tuesday   d) 12   c) 13

d)

Sunday	Monday	Tuesday	Wednesday	Thursday	Friday	Saturday
1	2	3	4	5	6	7
8	9	10	11	12	13	14
15	16	17	18	19	20	21
22	23	24	25	26	27	28
29	30	31				

e)

Sunday	Monday	Tuesday	Wednesday	Thursday	Friday	Saturday
			1	2	3	4
5	6	7	8	9	10	11
12	13	14	15	16	17	18
19	20	21	22	23	24	25
26	27	28	(29)			

Test 83
Page 367

1. a) 45   b) 60   c) 35   d) 25   e) 10
   f) comic books, science fiction books,
   horror books, adventure books,
   romance books

Exercises
Page 368

1.

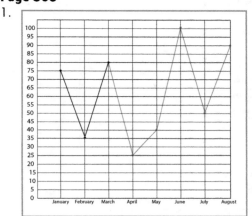

Exercises
Page 369

1. a) June   b) April   c) 495   d) 65   e) 65
   f) April, February, May, July, January, March,
   August, June

Exercises
Page 370

2. a) 10   b) 20   c) 25   d) 5   e) 15
   f) Answers will vary.

Test 84
Page 371

1. a) 45   b) 40   c) sunflower   d) rose   e) 13
   f) 197

Exercises
Page 372

1. Answers will vary

Exercises
Page 373

2. Answers will vary

Exercises
Page 374

3. a) Paris b) London c) 30
   d) Answers will vary.
   e) London, Tokyo, Venice, New York, Paris

Test 85
Page 375

1.

	Certain	Possible	Impossible
I can watch a movie.	X		
I can fly like a bird.			X
I can drive a school bus some day.		X	
I can scratch my nose.	X		
I can help my mother bake cookies.	X		
I can sleep.	X		
I can participate in the Olympic Games some day.		X	
I can finish my homework.	X		
I can talk.	X		

Exercises
Page 376

1.

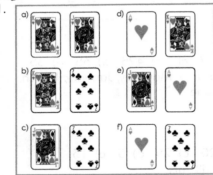

Exercises
Page 377

2. Answers may vary. Most common numbers are 5 and 1. Least common number is 4.
   Combination of 5 and 2 was rolled twice.

3.

Exercises
Page 378

4. a) 24 b) (6), (1) c) (5) d) (3)

Test 86
Page 379

1. Answers may vary.

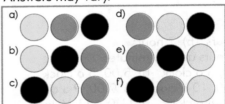

2.

		Certain	Possible	Impossible
a)	I can visit the planet Mercury some day.			X
b)	I can drink two small glasses of water	X		
c)	I can eat a whole cow at breakfast.			X
d)	I can recite the alphabet.	X		
e)	I can win a card game.		X	

Exercises
Page 380

1. Answers will vary.
2. c), largest yellow target

Exercises
Page 381

3. a) Answers will vary.
   26, 25, 24, 27, 21, 12,
   65, 64, 67, 61, 62, 16,
   54, 57, 51, 52, 56, 15,
   47, 41, 42, 46, 45, 14,
   71, 72, 76, 75, 74, 17
   b) Answers will vary.
   265, 264, 267, 261, 262, 126,
   654, 657, 651, 652, 656, 125,
   547, 541, 542, 546, 545, 124,
   471, 472, 476, 475, 474, 127,
   712, 716, 715, 714, 717, 165
4. a) Answers will vary.
   63, 62, 64, 32, 34, 36,
   24, 26, 23, 46, 43, 42
   b) Answer will vary.
   632, 634, 324, 326, 246, 243,
   463, 432, 624, 346, 263, 462

Exercises
Page 382

5. a) 25 b) 7 out of 25 c) 3 out of 25
   d) 9 out of 25 e) 6 out of 25 f) kiwi, pear

Test 87
Page 385
1. Answers will vary.

Exercises
Page 386
1. Answers will vary.

Exercises
Page 387
2. Answers will vary.

Exercises
Page 388
3. Answers will vary.

Test 88
Page 389
1. Answers will vary.

Exercises
Page 390
1. Answers will vary.

Exercises
Page 391
2. Answers will vary.

Exercises
Page 392
3. Answers will vary.

Test 89
Page 393
1. Maps will vary.

Exercises
Page 394
1.

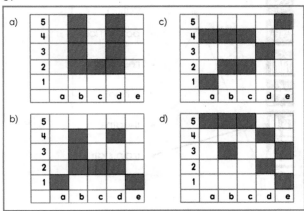

Exercises
Page 395
2. Answers will vary. For example:

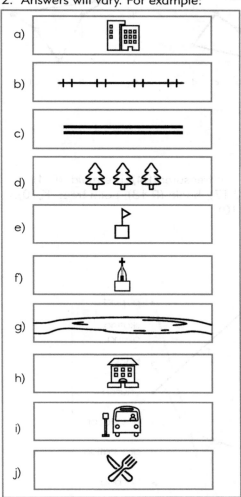

Exercises
Page 396
3.

Answers

Social Studies

4.

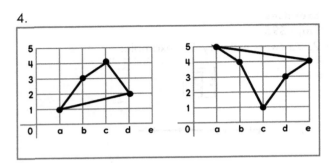

Exercises
Page 397

5. fish: (D,13); treasure: (P,4); mermaid: (C,4);
   island: (J,17); hook: (R,18); palm tree: (K,10),
   flag: (C,10)

Exercises
Page 398

6.

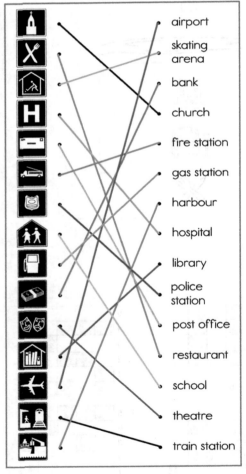

airport

skating
arena

bank

church

fire station

gas station

harbour

hospital

library

police
station

post office

restaurant

school

theatre

train station

Test 90
Page 399

1.

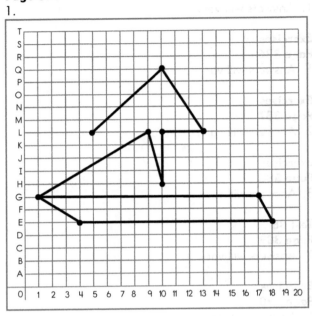

Exercises
Page 400

1.

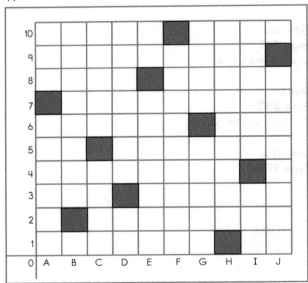

Exercises
Page 401

2.

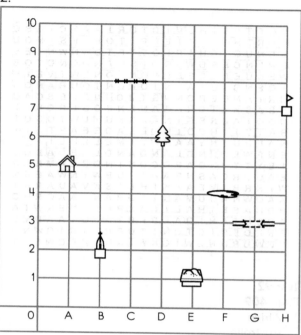

Exercises
Page 402

3.

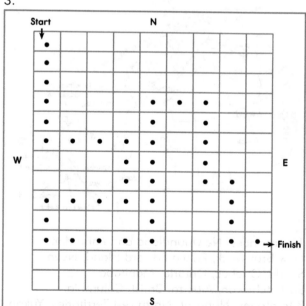

Test 91
Page 403

1. Colouring may vary.

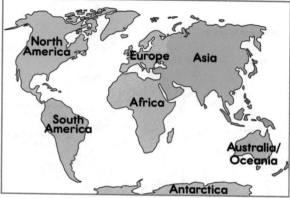

2. Answers will vary.
3. Antarctica
4. Asia
5. French and English
6. South America
7. Europe

Exercises
Page 404

1.

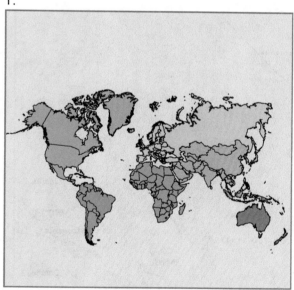

a) to c) Answers will vary. — Any 3 of:
Arctic Ocean, Atlantic Ocean, Indian Ocean,
Pacific Ocean, Southern Ocean

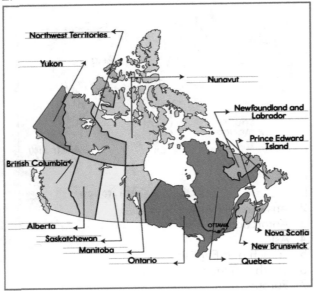

Exercises
Page 405

2.

Exercises
Page 406

3.

Exercises
Page 407

4. a) Mexico   b) Brazil   c) Mediterranean Sea
   d) Answers will vary. For example: France, Spain
   e) Arabian Sea   f) Equator   g) Antarctica
   h) Madagascar   i) Answers will vary.
   For example: Mali, Uganda, Kenya   j) Pacific Ocean

Exercises
Page 408

5.

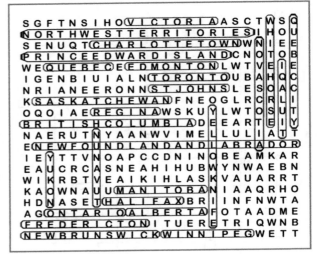

Test 92
Page 409

1. Africa
2. Australia
3. & 4.

10 provinces: Newfoundland and Labrador, New Brunswick, Prince Edward Island, Nova Scotia, Quebec, Ontario, Manitoba, Saskatchewan, Alberta, British Columbia.
3 territories: Nunavut, Northwest Territories, Yukon.
5. Answers will vary.

Exercises
Page 410

1.

Exercises
Page 411

2. Maps will vary.

Exercises
Page 412

3.

4.

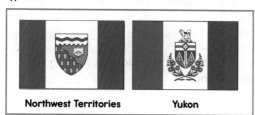

Northwest Territories **Yukon**

Nunavut

Exercises
Page 413

5. a)

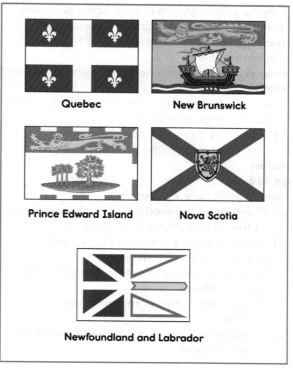

Exercises
Page 414

5. b)

Test 93
Page 417
1. A tree
2. Having a compost bin in your home promotes composting, thus reducing the amount of garbage you produce and helping to protect the environment.
3. Answers will vary. For example: glass, plastic and metal.
4. Answers will vary. For example: eggshells, apple cores and vegetable peels.
5. a) leaves   b) roots   c) flower   d) stem

Exercises
Page 418
1. Answers will vary. For example:
   a) Plants need to breathe in the carbon dioxide in the air and then release oxygen.
   b) Water nourishes the plant by carrying nutrients to its various parts.
   c) Light is necessary to create energy through photosynthesis.
   d) Many plants need warm temperatures to survive.
   e) Plants need space for their roots, stems and leaves to grow.

Exercises
Page 419
2. Drawings will vary.
3. Drawings will vary.

Exercises
Page 420
4. Answers may vary by municipality.

	Yes	No
a) peel from vegetables and fruits	X	
b) egg shells	X	
c) coffee grinds and filter	X	
d) meat leftovers	X	
e) tea bags	X	
f) oil	X	
g) lawn clippings	X	
h) milk products	X	
i) hay	X	
j) hair and animal's fur		X

	Yes	No
k) wilted flowers	X	
l) kleenex and paper towels	X	
m) animal waste	X	
n) leaves	X	
o) branches cut into small pieces	X	
p) metal		X
q) nut shells	X	
r) sick plants	X	
s) fish leftovers	X	
t) wilted herbs	X	

Exercises
Page 421
5. Drawings will vary. Examples of trees to draw include: maple, birch, fir and oak.

Exercises
Page 422
6. Answers will vary.

Test 94
Page 423
1. Answers will vary.

Exercises
Page 424
1. Answers will vary. Use a book or the Internet to help you.

Exercises
Page 425
2. a) crown   b) leaves   c) branch   d) trunk
   e) roots
3. a) stamen   b) petal   c) pistil   d) stem

Exercises
Page 426
4. Trees produce oxygen and keep our air clean.
5. Trees help keep temperatures cooler in summer by providing shade.
6. Trees help keep homes warm during the winter by providing insulation.
7. Drawings will vary.

Exercises
Page 427
8. Answers will vary. The plant with one need removed will not grow as much as the other plant.

Exercises
Page 428
9. Answers will vary, but the plant in potting soil will grow the most.

Test 95
Page 429
1. Answers will vary depending on the dictionary used.
2. Answers will vary depending on the dictionary used.
3. a) hot   b) heavy   c) hard
4.

5. Drawings will vary. For example: door, soccer ball.
6. Drawings will vary. For example: zipper, wagon.

Exercises
Page 430
1. a) dry b) cold c) furry d) soft e) wet
   f) light
2.

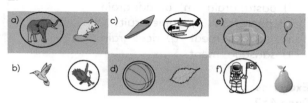

Exercises
Page 431
3. Answers will vary. Use a book or the Internet to help you.

Exercises
Page 432
4. Answers will vary.

Exercises
Page 433
5. Answers will vary. Use the Internet to check weather data published online.

Exercises
Page 434
6. Answers will vary. Each thumbprint pattern will be unique.

Exercises
Pages 435 & 436
7. Descriptions will vary. Objects are moved through static electricity.

Test 96
Page 437
1. Answers will vary.
   For example: a table and a fridge.
2. Answers will vary depending on the dictionary used. For example: pushing a door and kicking a ball.
3. Answers will vary depending on the dictionary used. For example: pulling a door and climbing up a rope.
4. Answers are approximations.
   a) 25°C b) 15°C c) 5°C d) -15°C

Exercises
Page 438
1. Drawings will vary.
2. Answers will vary.

Exercises
Page 439
3. a) -5 b) 10 c) 25 d) -15 e) -10 f) 20
4.

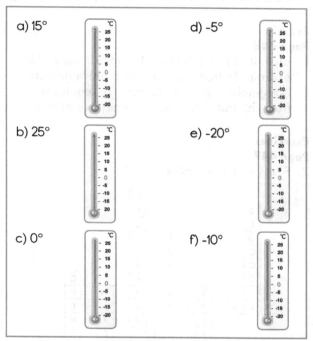

Exercises
Page 440
5. a) Water becomes colder as depth increases.

Exercises
Page 441
5. b) Answers will vary.

Exercises
Page 442
6. Answers will vary.

Exercises
Pages 444 & 445
8. Answers will vary.

Exercises
Page 446
9. The pockets of air in the Ivory soap expand and pop in the microwave.

Test 97
Page 447

1. Drawings will vary. Don't forget to label your fruits!
2. Drawings will vary. Don't forget to label your vegetables!
3. Answers will vary. For example, grains: rice, noodles, bread; fruits and vegetables: apple, carrot, orange; meat and alternatives: chicken, baked beans, ham; dairy: cheese, milk, yogurt.

Exercises
Page 448

1. a) fruit b) vegetable c) fruit d) vegetable
   e) fruit f) fruit g) vegetable h) vegetable
   i) vegetable j) fruit k) fruit l) vegetable m) fruit n) fruit o) fruit p) vegetable q) vegetable

Exercises
Page 449

2. Fruits and vegetables

Exercises
Page 450

3. a) cheese: dairy b) celery: fruits and vegetables
   c) rice: grains d) eggs: meat and alternatives
   e) cereal: grains f) apple: fruits and vegetables
   g) chicken: meat and alternatives
   h) pasta: grains i) lobster: meat and alternatives
   j) peas: fruits and vegetables
   k) broccoli: fruits and vegetables
   l) ice cream: dairy m) milk: dairy
   n) peanuts: meat and alternatives
   o) orange: fruits and vegetables

Test 98
Page 451

1. a) banana: fruit b) cucumber: vegetable
   c) carrot: vegetable d) celery: vegetable
   e) cereal: grain f) cabbage: vegetable
   g) green beans: vegetable h) grapes: fruit
   i) cheese: dairy product
   j) milk: dairy product k) strawberry: fruit
   l) pasta: grain m) bread: grain
   n) pear: fruit o) apple: fruit
   p) chicken: meat q) rice: grain
   r) sausage: meat

Exercises
Page 452

1.

L	M	E	R	C	M	L	R	A	E	R	E	T	G
C	A	A	O	A	E	A	N	T	O	P	O	E	R
O	E	A	A	R	W	P	B	A	N	A	N	A	E
C	A	Y	W	R	T	P	O	T	A	T	O	O	E
L	L	E	N	O	G	R	A	P	E	R	R	R	N
R	A	B	N	T	R	Y	O	P	G	P	N	A	B
R	W	A	T	E	R	M	E	L	O	N	L	N	E
E	E	E	A	E	A	P	P	L	E	R	A	G	N
S	A	S	T	R	A	W	B	E	R	R	Y	E	N
B	E	L	L	P	E	P	P	E	R	C	P	Y	S
T	O	C	H	E	R	R	Y	N	A	A	E	P	A
R	C	A	B	B	A	G	E	E	L	T	A	A	O
E	A	O	N	I	O	N	C	E	L	E	R	Y	B
R	A	B	R	O	C	C	O	L	I	E	E	N	A

Exercises
Page 453

2. a) watermelon: fruit
   b) eggplant: vegetable
   c) apple: fruit
   d) carrot: vegetable
   e) onion: vegetable
   f) cherry: fruit
   g) cabbage: vegetable
   h) celery: vegetable
   i) turnip: vegetable
   j) orange: fruit
   k) blueberry: fruit
   l) green beans: vegetable
   m) pear: fruit
   n) grapes: fruit
   o) banana: fruit

Exercises
Page 454

3.

CELERY PEAR

BROCCOLI APPLE

ORANGE BANANA

Test 99
Page 455

1. Drawings will vary.
2. Drawings will vary.
3. Answers will vary. For example: cows, giraffes and squirrels.
4. Answers will vary. For example: ducks, chickens and snakes.

Exercises
Page 457

1. a) Their babies hatch from eggs.
   b) Amphibians c) Answers will vary.
   d) Drawings will vary.

Exercises
Page 458

2.

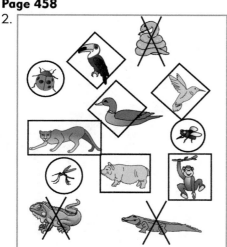

Test 100
Page 459

1. a) bird b) bird c) mammal d) reptile
   e) mammal f) mammal g) amphibian
   h) reptile i) fish j) fish k) mammal
   l) bird m) reptile n) amphibian o) fish
   p) insect q) insect r) reptile s) insect

Exercises
Page 460

1. Drawings will vary. Don't forget to label your animals!

Exercises
Page 461

2. a) swan: bird b) swordfish: fish c) eel: fish
   d) snake: reptile e) turtle: reptile
   f) moth: insect g) ostrich: bird
   h) kangaroo: mammal i) ant: insect
   j) tiger: mammal k) iguana: reptile
   l) penguin: bird m) frog: amphibian
   n) seal: mammal o) bee: insect

Exercises
Page 462

3.

S	I	O	N	S	E	R	E	S	A	O	L	L	S	S
E	R	L	I	E	L	A	D	L	S	Q	U	I	D	T
A	P	A	S	A	T	A	U	P	S	S	S	E	N	A
T	H	T	W	L	W	H	A	L	E	B	S	T	R	R
U	A	K	O	C	L	A	M	H	C	C	R	A	B	F
R	L	S	T	W	L	O	B	S	T	E	R	O	S	I
T	R	C	W	K	U	C	O	J	I	C	D	L	E	S
L	S	H	A	R	K	T	A	E	I	B	O	U	A	H
E	L	O	E	I	P	O	A	L	E	A	L	C	H	Q
L	A	A	M	L	N	P	O	L	E	P	P	O	O	L
L	H	L	O	O	I	U	T	Y	L	E	H	H	R	S
S	I	A	T	L	C	S	R	F	P	L	I	A	S	S
P	S	H	R	I	M	P	K	I	Q	R	N	Q	E	R
S	B	L	K	R	M	S	U	S	Q	S	I	T	C	H
C	L	O	W	N	F	I	S	H	L	L	U	I	P	D